"I have always wondered—perhaps somewhat jealously—why the food at
The Publican in Chicago is so delicious. Then, one lovely April morning I sat down
with my cappuccino and began to read Paul Kahan's first cookbook. I couldn't stop
reading—and now I know how Paul packs so much flavor into his food. The effort he
puts into sourcing and his balance of seasoning, marinating, cooking, and saucing
is what turns his cooking into a concert of flavor. These recipes are so clearly written
they will be easy to make at home. This is the most delicious book I've ever read."

—NANCY SILVERTON, co-owner of The Mozza Group and author of
Mozza at Home

"Paul Kahan is a Midwestern culinary wizard. He's my type of chef—strong-willed,
inquisitive, funny, and hungry—and I adore him for his stubborn 'Why not?' response
to anything difficult. Cosmo Goss is the perfect cohort for Paul. Together, they have
created a new paradigm of American cooking, an amalgam of all the bounty the
country has to offer, served lustily and with reverence. A terrific cookbook."

—JONATHAN WAXMAN, chef/owner of Barbuto and author of *Italian, My Way*

"My first stop when I arrive in Chicago—without exception—is The Publican.
It's thrilling to read the amazing stories that represent so much more than just
the recipes and see the inspiration that comes from the community of growers
and friends who support the restaurant. Cheers to Paul Kahan and Cosmo Goss
for this long overdue book!"

—STUART BRIOZA, co-chef/owner of State Bird Provisions and coauthor of
State Bird Provisions: A Cookbook

"This is a fascinating glimpse into what makes The Publican tick, filled with
invaluable lessons in respect and responsibility plus pure deliciousness."

—SEAN BROCK, chef/owner of Husk and author of *Heritage*

"Paul Kahan has mastered simplicity in cooking, and The Publican
cookbook is quite simply as honest and authentic as a cookbook gets.
Cheers to The Publican, indeed!"

—MARC VETRI, chef/owner of Vetri and author of *Mastering Pasta*

cheers to the
PUBLICAN
REPAST AND PRESENT

cheers to the PUBLICAN

REPAST AND PRESENT

Recipes and Ramblings from
an American Beer Hall

PAUL KAHAN

and Cosmo Goss with Rachel Holtzman

PHOTOGRAPHS
Peden + Munk

POEMS
Jason Pickleman

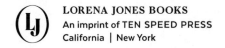

LORENA JONES BOOKS
An imprint of TEN SPEED PRESS
California | New York

THE PERFECT PUBLICAN

A PUBLICAN must be a Democrat, an Autocrat, an Acrobat,
a Doormat. He must be able to entertain Prime Ministers, Pick-Pockets,
Pirates, Philanthropists, and Ponces—
and be on both sides of the Political Fence—a Footballer, Golfer,
Bowler, Tennis Player, Darts Champion, and Pigeon Fancier.

He has to settle arguments and fights; he must be a Qualified Boxer,
Wrestler, Weightlifter, Sprinter, and Peacemaker.

He must always look immaculate when drinking with Bankers,
Swankers, Commercial Travellers, and Company Representatives,
even though he has just stopped a "beer-throwing" contest in the Public Bar.

To be successful he must keep the Bars Full, the House Full,
the Tanks Full, the Storeroom Full, and NOT get himself Full.

He must have Barmen who are Clean, Honest, Quick Workers
and Thinkers, Non-Drinkers, Mathematicians, Technicians,
and at all times to be on the Boss's side, the Customer's side,
and stay on the inside of the Bar.

IT IS SAID THAT THE PUBLICAN:
Home-Wrecks, takes Weekly Wage Cheques, in other words
Saturates, Confiscates, Deteriorates, and Propagates.

To sum up: He must be Outside, Inside, Offside, Glorified,
Sanctified, Crucified, Stupefied, Cross-eyed, and Paralyzed.

SO DRINK PLENTY AND LOOK TWENTY AT
The PUBLICAN

—*Unknown Author*

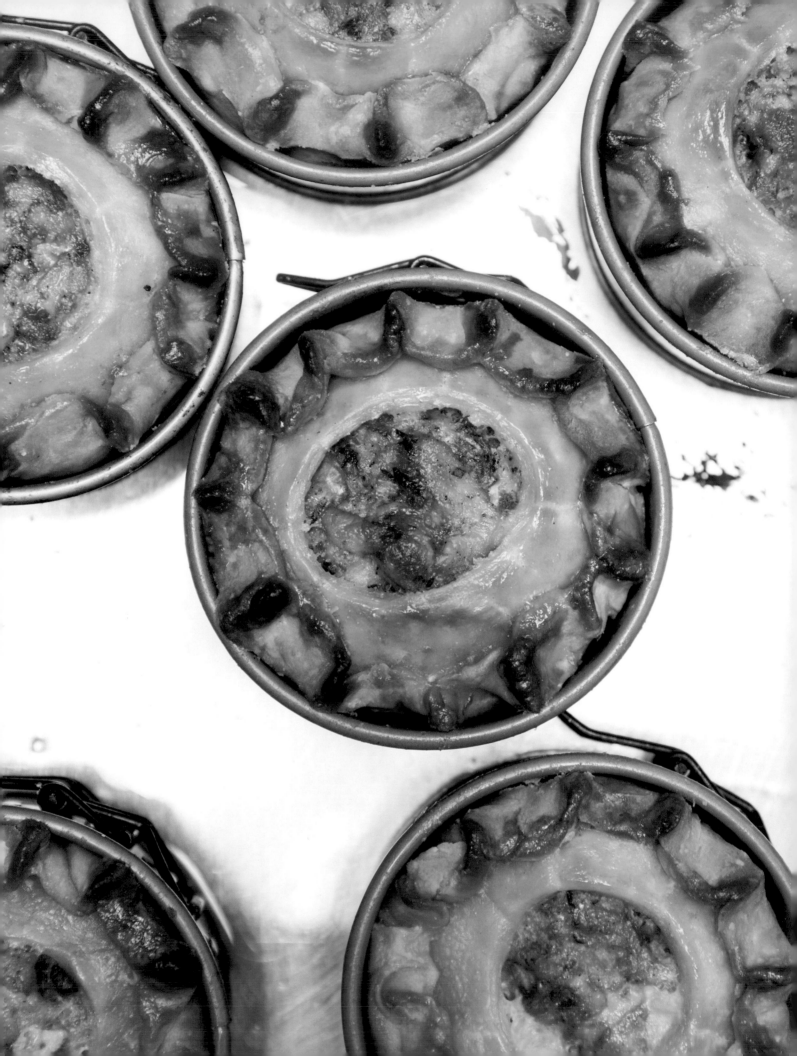

contents

recipe contents

introduction

When we built The Publican in Chicago in 2008, it was to offer homage to life's simplest pleasures: oysters, pork, and beer. That was our sound bite from the beginning. When people asked me what I was going to do next—after opening our first two restaurants, Blackbird and avec—that was all I'd say, "Oysters, pork, and beer." And to that people would respond, "How could *that* be bad?"

My business partners—Donnie Madia, Terry Alexander, and Eddie Seitan—and I thought of it as a kind of modern American beer hall, informed by those who had done it right for centuries in northern France and Belgium. But it wasn't meant to be a European theme park nor was it necessarily intended to be a James Beard Award–winning restaurant drawing in steady crowds day after day (though those things might be what we hoped for and, amazingly, also what ultimately happened). It was just supposed to be a good restaurant—a place for people to sit, eat, and drink, whether it was with ten buddies throwing back oysters and tearing through plates of Grilled Cucumbers and Zhoug with Burrata, Pickled Beef Tongue and Smoked Salmon Roe on grilled bread, and Lamb Leg "Ham Steaks" or a simple dinner for one of Publican Chicken and fries.

We wanted to share what inspired us so profoundly during our trips to Belgium, from the small hams simply brined with juniper, black pepper, and thyme and then strung from strands of garlic affixed to the ceiling and smoked; to the brown bread topped with Trappist cheese and celery salt and shared around a fire over chalices of Orval; from the white asparagus that had just come into season and graced the menus of every restaurant, places with three Michelin stars and rundown taverns alike; to the cold brains with tartar sauce, pots of mussels, and foamy glasses of beer that I would enjoy after an epic night of drinking with my wife and friends as I watched people drift through the alleys. It was food for sharing, food for comforting, food for contemplating, and best of all, food for feasting. It was the same dishes that weighed down the massive communal tables that farmers and laborers and townspeople would gather around in the squares and beer halls to revel in their triumphs and toast to their toils.

It's no mistake that at the heart of The Publican are the large walnut tables that would have been right at home in one of Bruegel's paintings. The dishes never match, and the food is served right out of the oven and heaped onto plates. It's a little rough around the edges, a little (or a lot) less than perfect. But to us it's just right. Replace those peasants with chefs huddled around the pass belting out Night Ranger songs while cooking up an end-of-harvest feast and pouring pre-'Hawks game pints, and what you have is The Publican. It's as familiar as the family joints you went to as a kid, but kind of pumped up—a sort of parallel universe where you can just as easily order headcheese and guinea hen as you can chicken, ribs, and overdressed Caesar salad (just the way we like it). We didn't want to just sling bowls of ordinary steamed mussels—we wanted them to be the best damn mussels you can imagine. So we challenged ourselves to make food out of what was around, what was well raised, and what tasted especially good. We started each week with a whole organic pig and the subsequent portioning, curing, and smoking would make up the right-hand column of our menu. We made the underdogs king—smelt, pig ears, pork rinds—and paired them with house-made pickles, fresh-baked bread, vegetables that local farmers brought to our back door, and some of our favorite ales, lagers, stouts, and ciders. It harkened back to the time of family-run businesses and traditional food craft—something we Americans had down pat until our bread stopped coming from the bakery down the street, our vegetables started coming from South America, and butchers went the way of the milk man. So while we started this place with simple aspirations, it has evolved into a mission of sorts: How do we keep it simple but raise the bar?

Cheers to The Publican is the story of how The Publican has become what it is today, but more important, it's our way of raising a glass to the food we love so much to make and share, and to the dishes that have earned a spot on our "best of" list. There's our signature Publican Chicken, made so simply with olive oil, brown sugar, oregano, and piment d'Espelette; the ever-present Little Gem Salad, our take on the (slightly overdressed) classic Caesar; and crowd-favorites Mussels Steamed in Sour Beer, and The Publican Waffle (an incredible mash-up between yeasty, fluffy Bruges-style and gooey, sugar-crusted Liege-style waffles). And—maybe you'll be surprised by this—there are lots of vegetables, from Barbecued Carrots and Roasted Beets in Green Garlic Labneh to Grilled Chicories and so on.

There's also those dishes that bring us back to a special time or place. The Ham Chop in Hay—or ham roasted in hay, a smoky, buttery, grassy preparation that had a table of world-renowned chefs chanting, "Ham Chop in Hay, Ham Chop in Hay" after dinner one night—is directly inspired by peasant preparations in sixteenth-century Europe. The Alm Salad is something I learned to make in Austria at an *alm*, or hiker's hut, where the proprietress—coincidentally, my college buddy's wife's sister—layered beautiful red tomatoes with pumpkin seeds; a homemade cheese consisting of not much more than raw milk; and then pumpkin seed oil, vinegar, salt, and pepper. I mean, it completely exploded my brain. To this day, that salad evokes big bottles of German beer chilling in a trickling mountain stream. It's a dish I consistently like to make at home (the cheese keeps for days in the fridge and is good crumbled over just about anything—meat, salad, pasta). We also threw in a few "food projects," especially for those elements where store-bought substitutions just won't cut it. After all, if you want it done right, do it yourself.

Let's go back to that overzealous moment in 2013 when my partners and I decided to open our butcher shop, Publican Quality Meats. It partially came out of necessity because we needed more space than we had at The Publican to break down whole animals. The chefs were getting more and more fanatical about preservation and trying cool stuff with charcuterie, dry curing, and other things you do with large chunks of animal. We actually had a shed in a borderline-legal "off-premise location" full of thousands of salamis. So we took over a ground-floor space across the street from The Publican, opened a butcher shop, started selling sandwiches, and used the basement as a private-event space. Then we thought, *why don't we bake bread here, too?* We wanted to do it on our own terms, using locally milled flour with an extra-long fermentation time and super-high hydration. Publican Quality Bread was born. At first it was a total mess—a butchery kitchen mixed with flour and baking . . . logistically, none of it worked. It was ultimately a decision gone wrong that turned into a decision gone right in the long run.

It's not that we set out to have this insane charcuterie program or bread operation; we were just excited about these things. Take jam and pickles— we make them all year with whatever's in season because it means we get to cook with these things year-round. Plus, we've always been into doing things ourselves, just like the good old times when that was what everyone did.

Is doing it all yourself more work? Absolutely. But it makes cooking off-the-cuff at home so much more fun. Putting together a meal doesn't have to be a super-complicated event if you have those great building blocks in your kitchen. The right projects at the right time of the season will give you stuff to rely on year round and make your cooking much easier and faster. It could be a loaf of Sourdough, a jar of Bread and Butter Pickles, a batch of my mom's Icebox Tomatoes, a container of Flaxseed Vinaigrette, a couple links of Mettwurst or round of Pancetta, or even just some cooked quinoa to fry up. If your pantry is stocked with all the essentials—olive oil, capers, lemon, anchovies, great salt, and piment d'Espelette (plus Parmesan or pecorino in the fridge)—then all that's left to do is get something fresh from the garden, market, or store.

In addition to being a guide for people to bring our food home, *Cheers to The Publican* is also a way for us to thank the myriad people who have helped us get where we are. That's because The Publican is as much informed by the people who cross its threshold as it is by the food we make. Our original chef de cuisine, Brian Huston, a Blackbird alum who spent time cooking out West, brought a real passion for creating relationships with the men and women growing and raising our produce and meat. Erling Wu-Bower, The Publican's first sous chef, infused what could have been a meat-centric menu with loads of fresh seafood, connecting us directly to the guys and gals whose daily catch we could get fresh off the boats. And Erling's willingness to teach himself just about anything when it came to charcuterie didn't hurt either. Everyone from a prison warden-turned mushroom hunter to a redneck boat captain waxing poetic about shore lunch has made a big impression on what we do. This collection of bakers, butchers, farmers, fishermen, libation-enthusiasts, trailblazing eaters, plus one spice guru have lent their wisdom on everything from curing bacon and hunting down the perfect hazelnut, to slathering fish in mayo before grilling it and dredging clams in salt and vinegar chips before frying them. When our now-executive chef Cosmo Goss joined The Publican clan—bringing his expertise gleaned from a childhood spent fishing in the kelp beds off California's Catalina Island and honed in some of the country's best kitchens—he brought a new chapter in our seafood and charcuterie offerings, owing majorly to his hunger for tracking down the very best ingredients. I've never seen someone get so excited about the most succulent plum from Penryn Orchards or the fact that there are sixteen varieties of avocados to choose from at Mud Creek Ranch. And then there are chefs like Chris Bianco, Suzanne Goin, Marc Vetri, and Jonathan Waxman, who are our culinary heroes at The Publican (but more on them later). These people are paramount to what The Publican is, which is why it's only fitting that we also toast to them in *Cheers to The Publican*. Their stories appear on these pages among the recipes they have inspired.

Ultimately, *Cheers* is about giving back—especially to all the chefs, bloggers, writers, and, well, everyone who has pulled up a chair in our restaurant—or wanted to—and asked for our recipes. We've never been shy about sharing, but now we can officially pay it forward after "borrowing" from so many people through the years. . . . You could say we created this book so people can bring The Publican home, without even having to buy it a drink.

And that's just about all there is to say about that.

—PAUL KAHAN

The partners (left to right): Donnie Madia, Eddie Seitan, and Terry Alexander

CHEERS TO THE PARTNERS

So much of my relationship with my partners is built on mutual admiration. Donnie and Terry had respect for what the other was doing, the restaurants they were behind, and the boundaries they were pushing. And they thought I could put out a decent plate of food. The three of us got together—and looped in Eddie Seitan, who runs The Publican's beverage program— and put our faith in this idea we had for the restaurant. There was never a moment when we sat down and defined our roles, when one of us said "You take this" and "I'll take that." It was just innate to our partnership— and still is at One Off Hospitality, our restaurant group—that we would be collaborators and equals. Front of house was just as important as back of house, which was just as important as the business deals that were being made. We all counted on one another to have each other's backs. And the great hospitality, that genuine warmth that you feel when you come into The Publican, that's not something we sat down and plotted. It was a natural extension of us working together the way we do and our team sharing in that vibe.

Sometimes our emotions get in the way, and we get into arguments about things—like which chair we like the best for a certain space. That emotion comes from the fact that we love what we do, and we are passionate about it. But at the end of the day, we know that it's not really about us; it's about the guests.

the publican pantry

The ingredients that we're always reaching for evolved from the idea that you start with really great product and then use great tools to enhance that flavor. So here's our go-to list. If you have all this stuff—and none of it goes bad if you store it properly—then all you need is a perfect piece of fish or meat and some fresh vegetables, and you have dinner.

Nowadays, you can find some of these things (especially finishing salts, oils, and spices) at just about any store, especially specialty shops. To help you out, though, we've included our favorite purveyors on page 316.

Espelette Pepper (piment d'Espelette): One of our absolute favorite ingredients at The Publican. It's like paprika, but smokier and richer. Aleppo is like the poor man's Espelette. We get a declassified version (it's an AOC product) that's way cheaper but still has about 99 percent of the same flavor and texture as the fancy stuff.

Finishing Vinegars: We primarily use two that Erling Wu-Bower is obsessed with: a 12-year-aged moscatel grape vinegar and 25-year-aged sherry vinegar. Aged vinegars, including saba and aged balsamic (two other favorites of ours) are more "round" than lemon juice, and a little softer at the edges. Every one of our cooks has these two bottles at their station, and most go through it all in one service. We also love Agro di Mosto, a balsamic condiment, or thin saba, which balances the bite of chicories with its sweetness.

Fishy stuff: Fish sauce, shiro dashi, and neonata (see page 28) for their salty, umami flavor.

Hardwood charcoal: Not really a pantry item, but we prefer using this when we grill because it burns hotter and cleaner.

Herbes de Provence: For marinating or seasoning just about anything, including bread crumbs.

High-quality black peppercorns: We're hardcore black pepper guys. (Unless we're cooking with other peppers like red pepper flakes or Urfa pepper because peppercorns can't compete with them.) We get great, oily tellicherry peppercorns and use them on just about everything.

Hipster peppers: Urfa, Marash, and Aleppo for smoky spice—and because no one said you have to finish every dish with black pepper.

Honey and sugar in the raw: To balance too-sharp vinaigrettes, infuse with spices (see page 29), or season root vegetables for roasting to balance out any bitterness.

Indian dried coriander seed: Super-floral; we have a whole vinaigrette dedicated to it (see Watermelon and Sungold Salad, page 178).

La Boite spice blends: These are less pantry items and more actual ingredients, but we're using them for just about everything in the kitchen. More about these on page 32.

Lemon juice and olive oil: The essential duo. Always freshly squeezed lemon juice. Store the olive oil in a cool place.

Nut oils: Hazelnut, walnut, pistachio, Austrian pumpkin seed, because olive oil shouldn't get all the credit. Store nut oils in the fridge.

Pickled, cured, and preserved: Great capers, caper berries, anchovies, olives, and preserved lemon because no one said you have to use purely salt to flavor a dish.

Salt: We use sea salt for everything except seasoning blanching and cooking water. We use kosher for that and enough to make the water taste salty, like the sea. People tend to under-season blanching water, which is a mistake because we don't want the water to just cook the vegetables, we want it to season them, too. We use Maldon salt as a finishing salt.

Wine: Make sure you don't cook with any wine you wouldn't drink. Crappy wine makes crappy food.

THE ANTI-TWEEZER MANIFESTO

The Publican is a revolt against the fussy, the frilly, and the frivolous. From the beginning, we've been set against the notion of precious, perfectly plated food—which has its place, just not at our table—and Michelin star-chasing. So what do we stand for? The celebration of great product, great cooking, great wine, great beer, great friends, and most important, collaboration—the belief that no idea is a bad idea. To me, a beautiful piece of California white sea bass that we cook perfectly and don't do much else to is much more interesting than some sous vide baby carrots and a pesto made from their fermented and dehydrated tops. I'm not in the least bit concerned that all our food is essentially big piles of brown stuff. And if you take a look in our kitchen, you'll see we're using the tweezers God gave us—our hands.

To the Mighty Vegetable

Carrot, Turnip,
     or Leafy Green,
From Farmyard Dirt
     Deep With'een,
Where Roots Do Spread
—nake'd, un'seen—
'Til Yanked & Rinsed,
     Now Fresh, Now Clean;
A Gentle Snap,
     Roasted, Steamed.

People think of The Publican as this big, meaty restaurant and so often I hear things like, "We don't go to The Publican because I'm a vegetarian." That's a shame because we believe in putting vegetables front and center. Sure, there are pigs on the wall, but we've evolved since we started out with the intention of highlighting gastropub staples like oysters, pork, and beer. In the beginning, we basically had two categories on the menu—meat and seafood—and dishes that progressed from zero manipulation (artisanal hams, oysters) to our "big box" items like Porchetta with Chicories and Ham Chop in Hay. The vegetable category was in the bottom right-hand corner of the menu, and it was kind of an afterthought. I was younger, and I was all about being bold. But then, to be perfectly honest, when we were getting ready to first open, I got really fat. I had a whole summer of R & D, just working through the menu, perfecting our now-staple dishes, eating country ribs and chicken and mussels and, of course, drinking beer like crazy. I felt sluggish and horrible (and the black circles under my eyes were blacker than usual). Part of what helped me make a change in my life was standing outside, checking in produce, and seeing all these people running through the alley carrying tires and realizing that it was time to join Mike Madonis's gym, Fulton Fit House, which had opened about a year before The Publican. But what made the biggest difference was that my wife and I completely changed the way we ate at home, adding more and more vegetables to our rotation. And in time that change was reflected at the restaurant, too.

Offering great vegetable dishes on our menu wasn't just about health. People would come to The Publican and get so excited about the food that they'd over-order and just get destroyed. The first twenty times I ate there, I felt as if I was going to die at the end of the meal, and the kitchen would be like, "There's still a Ham Chop in Hay coming!" So I started pushing for more vegetables on the menu to balance things out. Brian Huston got the ball rolling with his California-inspired market connections, and by the time Cosmo came to The Publican—with all his ties to the West Coast and his passion for finding really special produce, including stuff you'd never get in our market, like kinjoki grapefruits, puntarelle di galentina (a kind of chicory), and avocados with more fat content than most cheeses—we were putting out many more plant-forward dishes that were way more interesting and complex than the usual sautéed spinach.

Of course, the quality of our produce is what makes all the difference. The number-one thing for us at all our restaurants, and especially at The Publican, is that our food is driven by the market. (Within reason: There once was a restaurant in Chicago that aimed to be 100-percent seasonal. It went out of business.)

While we buy everything we possibly can from our local vendors—seriously, you wouldn't believe the pile of stuff sitting outside our back door as soon as asparagus and ramps pop up in the spring—we've expanded to bring in produce from warmer climes. It's important for keeping the restaurant vital and interesting, plus we can get a jump on the season with things like English peas and fava beans because they're picked in California about two months before we get the first inklings of a pea here.

Even though we buy specific ingredients from other locales, supporting local growers really is everything to us, and I pat myself on the back for helping plant the seeds for the now-thriving farmers' market system here in Chicago. I wouldn't say I was *the* first chef to shop at the Green City Farmers' Market, which was our city's first mostly organic market, opened in 1998 by Abby Mandel—chef and author, friend of Alice Waters and Craig Claiborne, author of my wife's favorite ratatouille recipe, and Chicago Grand Dame— but I was one of the first chefs to shop there. For the first three or four years, the market wasn't doing so well. Local and seasonal was the talk, but no one was doing it. Abby reached out to Sarah Stegner, Rick Bayless, and me to see if we could get it to work. She believed that people would buy what we bought. And sure enough, our meetings went from five people to fifteen to twenty to all these committees that helped the market pick up steam and find a permanent location.

Our faith in the great work that these local farmers were doing led to some of the most crucial relationships that we have at The Publican, which continue to shape the food that we serve. Dave Cleverdon at Kinnikinnick Farm, who I've known for about a hundred years, switched from growing mostly mesclun to baby heads of Little Gem and oak leaf because I wanted those beautiful and tender lime-green heads. He also grows rare varieties of Italian braising greens like spigariello, bietina, and minestra nera; and he's got the best asparagus I've ever tasted. Tim Burton of Burton's Maplewood Farm, our maple syrup guy, brings us ramps that he forages from the woods near his house in southern Indiana. He drops them off at our butcher shop, Publican Quality Meats, has a sandwich and a beer, and all the other chefs in town come by for their pick-ups. We started giving him bourbon barrels that he now uses to age his maple syrup, which in turn makes a better product for us. Henry Brockman of Henry's Farm, in the Mackinaw River Valley, grows things we can't find anywhere else—burdock root, bok choy, tatsoi. He's the reason (along with Ed Gast and J. W. Morlock & Girls Fruit Stand) someone from The Publican team drives up to the Evanston Farmers' Market every Saturday. You can't pre-order with him; you get what you get. We're always sure that someone's there at 8 AM so we don't miss anything. That's a really good example of what The Publican is about.

I would of course love to say that everything we serve is organic, but it's just not feasible. I always say that if you're out of business, you can't serve any organic food. Whether you're sourcing food for a restaurant or for your home kitchen, there does have to be balance, but it doesn't mean compromising on quality. We can guarantee that every farmer we source from is a responsible, conscientious grower. That's paramount to our philosophy.

THE VEG PLATE EVOLVES

COSMO The biggest transition I saw at The Publican was about five years after we opened. We'd never had a vegetable entrée, only what we'd call a "veg plate." If someone came in and requested something vegetarian, every cook on the line had about ten minutes to put up something from their station. Then we'd pass the plate around, and each of us would contribute one element. We'd be doing three to five of those a night, and guests really loved them, so it became pretty clear that we needed more vegetables on our menu. As we added hearty, balanced, fully thought-out dishes, such as Radishes with Red Lentil Falafel, Asparagus and Avocado Salad with Fried Quinoa and Flaxseed Vinaigrette, and Maple-Roasted Winter Squash with Piri-Piri Sauce, the balance of our menu changed. We were giving people a chance to have a healthy, super-satisfying meal instead of coming in and getting hammered with food. Paul is always telling us not to overfeed people, and I know what he means. When I go out to dinner, I want to be able to go have a drink afterward or take a walk and not feel like I never want to eat again.

barbecued carrots

I don't think there's ever been a dish at The Publican that people have freaked out about so much. Even chefs. We did a charity event last year and served these, and there was a table of twenty-five big-name chefs just losing their minds over them. We've tried new variations, adding different spices, experimenting with other preparations, but it always comes back to this recipe. We use a barbecue rub that I "borrowed" from Chris Lilly, the owner of Big Bob Gibson's in Georgia and a world champion of barbecued pork shoulder. He came in to eat once, and we got embarrassed about ripping him off, so we quickly changed the name of these to Chris Lilly Carrots.

We like to serve them with pecans that we get from Blain Farms in California, which are creamier than any other pecan, and then we top it off with an herbed dressing.

Makes 4 servings

1 gallon water

**1 cup plus
1 tablespoon BBQ Rub
(recipe follows)**

¼ cup kosher salt

**1 pound carrots,
cleaned and halved**

**1 tablespoon extra-
virgin olive oil**

1 teaspoon sea salt

**1½ teaspoons freshly
squeezed lemon juice**

**¼ cup pecans,
coarsely chopped**

2 sprigs dill, torn

**1 batch Ranchovy
Herb Dressing
(recipe follows)**

In a large pot, combine the water with 1 cup of the BBQ Rub and the kosher salt. Bring to a boil, add the carrots, and cook until they're just about fully cooked, about 5 minutes. Drain the carrots and set aside.

Build a fire on one side of a charcoal grill and let it burn down to embers.

Toss the blanched carrots with the remaining 1 tablespoon of BBQ Rub and the olive oil in a large bowl.

Arrange the carrots on the grill over direct heat and cook, moving them around a bit, until they have some char marks and are finished, about 5 minutes.

Pile the carrots on a serving plate, season with the sea salt, drizzle with the lemon juice, and garnish with the pecans and dill. Taste and add more salt or lemon juice, if needed. Dress the carrots with the Ranchovy Herb Dressing and serve.

cont'd.

BBQ RUB

This is just as good on carrots as it is on meat.

Makes 1 1/2 cups

½ cup firmly packed dark
brown sugar

½ cup kosher salt

¼ cup pimentón de la Vera
(hot smoked Spanish paprika)

1 tablespoon freshly ground
black pepper

1 tablespoon granulated garlic

1 tablespoon onion granules

1½ teaspoons celery salt

1 tablespoon ground cayenne pepper

1 tablespoon ground cumin

Combine the brown sugar, salt, pimentón, pepper, granulated garlic, onion granules, celery salt, cayenne, and cumin in a bowl. Mix well. Store in an airtight container at room temperature for up to 1 month.

RANCHOVY HERB DRESSING

Never use store-bought dressing again.

Makes about 1 quart

2 cups mayonnaise
(we like Hellman's/Best Foods)

1 cup buttermilk

1 tablespoon garlic powder

1 tablespoon onion powder

1 tablespoon Worcestershire sauce

1½ teaspoons white vinegar

1½ teaspoons Tabasco sauce

1 teaspoon Dijon mustard

1½ teaspoons granulated sugar

1½ teaspoons fish sauce

1 tablespoon freshly squeezed
lemon juice

2 tablespoons chopped parsley

1 tablespoon chopped chives

1½ teaspoons chopped tarragon

1½ teaspoons chopped oregano

Sea salt

Freshly ground black pepper

Whisk all the ingredients in a bowl and season with the salt and pepper. Taste and add more salt and pepper. Transfer the dressing to a glass container with a lid and refrigerate. The dressing will keep in the fridge for up to 1 week. Give the jar a good shake before using.

jared van camp's bread-and-butter pickles

Jared Van Camp, who was a sous chef at Blackbird, came up with this recipe. We use these pickles for *everything*—in remoulade, on sandwiches, in dressings, and, obviously, by themselves. They're our workhorse pickle. And because we don't want to waste the juice, we use it in things like brine for fried chicken or instead of vinegar in salad dressings. I highly recommend keeping a jar of them in your fridge.

In a large pot, combine the salt and water and stir to dissolve the salt. Add the cucumbers and place the pot in the fridge to brine for 24 hours.

In a small bowl, combine the vinegars, onion, garlic, allspice, celery seeds, cinnamon stick, and mustard seeds. Let the mixture sit in the fridge for 24 hours.

Add the vinegar mixture to a heavy pot and stir in the sugars and turmeric. Bring the pot to a boil.

Meanwhile, remove the cucumbers from the brine and put them in a large tub or pot. Discard the brine. Pour the boiling mixture over the cucumbers and set aside to let everything cool. Transfer the pickles to an airtight container and store in the fridge—they'll keep for 6 months.

Makes 5 pounds of pickles

½ cup salt

6 cups water

5 pounds pickling cucumbers, cut in ¼-inch-thick slices, stems discarded

2½ cups white wine vinegar

2½ cups cider vinegar

1 white onion, sliced

3 cloves garlic, sliced

½ tablespoon allspice berries

2 tablespoons celery seeds

cinnamon stick

2 tablespoons mustard seeds

2 cups granulated sugar

2 cups firmly packed brown sugar

½ tablespoon turmeric

BREAD-AND-BUTTER PICKLING RATIO

Whereas a lot of pickle recipes are 3-2-1 (three parts water, two parts vinegar, and one part sugar), a bread-and-butter version is half vinegar, half sugar, making them sweet and sour. Adding in seasonings such as turmeric, celery seed, and mustard seeds, also gives them a yellow color.

mom's icebox tomatoes

During tomato season, my mom would always slice up beefsteak tomatoes and marinate them in red wine vinegar, olive oil, thyme, white onion, salt, and pepper. She'd keep them in the fridge just like that, and we'd go in there and yank 'em out. Maybe grab a slice of bologna, too, toast up some white bread, and put a tomato on top. Now you'll see these on our menu, which we particularly like with burrata. The tomatoes will keep for a couple of days in the fridge, then they get a little soggy. Still good, but soggy.

In a large bowl, mix together the onion, olive oil, vinegar, and thyme. Add a pinch of salt and a few grindings of pepper. If the tomatoes aren't at peak season, you might want to add a pinch of sugar, too.

Make a single layer of tomato slices in the bottom of a shallow dish or pan and pour over some of the marinade. Make a new layer of tomatoes and repeat until you've used up all the tomatoes and marinade. Chill before serving. The tomatoes will last in the fridge for about 1½ days before they start to break down.

Makes 4 servings

½ white onion, julienned

¼ cup extra-virgin olive oil

¼ cup red wine vinegar

½ teaspoon fresh thyme leaves

Sea salt

Freshly ground black pepper

Sugar (optional)

4 beefsteak tomatoes, sliced ½ inch thick

BUYING TOMATOES

Buying good tomatoes is crucial, especially if you're eating them raw. Start with the best at the height of tomato season. Get the tomatoes from the guy whose prices are twice as expensive as every other guy's. Trust us; it's worth it. There's this guy at our market who's from Tomato Mountain Farm in Brooklyn, Wisconsin. He won't even let you *touch* his tomatoes because he's so proud of them. It's annoying—and they're not cheap—but they're the best. If we're serving tomatoes raw, we have to buy his.

WHAT WOULD SUZANNE GOIN DO?

Suzanne Goin and I were *Food & Wine's* "Best New Chefs" together, and our careers have, to some degree, been parallel—the number of restaurants, the cooking style. Lucques was her first; mine was Blackbird. Then she did AOC, and I did avec. We've traveled together and cooked together and, while she likes me just fine, we at The Publican *love* her. We're always asking ourselves, "Would Suzanne like this?" Whether it's adding green garlic to our labneh (her suggestion), adding suckling pig confit to our menu (her recipe), or tracking down the best possible ingredients (by badgering her to share her purveyors), she's always inspiring us to up our game—especially when it comes to honoring great product and keeping things simple. Seriously, one of the things we love most about her is that she always has a *guy*—a fig guy, a plum guy, a pistachio guy, a hazelnut guy. We get connections out of her a few at a time. As chefs, whenever we do an event with her or go to eat in her restaurants, we're always super jealous of at least one thing she has. It kind of ruins and makes your day at the same time. We've even shared a lot of talent between our kitchens over the years. What can we say? We're big fans.

elotes

Elotes—or traditional Mexican street corn—is usually an ear of corn that's been slathered in mayo, queso fresco, chile powder, and lime. That's how we do it at Big Star, another one of our restaurants, but Brian Huston came up with a mutation that we started serving at The Publican because, as I like to say, any culture is fair game here. We take the corn off the cob, sauté it in oil, and then finish it with salt, a little butter, and lime juice. Then we add freshly grated Parmesan cheese for its salty nuttiness, Espelette pepper, and our Garlic Aioli (page 24), which is like a mother sauce for us. We roast a ton of garlic in olive oil to make roasted garlic marinade, so we use the oil that we roasted the garlic in as the base for the mayo. There's not much more to it, besides salt, and it ends up tasting really savory, almost cheesy. We serve this dish in a casserole that you just scoop into, and it's like. . . . *oh my God!*

COSMO We start getting corn in late August, if we're lucky, so when we do eventually get great, super-sweet corn from our farmers, we hoard it. We feature it all over the menu, and it's one of our favorite things to preserve—as demonstrated by the 250 quarts of corn relish (also known as chow chow) that we put up last summer.

Heat a large sauté pan over medium-high heat. Add the oil and let it get to the point of almost smoking, it's so hot. Add the corn and sauté until it's tender, about 3 minutes. Stir in the butter and half the lime juice with a pinch of salt and a few cracks of pepper. Taste, and adjust seasoning if you think it needs it, adding more lime juice if you want.

Transfer the corn to a serving dish and spoon the aioli on top and sprinkle on the piment d'Espelette. Garnish with the cilantro. Grate about ¼ cup of Parmesan over the top (at the restaurant we always do this at the last second because it tastes better that way) and serve.

Makes 4 servings

1 teaspoon high smoking-point oil, such as rice bran, sunflower, grapeseed, or peanut

3 cups corn kernels (from 4 to 5 ears)

1½ tablespoons unsalted butter

Juice of 2 limes

Sea salt

Freshly ground black pepper

2 tablespoons Garlic Aioli (recipe follows)

1 teaspoon piment d'Espelette

4 springs cilantro, leaves picked from stems

Parmesan cheese

cont'd.

GARLIC AIOLI

COSMO Paul always refers to this aioli as one of The Publican mother sauces because we use it for so many things. We rub it on fish (instead of oil) to keep it moist, whisk it into salad dressings to thicken them, and, of course, serve it with our frites and other fried foods. It's simple, basic, and delicious.

Makes 1 quart

10 cloves Garlic Confit (page 28)	3 to 4 tablespoons ice water
Zest of 1 lemon	½ cup oil from Garlic Confit (page 28)
Juice of 2 lemons	3 cups grapeseed oil
4 large egg yolks	Salt
1 raw garlic clove, finely grated	Freshly ground pepper

In the bowl of a food processor, combine the garlic confit, lemon zest, lemon juice, egg yolks, grated garlic clove, and 1 teaspoon of the ice water.

With the food processor running, slowly stream in the garlic oil. Once the mixture is thick, add 1 tablespoon of the remaining ice water. With the processor running, slowly stream in the grapeseed oil, adding the remaining ice water a few drops at a time until the aioli is a little thinner than store-bought mayonnaise. Season the aioli with the lemon zest, salt, and pepper to taste. Transfer the aioli to a jar with a tight-fitting lid and store in the fridge for up to 2 weeks.

radishes with red lentil falafel, yogurt, and spiced honey

COSMO The pound of radishes in this dish adds spark to what would otherwise be a falafel plate (and gives us justification for sneaking this recipe into the vegetable section of our menu). After Paul came back from eating at Shaya in New Orleans and said he'd had "the best falafel ever," it was like the falafel challenge had been thrown down. I tried a hundred different variations to make one that even came close, but every time Paul just said, "You gotta go back to the drawing board." Paul even called Alon Shaya to ask for his recipe, and we *still* couldn't get it right. The taste was good, but the texture was off—you want falafel to be crunchy and crispy on the outside and herby and clean on the inside. Then I had this lentil croquette at Bar Tartine in San Francisco, and I thought about using lentils in the falafel instead of the traditional chickpeas. Sure enough, they made the falafel creamier, whereas chickpeas can be a little dry and crumbly. Paul finally let us put it on the menu and ten people told us it was the best thing ever. (Paul still said it was okay, or more specifically, "Do whatever you want, Cosmo . . . I would rework it if I were you.") We refined the recipe a bit more and twenty people said it was the best ever the next night, and so on. We just kept trying to improve it every time, and Paul was always pushing us to make it better, too, which was how we knew we were on to something great.

———————

Strain the lentils and measure 5 cups. Set aside.

Toast the pimentón, cayenne, cumin, and coriander in a dry skillet over medium heat, 1 to 2 minutes. In the bowl of a food processor, combine the toasted spices and the seaweed, bonito flakes, Garlic Confit, scallions, neonata, baking soda, fish sauce, sugar, flour, onion granules, ricotta, cilantro, and parsley. Pulse into a coarse paste. Add the lentils and pulse until they just start to break up. Season with a healthy pinch of salt and pepper.

Heat the about 4 inches of oil in a deep fryer or a large heavy pot to 350°F on a deep-fat/candy thermometer.

Make a tester falafel by taking a couple tablespoons of the lentil mixture and forming it into a ball in your hand. Fry it for 3 to 5 minutes or until golden brown. It should be crispy on the outside and a great mix of creamy and coarse on the inside. If it's too coarse, pulse the mixture a few more times and test again. You can also adjust the seasoning.

Makes 6 to 8 servings

3 cups dried red lentils, soaked in hot water for 1 hour

1 tablespoon pimentón de la Vera (hot smoked Spanish paprika)

1½ teaspoons ground cayenne pepper

1 tablespoon ground cumin

1 tablespoon ground coriander

1½ teaspoons ground seaweed

1½ teaspoons bonito flakes

4 cloves Garlic Confit (recipe follows)

1 cup chopped scallions, white and green parts

2 scant teaspoons neonata (see note, page 28)

1½ teaspoons baking soda

1 tablespoon fish sauce

1½ teaspoons sugar

1 tablespoon all-purpose flour

1½ tablespoons onion granules

¾ cup ricotta

½ bunch cilantro

½ bunch parsley

cont'd.

Sea salt

Freshly ground black pepper

High smoking-point oil, such as rice bran, sunflower, grapeseed, or peanut, for frying

1 lemon, cut in half

1 pound mixed radishes, cut into bite-size pieces

Extra-virgin olive oil

⅓ cup plain Greek yogurt

2 tablespoons Spiced Honey (recipe follows)

2 tablespoons chopped herbs, such as mint, parsley, dill, and cilantro

2 teaspoons sesame seeds

2 teaspoons sunflower seeds

Form the remaining falafel mixture into balls that are 3 to 4 tablespoons (1½ to 2 ounces) each, to make a total of 12 to 18 balls. Fry them, turning continuously, until they're golden brown and crispy, 3 to 5 minutes. Season with salt and lemon juice as they come out of the fryer. Set aside.

Toss the radishes in a small bowl with a generous amount of lemon juice and olive oil, plus a good pinch of salt. Set aside.

Spread the yogurt on the bottom of a serving plate. Place the crispy falafel on top and drizzle with the honey. Dance the radishes over the top, reserving any lemon juice and olive oil that has collected at the bottom of the bowl. Combine the herbs and sesame and sunflower seeds in a bowl. Pour the reserved lemon juice–oil mixture over the top and toss to coat. Place the dressed herbs and seeds on the radishes and serve.

GARLIC CONFIT

Garlic that has been slowly cooked in fat—the technique known as confit—takes on a whole new flavor and is sweeter and richer than it is raw or even sautéed. Use any leftover cloves in salad dressings or soups, or just slather it on bread. The leftover oil is great for cooking with—it's awesome when you're roasting root vegetables, and you can also use it to make Garlic Aioli (page 24).

Makes about 1 ½ cups

1 cup olive oil

2 heads garlic, separated into cloves and peeled

Place the oil and garlic in a small pot and cook over very low heat—it should gently bubble—until the garlic is tender, about 30 minutes. Let cool. Store the oil and garlic in an airtight jar in the refrigerator for up to 2 weeks.

NEONATA

Italian for "just born," this condiment is traditionally a mix of Calabrian chiles and baby eels. The fish makes it sweeter than using straight chiles, and the overall effect is a savory character with rich heat and great acid. We get ours from an Italian import company, but you can find it online. Since it's now illegal to fish for baby eels, most versions will substitute glass fish.

SPICED HONEY

This is great on gamey things like lamb and venison, and we always find ourselves frying vegetables and reaching for spiced honey to dip them in. In the restaurant we use The Publican Spice Blend for this recipe, which we get from Lior Lev Sercarz (page 32). But a good substitute is equal parts pimentón, cumin, and cayenne.

Makes about ¹⁄₄ cup

¹⁄₄ cup good farm honey

¹⁄₂ teaspoon salt

2 teaspoons Tapatio hot sauce

2 teaspoons water

1 tablespoon Publican Spice Blend or 1 teaspoon each pimentón, cumin, and cayenne

In a small pot over low heat, heat the honey until it's just warm. Stir in the salt, hot sauce, and water. Turn off the heat and let the honey steep for about 30 minutes. This will keep indefinitely at room temperature in a tightly closed jar.

LIOR LEV SERCARZ, LA BOÎTE

I met Lior about eight years ago when he had just opened his spice shop, La Boîte, in Manhattan. He was Michael Solomonov's spice guy—so I knew he was for real—plus he'd been a sous chef at Daniel, learned to cook in France, and most amazingly, did a rare externship with Olivier Roellinger in Cancale, France. (If you want a good read, look him.) And he's from Israel— he grew up on an olive orchard there, which his family still runs. He's just this total spice mastermind. We get our Shabazi Blend (see page 38) from him—which, is I think, my favorite spice that he makes—along with our namesake, The Publican Spice Blend (Lior had an avec blend, a Paul Kahan blend, and a Publican blend, which was originally called the Cosmo blend, but that name didn't make the cut). It's crazy, the way he gets inside your head to figure out how to customize these spices. He totally nailed the fact that even though we're clearly influenced by the Mediterranean and Mexico and Italy, we're not necessarily cooking Mediterranean or Mexican or Italian food. He could identify with my love of all things acidic in the name of balance, and we share the idea that not every recipe should end with the words "salt and pepper." (Saltiness is important and heat is important, but that doesn't have to come from salt and pepper.) Plus, he's a really cool dude, a T-shirt junkie, and a good-looking man.

roasted beets with green garlic labneh

Beets have always been on our menu 365 days a year. There's merit to that—young beets are amazing, but so are the big overgrown ones that have been in cold storage for months. They have a ton of sugar, and they retain that sugar as they sit. It's one of the few vegetables that can be just as good out of cold storage as it is fresh out of the ground. We've always made them the same way, too: First we toss them with olive oil, garlic, thyme, and orange peels to get them even more aromatic and flavorful. We throw 'em in the oven with the skins on and then, when they're good and roasted, we just slip off the skins and marinate them in olive oil, vinegar, shallots, and honey. Forget the rubber gloves; your hands will be pink for a little while, but who cares.

For this dish, we pair the beets with thick and tangy labneh, which is basically just Greek yogurt that has been strained. When Suzanne Goin recommended using green garlic paste, which she loves more than pesto, we were immediately into it. We did it just like she did it—Little Miss Mortar and Pestle—and mashed it into a paste, seasoned it with salt and pepper, and folded it into our labneh. The result is herbaceous and bright; just the action you want for earthy roasted beets.

Preheat the oven to 350°F.

To make the beets: Add the beets to a glass or metal pan with sides, along with the thyme, chiles, and garlic. Squeeze the orange wedges over the whole lot and toss in the rinds. Lightly season with salt and pepper and then coat with the olive oil.

Pour in just enough water to make a shallow pool in the bottom of the pan; it'll help create steam as the beets cook. Cover the pan with aluminum foil and transfer to the oven.

Set a timer for 1 hour, then start checking the beets every 25 minutes until they're tender all the way through. If a fork can easily pass through the skin into the center of the beet, they're done.

Remove the foil and let the beets cool to room temperature.

While the beets cool, make the marinade: Combine the shallots, salt, pepper, vinegar, honey, thyme, and olive oil in a bowl and whisk them together. Taste to see if the acidity or sweetness need balancing. No two vinegars are exactly the same, so adjust accordingly by adding more vinegar, honey, olive oil, salt, or pepper.

Makes 8 to 10 servings

BEETS

3 pounds red beets, rinsed

3 sprigs of fresh thyme, leaves picked from the stems

3 dried chiles de árbol

4 cloves garlic, skin-on and smashed

1 orange, quartered

Sea salt

Freshly ground black pepper

3 tablespoons extra-virgin olive oil

MARINADE

2 shallots, haché (see note, page 178)

Sea salt

Freshly ground black pepper

⅓ cup red wine or champagne vinegar

2 tablespoons honey

1 tablespoon chopped fresh thyme leaves

½ cup extra-virgin olive oil

cont'd.

roasted beets with green garlic labneh, *continued*

Green Garlic Labneh (recipe follows)

1 hefty bunch mixed greens, such as dandelion, arugula, and watercress (optional)

Extra-virgin olive oil

½ lemon

2 tablespoons slivered red onion

2 tablespoons slivered mint leaves

Once the beets are cool enough to handle, take off the skins. They should slip off very easily.

Cut the beets into bite-size pieces and toss them in a large bowl with enough marinade to lightly coat. Don't feel like you need to use all the marinade. (You can store any leftover marinade in the fridge and use it for a simple salad dressing, which we do all the time for our staff meals.)

Taste the dressed beets and adjust the seasoning if necessary. You can store the dressed beets in your fridge for up to 1 week.

To assemble the dish, place a mound of Green Garlic Labneh on each plate and top with a nice scoop of beets along with a drizzle of marinade. Garnish with the onion and mint. Place the greens in a bowl, drizzle with olive oil, and add a squeeze of lemon juice. Toss to coat. Mound the greens on the beets and serve.

GREEN GARLIC LABNEH

We like our labneh, which is essentially yogurt cheese, a little thinner than the commercially made kind. The green garlic we use comes from California and is almost woody and sweet. The paste we make with it and blend into this lebneh makes it aromatic, not spicy.

Makes about 1½ cups

2 cups high-quality Greek yogurt

1 head green garlic or 1 bunch scallions

Sea salt

Freshly ground black pepper

Line a strainer or funnel with cheesecloth, add the yogurt, then gather up the ends of the cheesecloth to form a ball. Tie the ball closed with kitchen string and hang it from a rack in your fridge with a small bowl or plate underneath to catch the drippings. Aim to keep it in your fridge for 5 to 10 days (we go for 7 at The Publican). The longer the yogurt strains, the more tangy and rich it gets. Remove the cheesecloth and use the strained yogurt right away or store it in your fridge for up to 1 week longer.

Cut the green garlic or scallions into small pieces and beat them into a paste using a mortar and pestle. It should take 5 to 10 minutes.

Tasting as you go, add the paste to the yogurt until it tastes good to you. Adjust the seasoning with salt and pepper.

MATCHING YOUR VINEGAR TO YOUR BEETS

Use any variety of beets, but change the type of vinegar you use for the marinade: match light-colored beets with champagne vinegar, match dark red beets with dark vinegar. For example, use red wine vinegar for red beets and champagne vinegar for yellow or Chioggia beets. We like to serve this with some nice greens on top—dressed with lemon juice and olive oil—but it's up to you.

baby turnips and chocolate persimmon salad with cosmo's magic bacon dressing

COSMO This dish is kind of an excuse to showcase our Magic Bacon Dressing, a buttermilk and bacon fat–based miracle that can be served cold without congealing. We don't quite know why it works (probably because it's emulsified into a mayonnaise). Regardless, it's awesome on vegetables, salads, and sandwiches and for dunking fried fish.

Chocolate persimmons are really special. We get ours from Penryn Orchards in Penryn, California. They grow fifty-six varieties of fruit on just over four acres of land (most commercial growers have hundreds), and their produce is like no other (see green gauge plums, page 77.) These persimmons are essentially pure sugar, to the point that you can also eat the skin. You could definitely substitute a different kind of persimmon, like a fuyu, but you'll need to peel it.

Start by making the dressing: In a large sauté pan over medium heat, heat the grapeseed oil and add the bacon. Stir every few minutes, rendering as much fat out of the bacon as possible and crisping it on all sides, 5 to 8 minutes. Transfer the bacon and all rendered fat to a blender. Add 1 cup of the buttermilk. While the bacon is still warm (before the fat can congeal), blend on high speed for 45 seconds.

Pass the bacon and buttermilk mixture through a fine-mesh strainer into a medium bowl. Finely grate the zest of the lemon, and then cut in half. Whisk in the zest, squeeze in the juice of the lemon, and then whisk in the mayonnaise and the remaining 2 tablespoons of buttermilk. Season to taste with salt and pepper.

To make the salad: Heat the olive oil in a large sauté pan over medium heat. Add the quartered turnips and sauté for 2 to 4 minutes, until they are almost tender. Season with a squeeze of lemon, salt, pepper, and sugar to taste. (The sugar offsets the bitterness of the turnips.) Spread the turnips in a single layer on a serving platter.

In a medium bowl, combine the shaved turnips, persimmon slices, and onion and season with salt and pepper. Top with a drizzle of olive oil and a squeeze of lemon juice. Toss the salad to combine and spread it over the sautéed turnips. Pour about ¼ cup of the bacon dressing evenly over the whole dish. Garnish with the chervil or parsley leaves and serve. Leftovers can be stored in the fridge for up to 1 week.

Serves 4

MAGIC BACON DRESSING
1 teaspoon grapeseed oil

8 ounces bacon, diced

1 cup plus 2 tablespoons buttermilk

1 lemon zested and juiced

½ cup mayonnaise (we like Hellman's/ Best Foods)

Sea salt

Freshly ground black pepper

SALAD
1 tablespoon extra-virgin olive oil, plus more for drizzling

3 cups washed and quartered raw baby turnips

½ lemon

Sea salt

Freshly ground black pepper

Sugar

½ cup shaved raw baby turnip

2 persimmons quartered then cut into ⅛-inch-thick slices

1 cippolini onion, thinly sliced into rings

2 tablespoons chervil or parsley leaves

fried sweet potatoes with hazelnut mayo and shabazi vinaigrette

Serves 2 to 3

8 cups salted water

1½ teaspoons baking soda

2 sweet potatoes, peeled and diced into 1-inch cubes

High smoking-point oil such as rice bran, sunflower, grapeseed, or peanut

½ cup cornstarch

Sea salt

Freshly ground black pepper

2 cups Parmesan Tempura Batter (recipe follows)

1 lemon, cut in half

2 tablespoons pulverized salt (see note, page 40)

1 scallion, white and light green parts only, thinly sliced on the diagonal

¼ bunch mint, leaves picked from the stems

¼ bunch cilantro, leaves picked from the stems

2 tablespoons chopped toasted hazelnuts

Extra-virgin olive oil

3 tablespoons Hazelnut Mayonnaise (recipe follows)

2 tablespoons Shabazi Vinaigrette (recipe follows)

COSMO There's this Chinese dish I used to love as a kid called Crispy Walnut Shrimp. It was fried shrimp covered with walnuts and mayonnaise (okay, so it probably wasn't really Chinese), and it was that perfect mix of salty and sweet, creamy and crunchy, and right with a little bit of wrong. When Dan Snowden, the executive sous chef at Nico Osteria, another restaurant in our group, came up with an incredible Parmesan tempura batter, we answered with our sort-of grown-up interpretation of Crispy Walnut Shrimp. Instead of shrimp, though, we use sweet potatoes, which bring a similar sweet and meaty element. We cook them with a little baking soda in the water, drawing out their starch so they get crispier when you fry them in the tempura batter. We really like the Beauregard variety, which we get from Henry Brockman's farm in central Illinois, but in most stores you'll find Paul's favorite "sweet potato," which is the Garnet yam. Then we finish them with Shabazi vinaigrette, tons of toasted hazelnuts, and hazelnut aioli. Shabazi is one of the spice blends that we get from Lior Lev Sercarz (page 32). It's essentially the dry flavors of zhoug—a spicy Yemenite condiment—combined with green chiles, cilantro, and mint. You can order it from his Manhattan shop, La Boîte.

Bring the salted water to a simmer in a large pot. When simmering, whisk in the baking soda. Gently cook the sweet potatoes until they're tender all the way through, about 10 minutes. Strain them and let them cool.

Heat the oil in a deep fryer or a large heavy pot to 350°F on a deep-fat/candy thermometer. Line a baking sheet with paper towels.

In a medium bowl, combine the cornstarch with a pinch of salt and pepper. Dredge the cooled sweet potatoes in the mixture, shaking off any excess, then dunk in the tempura batter until completely coated. Drop a few of the sweet potato pieces in the hot oil at a time and fry until golden brown, 3 to 5 minutes. Using a slotted spoon, remove the pieces from the oil and transfer them to the paper towels to drain. As they come out of the fryer, give them a squeeze of lemon juice and season with the pulverized salt and the pepper.

cont'd.

In a small bowl, make a salad of the scallions, mint, cilantro, and hazelnuts. Dress it with a squeeze of lemon juice and just enough olive oil to coat everything well.

Arrange the sweet potatoes on a plate and drizzle the mayo and Shabazi dressing. Top with the salad and serve.

PARMESAN TEMPURA BATTER

This recipe makes about double what you need for the potatoes, so save the extra for frying other veggies, such as broccoli or cauliflower, or fish (especially white, flaky fish).

Makes about 5 cups

1 (16-ounce) box cornstarch

1 cup grated Parmesan cheese

1 cup all-purpose flour

1 teaspoon baking soda

1 teaspoon baking powder

1 teaspoon coarse sea salt

1 cup vodka

2 cups seltzer water

1 large egg

Whisk together the cornstarch, Parmesan, flour, baking soda, baking powder, salt, vodka, seltzer, and egg and refrigerate until ready to use, for up to 2 hours.

PULVERIZED SALT

I first saw pulverized salt—or sea salt that has been blended into a fine powder—when I was in Japan at a restaurant called Den. I thought it was genius because the salt just dissolves when it hits the food, making for a really evenly seasoned and really clean bite because you don't get any salty residue on your hands when you're eating. Coarse salt is awesome for some fried things—there's something pretty satisfying about licking your salty, French fry–covered fingers after eating a burger—but sometimes you want something that's a little more refined.

HAZELNUT MAYONNAISE

The lemon vinegar that we use for this recipe is Jean-Marc Montegottero's Citron/Lemon vinegar. It's small-batch vinegar made from in-season fruit and is honestly the best vinegar in the world. We get ours from Rod Markus at Rare Tea Cellar in Chicago and encourage you to do the same. But if you're not willing to set yourself back fifty dollars a bottle, you could substitute a mixture of $\frac{1}{2}$ lemon juice and $\frac{1}{2}$ rice wine vinegar. Honestly, though, just buy some. You can use it on almost anything—seafood, meat, soups, salads; it's really versatile. You could even substitute it for lemon juice, if you're feeling fancy.

Makes about 2½ cups

1 cup mayonnaise
(we like Hellman's/Best Foods)

½ cup Garlic Aioli (page 24)

¼ cup hazelnut oil

3 tablespoons lemon vinegar

3 tablespoons sweetened
condensed milk

2½ tablespoons honey

¼ cup buttermilk

Sea salt

LOTS of freshly cracked black pepper

Whisk everything together and store in an airtight container in the fridge for up to 10 days.

SHABAZI VINAIGRETTE

I walked into the restaurant one day, and Cosmo was tasting like eight different shiro dashis, which is basically like ready-made broth that's flavored with bonito flakes and white soy, so it's got a real mushroomy, umami flavor. All I know is that I tasted one and immediately took a bottle to everyone in the company. Now it's like The Publican secret ingredient #486.

Makes 1½ to 2 cups

Zest and juice of 1 orange

Zest and juice of 1 lemon

1 teaspoon Calabrian chile paste

6 tablespoons minced shallots

2 tablespoons Shabazi spice blend
(see page 38)

5 tablespoons shiro dashi

½ cup olive oil

2 tablespoons sugar

Whisk everything together and store in an airtight container in the fridge for up to 3 days.

frites [with an egg on top]

We certainly had Belgian fries on the mind when we created this dish, so the fries are a thicker cut that's not just all crunch but creamy on the inside. It's a simple process of cutting, soaking, blanching, chilling, and then frying when you're ready to serve. So it's all about paying attention to the details—using the right potatoes (we have the best luck with Kennebec, but any baking potato will work), hitting the right blanching temp, and cooking the fries completely through before refrying them. You know they're right when you put 'em in a metal bowl, toss them with salt, and they make a loud clanking noise. We serve them under a blanket of fried eggs, but you can skip the eggs or serve them with Garlic Aioli (page 24) instead.

Makes 4 servings

2½ pounds Kennebec, Idaho, or Russet potatoes

Vegetable oil, for frying

Sea salt

4 Fried Eggs (recipe follows)

Fill two large bowls with cold water.

Peel the potatoes, placing the finished ones in one bowl of water to prevent them from turning brown. Slice the potatoes into ½-inch-wide sticks, adding the pieces to the second bowl of water while you work.

Heat a few inches of oil in a large pot or deep fryer to 275°F on a deep fat/candy thermometer.

Rinse the sliced potatoes under running water to wash off all the excess starch. You know you're done when the water starts to run clear. Dry the potato slices well with a clean kitchen towel.

Line a baking sheet with paper towels or parchment paper. When the oil is at the right temperature, add one-third to one-half of the potato sticks, depending on how large your pot is. (If you crowd the potatoes in the oil, they break up and you get fry nubbins. We hate fry nubbins.) Blanch the sticks in the oil until they are light golden, 7 minutes. Using a slotted spoon, transfer them to the baking sheet to cool and drain. Repeat for the remaining potato sticks.

Turn up the oil to 350°F. When the oil is at the right temperature, fry the potatoes in batches until golden brown, 3 to 6 minutes. Using the slotted spoon, transfer them to the baking sheet. Season with sea salt, pile them on a platter, drape the fried eggs over the top and serve immediately.

FRIED EGGS

COSMO Most chefs don't want their fried eggs with any color on the whites. But Paul isn't one of those chefs. We fry ours in really hot oil so the whites puff up, then pull 'em off just in time for the yolks to stay nice and runny—so they act kind of like an aioli on the frites. Don't skimp on the eggs—get some nice farm eggs from a local farmer. They cook better, look better, and taste better than the supermarket kind.

Makes 4

¼ cup olive oil   **4 farm eggs**

Add half of the oil to a nonstick pan so that it completely coats the bottom and heat oil on a medium-high heat until it's almost to the point of smoking. Crack 2 of the eggs into the pan and let the edges fry and caramelize until they are GBD—golden-brown-delicious. This is quick because you want bubbly, crispy edges with runny yolks. Once the whites are golden brown, use a perforated spatula to carefully transfer the eggs to the serving plate and repeat for the remaining eggs.

CHOOSING POTATOES

Keep in mind that the crispiness and color of the fries depends not as much on their cooking time as when the potatoes were harvested. Once potatoes are dug from the field, they're put into cold storage (farmers aren't digging potatoes every day). In cold storage, a process called recrystallization starts, during which the starches in the potato convert to sugar. So at certain points of the year, you get a very crispy, very blond potato that won't ever turn golden brown no matter how long you fry them, or on the other end you get a dark brown, soggier potato, no matter how long it is in the oil. French fries are tricky to make at home, but at least they are a delicious experiment.

baby squash with chickpea pesto

COSMO We're lucky to get our summer squash—patty pans, zucchini, crooknecks—about a month and a half before everyone else, because Nichols Farm and Orchard in Marengo, Illinois, grow theirs in a hoop house. We showcase them with a combination of roasted and raw, tossed together, and topped with Chickpea Pesto, which we invented by accident. We didn't have enough basil one day, so we threw in all kinds of greens—sorrel, kale, ramp greens (or scallion greens). It's incredibly delicious. You don't have to add pine nuts because the chickpeas give that thick texture and nutty flavor, and the vitamin C from the kale keeps the mixture super-bright green. In Chicago, we find fresh chickpeas in Mexican markets and year-round at the farmers' markets. Spoon any leftovers over burrata with a little good salt, a grating of Parm, and you're done.

To make the pesto: Start by placing the olive oil and—if you have room—the bowl of your food processor in the freezer. This will help the pesto stay cold, which will help keep its bright green color.

Bring a large pot of water to a boil. Fill a large bowl with ice water. Blanch the chickpeas in the boiling water for 20 seconds, then drain and transfer them to the ice water. When the chickpeas are cool, drain them and set aside.

Remove the oil and food processor bowl from the freezer. Combine the fish sauce, arugula, basil, ramp leaves, lemon zest and juice, and ½ cup of the oil in a food processor. Pulse in 20-second intervals until you have a smooth green paste. Add the cheese and blend until smooth. Add the chickpeas and, while pulsing, drizzle in the remaining olive oil until you get the desired texture. You want the chickpeas to still be chunky. Season with salt and pepper, and if necessary, adjust the seasoning with more lemon juice or, if the greens are bitter, a touch of sugar. Set aside.

To make the squash: Cut half of the squash into bite-size pieces and set aside. Cut the other half lengthwise into ⅛-inch-thick slices. A mandoline works well here.

Add the olive oil to a large sauté pan over medium-high heat. Sauté the bite-size squash pieces. As they begin to get tender and turn golden brown, season them with a good pinch of salt, a few cracks of pepper, and a squeeze of lemon.

Add the butter to the pan and let it lightly grab the squash. Transfer the cooked squash to a bowl and toss with the raw squash and about ½ cup of pesto. Season with salt and pepper to taste, give the salad a good grating of Parm, and serve.

CHICKPEA PESTO

1 cup extra-virgin olive oil

2 cups fresh chickpeas, shucked

2½ tablespoons fish sauce

1 cup packed arugula

1 cup packed basil leaves

1 cup packed ramp leaves

Zest and juice of 2 lemons, or more juice as needed

½ cup grated Parmesan

Sea salt

Freshly ground black pepper

Sugar (optional)

SQUASH

1½ pounds baby summer squash, any varieties or mix thereof

1 tablespoon extra-virgin olive oil

Sea salt

Freshly ground black pepper

1 lemon

2 teaspoons unsalted butter

1 chunk good Parmesan cheese, for garnish

maple-roasted winter squash
with piri-piri sauce

Makes 4 to 6 servings

**2 medium or large
delicata squash**

**1 tablespoon high
smoking-point oil,
such as rice bran,
sunflower, grapeseed,
or peanut**

**1 tablespoon
unsalted butter**

**1 teaspoon
red pepper flakes**

**2 teaspoons slivered
fresh garlic**

**2 teaspoons chopped
fresh thyme**

Sea salt

**2 tablespoons
maple syrup**

**1 tablespoon 25-year-
aged sherry vinegar or
1½ teaspoons un-aged
sherry vinegar (see
note, page 47)**

**3 tablespoons
feta cheese**

3 tablespoons cashews

**2 sprigs parsley,
leaves pulled
from stems**

**3 tablespoons Piri-
Piri Sauce (recipe
follows)**

I have a compost pile in my backyard, and one summer when I left for my vacation house up in Wisconsin, I came back to *fourteen* delicata squash coming up through the compost. I was pretty damn excited, especially because then I could make this recipe, which Brian Huston came up with. He cuts the squash into half-moons, about a half-inch thick, and sears one side in oil. Then he flips them, sprinkles them with red pepper flakes and fresh thyme, and adds some slivered garlic and maple syrup just as they're done so they burn just the right amount. We leave the skin on, too, which is delicious, and no matter how hammered the squash gets in the pan, the skin helps hold everything together. This recipe has essentially gone untouched. There's just no way to make it better.

———————

Start by cleaning the squash: Cut off the stems, then halve the squash lengthwise so the seeds are exposed. Scoop them out and discard. Cut the squash into thin, half-moon slices that are ¼ to ⅓ inch thick.

Heat the oil in a large sauté pan over medium heat. Once the oil begins to shimmer, add the squash in a single layer, working in batches if necessary. Make sure the pan isn't smoking hot as you do this because you don't want the outside of the squash to burn before it's fully cooked through. Gently roast the squash until it starts to get tender, 5 to 7 minutes.

Add half of the butter plus the pepper flakes, garlic, thyme, and a pinch of salt. Agitate the pan—either by shaking or mixing things with a large spoon—to make sure the garlic and pepper flakes don't burn. After about 1 minute, add the rest of the butter and the maple syrup, cook another minute, then finish by adding the vinegar to the pan. It will steam right out, which is what you want. Remove the pan from the heat.

Taste the squash to make sure it's tender and seasoned, adding more salt if you want. Arrange it on a serving dish and sprinkle the feta, cashews, and parsley on top. Drizzle the Piri-Piri over and serve immediately.

PIRI-PIRI SAUCE

Piri Piri is a North African pepper sauce, almost like a fresh Sriracha. It's got a great sweet heat and very high acid. We like to drizzle it on fatty foods—like meat—to cut through the richness.

There's nothing to this recipe other than putting everything in a blender. We call for having some extra sugar and lime juice on hand since some chiles are hotter than others and adjusting the sugar and acid will help mellow out the spice.

Makes about 2 cups

5 Fresno chiles, stemmed and seeded

1½ teaspoons peeled and chopped fresh ginger

1 garlic clove

½ teaspoon sea salt

1 teaspoon white wine vinegar

1 tablespoon extra-virgin olive oil

2 teaspoons brown sugar

3 tablespoons lime juice

Add the chiles, ginger, garlic, salt, vinegar, oil, 1 teaspoon of the brown sugar, and 1 teaspoon of the lime juice to a blender or food processor and blend until smooth. If too spicy, add more of the remaining brown sugar and lime juice to taste. This will keep in a tightly closed jar in your fridge for about 1 week.

AGED SHERRY VINEGAR

At the restaurant we use a 25-year-aged sherry vinegar because it's a little sweeter and a lot less astringent than un-aged. It's okay to use regular sherry vinegar for this dish, just halve the amount called for if you do.

cauliflower caponata

Makes about 5 cups

2 tablespoons extra-virgin olive oil

1 head cauliflower, cut into florets

Sea salt

Freshly ground black pepper

1 lemon, cut in half

1 small white onion, halved and thinly sliced

4 stalks celery, sliced

2 cloves garlic, sliced

2 teaspoons red pepper flakes

1 bay leaf

2 tablespoons capers, rinsed

¼ cup toasted pine nuts

¼ cup raisins

¼ cup high-quality tomato paste

¼ cup red wine

2½ tablespoons red wine vinegar

1 tablespoon sugar

½ cup picholine olives

2 tablespoons unsalted butter

Caponata is kind of like a Sicilian vegetable stew or Italian ratatouille. Typically it's made from eggplant that has cooked down with things like onion, garlic, tomato paste, and anchovies; but because I always associate caponata with fall, we came up with a version that shows off the big-time texture of cauliflower. If you ordered caponata in an Italian trattoria, it would come out in a big bowl at room temperature with a spoon stuck in it, and that's exactly how we serve it at The Publican. It's super good on its own, but some grilled whole mackerel with caponata in the wintertime? Insane. Or in the summer, if you just skewer a coil of merguez, grill it, and serve it with this, you have an easy and awesome backyard kind of meal.

COSMO Our version of caponata has more great texture than you'd traditionally get. You want the cauliflower to still have a little bite to it and the celery to have a nice crunch to contrast the softer pine nuts and raisins, which give this more of a sour-sweet flavor than usual. The rest is just quality ingredients—good anchovies, good vinegar, and great tomato paste. We use Estratto di Pomodoro, a special sundried version from Sicily, which you can find online or in specialty markets. Its rich, deep flavor is no match for the cheap kind that tastes like the inside of a tin.

———————

Heat 1 tablespoon of the olive oil in a large sauté pan over medium heat. Add the cauliflower in a single layer, working in batches if necessary, and sear, agitating the pan until the florets start to get golden brown, 3 to 5 minutes. Add a pinch of salt and a few cracks of pepper and let them continue to cook until they're just about tender but not quite—they should still have some nice crunch to them—2 to 4 minutes. Add a squeeze of lemon to the pan and arrange the florets on a plate or tray to cool.

Heat a heavy saucepot over medium heat, add the remaining tablespoon of olive oil and start to sweat the onions, celery, and garlic with the pepper flakes and bay leaf. Stir constantly with a wooden spoon until the vegetables start to lightly caramelize and soften, 5 to 8 minutes. Add the capers, pine nuts, and raisins, and continue to cook for about 3 more minutes. Add the tomato paste and work it into the mixture for about 1 minute.

Deglaze the pan with the red wine and let it reduce until it's almost gone. Stir in the vinegar, sugar, and olives. Taste, adjust the seasoning if necessary, and cook for another two minutes. Add the butter, and when the base is nice and saucy, add the cauliflower and make sure it gets generously coated. Cool to room temperature before serving. Serve cold as an appetizer or hot over roasted pork or fish.

fava beans, english peas, and green garlic salsa verde with burrata

Burrata is basically mozzarella curds mixed with cream and wrapped inside a more mature, firm mozzarella shell, like a beggar's purse. So when you cut into it, the creamy center just oozes out. You can make your own, but we don't. We import ours from Puglia. They've been making it a lot longer than we have, and they do it better than we ever could.

Burrata is really special; you have to know how to treat it. You can't cut it two hours ahead. That ruins it—turns it into a puddle. Slice it at the last minute. Top it with some cold or room temperature stuff, such as peaches with lemon juice and olive oil or trout roe. Maybe some herbs. Though, you don't even really need to dress it up. It's pretty perfect from the get-go.

Bring a medium pot of water to a boil and fill a large bowl with ice water. When the water comes to a boil, season with the kosher salt and taste. It should be salty like the sea. Blanch the peas for about 20 seconds. Taste one, and if it is still starchy and not tender, cook for another 10 seconds until tender and sweet but still bright green and not mushy. If it's early in the season, you might want to add a pinch of sugar to the blanching water. Transfer the peas with a slotted spoon to the bowl of ice water. When just cooled, use the slotted spoon to transfer the peas to a colander and set aside to drain.

Blanch the fava beans in the same water used for the peas until their remaining skins start to soften, about 1 minute. Taste one, and if still starchy and not tender, cook for another 10 seconds until tender and sweet but still bright green and not mushy. Transfer the favas with a slotted spoon to the ice water and let cool. Pour the fava beans into a separate colander and drain, removing any remaining fava skins, and set aside.

Lay out the peas on a cutting board and run your knife through them once. (We hate things rolling around on the plate, so we cut all round things in half—the dish will eat better that way.) Combine the peas and favas in a medium bowl and toss with the salsa verde and herbs. Season to taste with the sea salt and pepper.

Spoon everything over the burrata and serve with the crusty bread.

Makes 2 to 4 servings

Kosher salt

1 cup fresh peas, shucked

Sugar (optional)

1 cup fresh fava beans, shucked

¼ cup Green Garlic Salsa Verde (recipe follows)

2 tablespoons chopped mint

2 tablespoons chopped chives

2 tablespoons chopped cilantro

Sea salt

Freshly ground black pepper

2 (4-ounce) balls burrata

Crusty bread, for serving

cont'd.

GREEN GARLIC SALSA VERDE

When spring comes around, we try to put this in almost every dish on our menu, from veg to meat. Green garlic is not only the first fresh thing to come out of the ground after winter, it also has a sweet, almost floral flavor that regular garlic doesn't have. It's pretty incredible.

Makes about 2 cups

2 shallots, minced

1 green garlic shoot, whites only, finely chopped

2 tablespoons rinsed and chopped capers

5 brown anchovy fillets, rinsed, patted dry, and chopped

¼ cup champagne vinegar

¼ cup extra-virgin olive oil

1½ tablespoons honey

½ jalapeño, seeded and minced

Sea salt

Freshly ground black pepper

Mix everything in a bowl, taste and adjust the seasoning, and serve. This will keep in an airtight container in your fridge for up to 1 week.

IT'S OKAY TO BUY IT

When it comes to deciding whether to make something in-house versus outsourcing it, I think about my great friend Chris Bianco, who owns Pizzeria Bianco, Pane Bianco, and Bar Bianco in Phoenix. He's a real philosopher, and whenever I go out to see him, I always end up listening to one of his monologues on something profound. One time, sitting in his old La-Z-Boys, drinking Miller High Life (this was before he got married), he starting waxing poetic about whether we as chefs should really be making all our products—bread, cured meat, cheese, preserves, etcetera—ourselves. We talked about how there's a little ego in wanting to make absolutely everything yourself, and a huge talent in recognizing the gifts of others. Sure, you could make your own sundried tomato paste and balsamic vinegar, but if somebody has been making them for generations, and they make it better than you ever could, what's the point? So unless you're going to raise the bar, sometimes it's better to leave it to the experts.

peaches, grilled green beans, and white balsamic dressing with burrata

Any stone fruit plus green beans says July and August to us. We favor peaches for this because they have sweetness and acidity all in one package.

———————

Makes 2 to 4 servings

1 large ripe peach, halved and pitted

1 teaspoon ground Aleppo pepper

½ teaspoon ground cumin

Sea salt

Extra-virgin olive oil

Kosher salt

1 small bunch of green beans (we prefer haricots verts; they're smaller and more tender than regular green beans)

2 tablespoons White Balsamic Dressing (recipe follows)

2 (4-ounce) balls burrata

4 or 5 basil leaves, torn

Prepare a grill.

Season both cut sides of the peach halves with the Aleppo pepper, cumin, and a pinch of sea salt. Drizzle with just enough olive oil to coat.

On a hot grill or in a grill pan over high heat, cook the peach halves, cut-sides down, until the flesh starts to caramelize, about 1 minute. Remove and let cool.

Bring a small pot of water to a boil and fill a large bowl with ice water. When the water comes to a boil, season with the kosher salt and taste. It should be salty like the sea. Add the green beans and cook until they just begin to get tender but still have a nice crunch, 1 to 2 minutes. Remove them with a slotted spoon or strainer and plunge them into the ice water to cool. Remove them and let them dry on a kitchen towel or paper towels.

Cut the green beans into 2-inch pieces and cut the peach into ½-inch-thick slices. Combine the green beans and peach slices in a medium bowl and toss with the White Balsamic Dressing. Spoon over the burrata, garnish with the basil leaves, and serve.

WHITE BALSAMIC DRESSING

Nice and tart, this dressing needs something to balance it out—like roasted vegetables, meat, or even a rich cheese.

Makes about 1½ cups

2 stems basil

⅓ cup sliced shallots

2 teaspoons thyme

1 tablespoon honey

½ cup white balsamic vinegar

Pinch of sea salt

Freshly ground black pepper

¾ cup extra-virgin olive oil

Using a mortar and pestle, grind the basil stems into a paste.

Combine the basil paste, shallots, thyme, honey, vinegar, salt, and a few grinds of pepper in a blender, food processor, or large bowl and pulse or blend to combine. While the machine runs on low, or while whisking, slowly add the olive oil until emulsified. Adjust the seasoning to taste.

grilled cucumbers and zhoug with burrata

We make this in the fall, but the grilled cucumbers are so smoky good that you should make it year-round—that is, if you live somewhere you don't have to stand in snow to grill 4 months out of the year.

Makes 2 to 4 servings

1 English cucumber, halved lengthwise (we like these because they have nice small seeds that add texture)

3 tablespoons Zhoug (recipe follows)

Freshly squeezed lemon juice

2 (4-ounce) balls burrata

2 tablespoons toasted pumpkin seeds

Prepare a hot grill.

Char the cucumber heavily on the grill or on a grill pan over high heat until the flesh side starts to turn black, about 2 minutes. A little burnt on the edges is good—we like that. Once cool, slice the cucumber into ½-inch strips that are 2 to 3 inches long and toss with the Zhoug and a little lemon juice to taste. Spoon the mixture over the burrata and finish with the toasted pumpkin seeds.

ZHOUG

This is our version of the classic falafel-stand spicy sauce. Think of it as a Middle Eastern pesto. Use it with red meat, such as sirloin or ribeye, or with any roasted veggies.

Makes about 1½ cups

1 jalapeño, seeded

1 cup cilantro leaves

2 cloves garlic

½ teaspoon freshly ground black pepper

1 teaspoon ground cumin, toasted

¼ cup pumpkin seeds, toasted

2½ teaspoons sugar

¼ cup extra-virgin olive oil

1 tablespoon sherry vinegar

Zest and juice of 1 lime

Combine the jalapeño, cilantro, garlic, pepper, cumin, pumpkin seeds, sugar, oil, vinegar, and lime in a food processor and pulse until only a few chunks remain. It should look like a pesto when it's done. Store in an airtight container in the fridge for up to 3 days.

brussels sprouts, pear, fried shallot, and balsamic onion with burrata

Whenever frost is on the ground, Brussels, kale, and cabbage get a lot sweeter.

Makes 2 to 4 servings

1 white onion, peeled and sliced into 1-inch-thick rings

Extra-virgin olive oil

Sea salt

Freshly ground black pepper

2 teaspoons balsamic vinegar

1 pint Brussels sprouts, shaved very thinly with a mandoline

½ cup diced Bartlett pear

2 tablespoons thinly sliced Parmesan shards

2 tablespoons Fried Shallots (recipe follows)

1 tablespoon chopped parsley

2 tablespoons Lemon Vinaigrette (recipe follows)

Freshly squeezed lemon juice

2 (4-ounce) balls burrata

In a mixing bowl, toss the onion rings with just enough olive oil to coat and season with the salt and pepper.

In a large sauté pan over high heat, char the rings on both sides until black and the onion is beginning to get tender, 3 to 4 minutes a side. Transfer to a medium bowl and toss with the balsamic vinegar. Cover with plastic wrap and let the onion steam to cook all the way through, 5 minutes. When the onion rings are completely cool, chop them into small pieces.

In a medium bowl, toss together ⅓ cup of the balsamic onions with the Brussels sprouts, pear, Parmesan, shallots, parsley, and Lemon Vinaigrette. Season to taste, adding a squeeze of fresh lemon juice if the salad needs a little brightening. (Save leftover balsamic onions to use in a salad dressing or toss in the pan with roasting vegetables, such as broccoli or cauliflower). Spoon the salad over the burrata and serve.

FRIED SHALLOTS

We always have a stash of these on hand, but a lot of Asian grocery stores carry a fried shallot product that's pretty good, and it's totally fine to use that instead. Frying shallots can be a little tricky because if they're cut only slightly too thick, they won't stay nice and crispy.

Makes 1 cup

High smoking-point oil such as rice bran, sunflower, grapeseed, or peanut, for frying	6 whole shallots, thinly sliced ¼ cup Wondra flour

Heat a few inches of oil in a large pot or deep fryer to 250°F on a deep fat/candy thermometer. Line a plate with paper towels.

Place the shallots in a mixing bowl. Add the flour and toss to evenly coat.

Add the the shallots to the oil and fry until they stop bubbling, 2 to 3 minutes.

Using a slotted spoon, transfer the shallots from the oil to the paper towels to cool and drain. When completely cool, store the shallots in an airtight container at room temperature for up to 2 days.

LEMON VINAIGRETTE

This is an all-purpose dressing—use it on just about any salad, especially with lots of raw vegetables. The kiss of rice wine vinegar really makes the lemon pop.

Makes about 1 ½ cups

½ cup minced shallots

2 teaspoons thyme

Zest and juice of 2 lemons, plus 1 more just-in-case lemon

1 tablespoon rice wine vinegar

½ tablespoons honey

⅔ cup extra-virgin olive oil

Sea salt

Freshly ground black pepper

Mix everything in a bowl. Taste and adjust the seasonings, adding more salt, pepper, or lemon juice as needed. The dressing should be sweet and acidic. It will keep in an airtight container in the fridge for about 3 days. After that, the lemon flavor will start to fade.

alm salad

My next-door neighbor—who also happens to be a college buddy of mine—married a Bavarian woman, and her sister Christina runs an alm (a small hiker's hut up in the mountains) near the town of Scharnitz in the Austrian Alps. Her alm has an outdoor café attached where you can sit year-round and drink beer that was chilled in the small stream nearby and eat food prepared from their self-sustaining farm. When we went there, we got to cook a lot—trout from the stream and venison they'd hunted. And then there was this salad that Kristina made, which just exploded my brain. It was beautiful red tomatoes from her garden, pumpkin seeds, Austrian pumpkin seed oil, cheese that's made from a mixture of goat and cow's milk, vinegar, salt, and pepper.

Makes 2 to 4 servings

2 large, red farm or heirloom tomatoes

2 tablespoons red wine vinegar

1 tablespoon extra-virgin olive oil

1½ tablespoons pumpkin seed oil

Coarse gray salt or fleur de sel

2 scallions, white and green parts, thinly sliced

2 tablespoons toasted pumpkin seeds

¼ cup Farmer Cheese (recipe follows, or store-bought)

2 to 4 small handfuls arugula, or any other greens, such as watercress or miner's lettuce

---

Start by cutting the tomatoes into slices that are ⅓ inch thick and laying them down on a serving platter. Sprinkle them with the red wine vinegar, then the olive oil, and then the pumpkin seed oil. Give the tomatoes a generous seasoning of the coarse salt. This not only seasons but also gives crunch to the salad. If you put the salt on first, the vinegar may start to dissolve the salt. Sprinkle the tomatoes with the scallions, then the pumpkin seeds and Farmer Cheese. Pile the greens on top and serve.

FARMER CHEESE

This cheese is really straightforward to make: you take high-quality milk, bring it just to a boil, add vinegar to curdle it, scoop out the curds, and season them. The seasoned curds are the farmer cheese, and the liquid that remains when you scoop out the curds is the whey and can be used as the cooking liquid for polenta or grits or even for braising meat. Farmer cheese is a simple, supple cheese that lasts for weeks in the fridge and is good crumbled over meat, salads, and pasta. This recipe is about quality—use great milk, amazing vinegar, and high-fat butter, and the cheese will come out perfectly. We try to use goat's milk whenever we can, but cow's milk works, too. Sure, you could buy feta or farmer cheese, but if there's a guy at the market selling great milk, or even raw milk, why not buy it?

cont'd.

We recently made a batch of this cheese with brown butter and horseradish. Super tasty.

Makes about 3 cups

1 gallon goat's or cow's milk or a blend of the two

¾ cup apple cider vinegar

½ cup unsalted butter

⅓ bunch sage, leaves picked from stems

Rice bran oil, for frying

Zest and juice of 3 lemons

Sea salt

In a heavy pot over medium heat, bring the milk to 195°F on an instant-read thermometer. Slowly whisk in the vinegar until small curds start to form. This should be fairly instant. Remove the pot from the heat and let it sit for 30 minutes.

Pour the mixture through a fine-mesh strainer and let it cool completely.

Heat a large sauté pan over medium heat and add the butter. Heat the butter while stirring until the milk solids separate and start to brown, 5 to 7 minutes. After the butter starts to bubble and turns a light almost-caramel color, remove the pan from the heat but continue stirring as you pour the butter into a nonreactive bowl. Set aside to cool.

Lastly, fry the sage. Heat the oil in a small pan over high heat, add the sage, and fry for 1 to 2 minutes or until all the moisture in the sage has been cooked out. You'll notice that the sage will bubble like crazy around the edges at first and then taper off—that's when you know to pull it out. Transfer the sage to a paper towel to cool.

Once the curds, brown butter, and sage are cool, mix them all together in a large bowl. Add the lemon zest and juice and season with salt. The cheese will keep in an airtight container in the fridge for up to 1 week.

little gem salad

So maybe a Little Gem salad is cliché at this point, but this has been on our menu from the very beginning, and it's the ultimate example of our mission to do the family-restaurant classics, like Caesar salad, in a bigger, better way. We take our croutons, crush 'em up, and toss 'em in the salad, so just about every bite has crunch. I love croutons—especially when they're fresh and soaked with olive oil and herbs—and a lot of them. So we indulge my crouton obsession by making small crumbles that get into every bite. And then we thought it would be novel—though, again, maybe a little cliché at this point (and completely optional)—to put a fried pig's ear on top, to make up for the hidden croutons. Then we drench the whole thing in buttermilk crème fraîche dressing so it's slightly gloppy, maybe even overdressed.

———————

To make the dressing: Add all the ingredients to a bowl and mix until combined. Season to taste with salt and pepper. Set aside.

To make the salad: Remove the leaves of lettuce from the heads and place in a large serving bowl. Add the fennel, radish, basil, and bread crumbs and mix together. Pour over the dressing and toss to coat—the salad should be heavily dressed. Top with the fried pig's ear and serve.

BREAD CRUMBS

We really like making our bread crumbs like this. Heating the herbes de Provence in the butter and oil brings out the herbs' aroma, which isn't too overpowering—just nice and toasty and great as a base for topping with other flavors. Toss them into salads or over anything that might need a little crunch, such as grilled meat or fish.

Makes 1½ cups

3 tablespoons unsalted butter

3 tablespoons extra-virgin olive oil

2 teaspoons herbes de Provence

Sea salt

6 slices Spence Sourdough (page 282, or store-bought sourdough bread)

Preheat the oven to 350°F.

In a large heavy-bottomed sauté pan over medium heat, combine the butter and olive oil. Add the herbes de Provence. Season with salt to taste.

Makes 4 servings

BUTTERMILK DRESSING

1 cup buttermilk

¼ cup crème fraîche

1 shallot, minced

2 tablespoons 12-year-aged moscatel vinegar

½ tablespoon extra-virgin olive oil

Sea salt

Freshly ground black pepper

SALAD

4 heads Little Gem lettuce, washed

1 small bulb fennel, halved lengthwise, cored, and thinly sliced

3 healthy-size watermelon or French breakfast radishes, thinly sliced

12 basil leaves, torn

Bread Crumbs (recipe follows)

1 Fried Pig's Ear (recipe follows)

cont'd.

Remove the crust from the Sourdough Bread (it doesn't have to be perfect; you can leave some on there) and tear the slices into bite-size pieces. Put the bread in the bowl and toss to coat with the herbed liquid. Place the bread on a baking sheet and toast in the oven for 10 to 12 minutes, until golden brown.

Transfer the bread to a food processer. Blend the bread into crumbs, then transfer them back to the baking sheet. Toast for 3 to 5 minutes, until golden brown and crunchy. The bread crumbs will keep for up to 3 days in an airtight container.

FRIED PIG'S EAR

We like to think of these as croutons. You can put them on almost any salad for a nice, meaty crunch. These take all day (or night) to cook, so plan ahead.

Makes 4 pig ears

1 fresh bay leaf or 2 dried bay leaves

4 raw pig ears

1 white onion, coarsely chopped

1 carrot, coarsely chopped

2 celery stalks, coarsely chopped

2 sprigs thyme

2 dried chiles de árbol

3 cups Pork Stock (page 65) or water (optional)

Vegetable oil, for frying

Sea salt

Preheat the oven to 300°F.

Using tongs, run the fresh bay leaf through the flame on your stove or toast in a dry cast-iron skillet over high heat for a few seconds, until it is aromatic and shiny. If using dried bay leaves, skip this step.

Add the bay leaf, pig ears, onion, carrot, celery, thyme, and chiles to a stockpot and add stock or water. Bring to a simmer over medium heat, then cover the pot first with plastic wrap then with aluminum foil and transfer to the oven. (Yes, the plastic wrap is fine to use in a 300°F oven.) Cook for 8 hours.

Line a plate with parchment paper, lay the ears on the prepared plate, and let cool.

cont'd.

Preheat a deep fryer or a few inches of oil in a heavy pot to 350°F on a deep-fat/candy thermometer.

Slice the ears into ¼-inch strips and fry until golden brown and crispy. Season with salt. Raw pigs' ears can be stored for up to 5 days in the fridge; once cooked, they should be eaten the same day.

PORK STOCK

We use this as our default stock. It has just the right amount of meatiness.

Makes 4 quarts

10 pounds pork bones

2 tablespoons water

4 yellow onions, large diced

3 carrots, large diced

1 bunch celery, large diced

4 bay leaves

5 sprigs thyme

2 tablespoons black peppercorns

Preheat the oven to 450°F.

Arrange the pork bones in a single layer on a baking sheet, dividing them between two pans if necessary. Place the bones in the oven for 60 to 90 minutes, turning every 20 to 30 minutes to ensure even browning. Transfer the bones to a large pot. Immediately deglaze the baking pan(s) with the water, scraping up the extra bits with a wooden spoon. Pour the deglazing liquid over the pork bones.

Add the onions, carrots, celery, bay leaves, thyme, peppercorns, and 6 quarts of cold water to the pot and cover. Bring the stock to a boil and immediately decrease the heat to a simmer. Simmer for 6 to 8 hours, skimming any scum from the surface of the stock and adding water as needed to keep the bones submerged. Strain through a fine mesh strainer and chill. Store leftover stock in the fridge for up to 1 week.

TOASTING FRESH BAY LEAVES

Fresh bay leaves are increasing available in the herbs section at markets and are what we prefer to use. To use a fresh bay leaf, hold it in tongs and run it through the flame on your stove or toast it in a dry cast-iron skillet over high heat for a few seconds, which will help bring out its oils and add a ton of flavor to whatever you're adding it to. You'll hear some popping as the leaf heats up, and that's okay.

FRIENDS OF THE PUBLICAN
Dave Cleverdon, Kinnikinnick Farm

Dave Cleverdon has been such an important part of our lineage at the restaurant, and in my career. And he says the same thing about us, which is pretty neat. Dave is sort of an accidental farmer—he retired from the Chicago Board of Trade in 1988, sent his last kid off to school, and in 1994 decided to buy a rundown farmstead with not much more farming experience than tending a backyard garden. He just wanted to work "where culture and nature met," as he puts it. The farm is a seriously beautiful plot of land overlooking the north branch of the Kinnikinnick Creek in northern Illinois, and even though it didn't have the sandy soil that's ideal for growing and he had no idea what he'd ultimately end up using the land for, as he says, he has "managed to get things out of the ground just fine."

That's pretty much the understatement of all time. Dave's produce—all certified organic—caught the eye of Brian Wolf at the Evanston's Farmers' Market, and by '98, Dave was selling to us directly at Blackbird. I loved that he focused on a really small palette of products—arugula, Italian braising greens (which are now my obsession), sunchokes, tomatoes, leeks, the best asparagus ever. . . . By the time we opened The Publican, I asked if he could maybe do his regular salad greens mix with a slightly tougher leaf, something that would really hold up to a creamy dressing. Sure enough, he came back to me with incredible Gem lettuces that have small, tight heads with crunchy leaves and all these nooks and crannies that just cradle the dressing without wilting down into nothing. He changed his entire style of production for us. On our end, it led to our menu staple, the Little Gem Salad, and for Dave, it led to selling thousands of these mini heads every week.

Dave and I have had our share of adventures over the years: We did an early California Outstanding in the Field dinner together (when Alice Waters calls to ask if you're interested, you say "Hell yes." . . . it's still the best OITF dinner EVER). He used to have these epic Labor Day parties at Kinnikinnick with tents and a giant bonfire. He always wanted it to be more than a farm, which is why you can now stay for the weekend in these elegantly rustic tents—or at least you can try, because they start booking on a Friday in February, and by the following Tuesday, they're full booked for the season.

chicories with pecorino and creamy anchovy vinaigrette

Serves 4 to 6

SALAD

1 head escarole

2 tablespoons fines herbes (see note, opposite)

3 tablespoons pecorino shards

¼ red onion, thinly sliced

CREAMY ANCHOVY VINAIGRETTE

1 egg yolk

⅓ cup freshly squeezed lemon juice

⅓ cup champagne vinegar

1 shallot, coarsely chopped

1½ tablespoons granulated sugar

1 tablespoon lemon zest

5 brown anchovies, rinsed and patted dry

5 white anchovies

1¼ cups grapeseed oil

Sea salt

Freshly ground black pepper

I'm kind of obsessed with chicories, so when I go visit friends of ours who have an olive oil farm in Pitigliano—in southern Tuscany—I always visit their sort-of Italian version of our home and garden store, Mills Fleet Farm, where I buy basic Italian country stuff like farm boots and a whole bunch of seeds to plant in my garden. I bring back all kinds of chicories, or bitter greens and lettuces, which I pick on the younger side—so I have lots of the tender light-green leaves that grow right at the heart—and then lightly dress with a creamy dressing that's heavy on anchovies. This recipe is our nod to that.

COSMO We're chicory-deprived in this country, and we're trying to change that. Why you would want any other kind of lettuce is beyond us—it's like romaine on crack. You don't need to do much more to it than add a little Parm or pecorino with lemon juice and olive oil, but we take things a step farther for this salad. The recipe differs depending on who you ask for it, though. I like a nice mix of gorgeous chicories, but Paul likes it with just one variety (using more than that reminds him of his disdain for mesclun mix). So for Paul's sake, we wrote this recipe with escarole hearts, his favorite. Then we give it a classic egg yolk–based anchovy dressing, like a Caesar. This is also great on top of Porchetta (page 187) or really rich pork belly, especially in the fall or winter.

———————

To make the salad: Start by cleaning the escarole. Fill a large bowl with cool water. Cut off the root end and pull apart the leaves and place in the water. Rinse the leaves well in the water, especially if they're from the farmers' market and not the triple-washed stuff from the store. Taste one to make sure it's not still gritty. To dry the leaves, lay them flat on dry towels or use a salad spinner. At the restaurant, we reserve all the heavier dark-green leaves for staff meal and only use the tender lime-green hearts for this salad, but you can use the whole head of lettuce if you want. Instead of using a knife to cut the leaves into bite-size pieces—which makes the lettuce wilt more quickly—tear it with your hands. You'll get a crisper, fresher salad. In a large bowl, combine the lettuce with the herbs, cheese, and the onion.

While the leaves dry, make the dressing: Combine all the ingredients except the oil, salt, and pepper in a food processor, blender, or large bowl. Mix well, and with the blender still running—or while whisking—slowly, drizzle in the oil until completely incorporated. Set aside.

Toss the salad with about ⅓ cup of dressing—it should coat the leaves a little more than a normal dressing would, as for a Caesar salad. Leftover dressing can be stored in an airtight container in the refrigerator for 5 to 6 days. Season the salad with salt and pepper to taste and serve.

FINES HERBES

Fines herbes is a fancy way of saying equal-parts mix of finely minced parsley, chives, tarragon, and chervil.

asparagus and avocado salad with fried quinoa and flaxseed vinaigrette

Makes 4 servings

2 small fennel bulbs, halved lengthwise and cored

Sea salt

2 lemons, cut in half

½ cup quinoa

1 cup water

2 bunches asparagus

Freshly ground black pepper

2 tablespoons extra-virgin olive oil

Vegetable oil, for frying

2 firm-ripe avocados

Maldon or gray salt

1 cup sliced spring onion

6 tablespoons sesame seeds, toasted

6 tablespoons sunflower seeds, toasted

Flaxseed-Tahini Vinaigrette (recipe follows)

2 bunches pea shoots

¼ cup coarsely chopped curly parsley

Finishing olive oil

This salad is basically a bunch of our obsessions on a plate: First there's my fixation on the combination of grilled and raw, so we grill some of the asparagus and shave the rest into thin ribbons. There's the creamy, spicy flaxseed vinaigrette, which we came up with at our butcher shop, Publican Quality Meats, as a dressing for one of our vegan sandwiches that we worked on for months, and we thought it ended up being pretty much the best thing ever. And I always have to have something crunchy, so we threw in some fried quinoa. Then we just layer everything up and let people dig through it.

COSMO This recipe was partially inspired by Nick Balla and Cortney Burns, when they were the chefs at San Francisco's Bar Tartine. They came out to do a dinner with us and served a layered salad with sweet potatoes and avocado—a combination that didn't seem like it would make any sense—and it blew our minds. Since then, we've always run some sort of layered salad, and this is one of our favorites. It's also partially inspired by the avocados we get at The Publican. I once asked Mud Creek Ranch, one of our citrus purveyors in Santa Paula, California, if they had any avocados, and they sent me a list of *sixteen different kinds*—Fuerte, Gem, Nabal, Rincon, even Bacon avocados. We ended up ordering a bunch of Pinkertons, which, unlike the Hass variety we're all getting from Mexico, don't turn brown after you slice them. They are insanely good, but pretty hard to find outside of California (unless, like Suzanne Goin, you know a guy . . .). If you're in California, look for them at restaurants and markets—you have to try them.

This salad has a bunch of components, but once you get each one prepped, it just takes a minute to put the whole thing together.

Start by marinating the fennel: Using a mandoline or your knife, shave the fennel as thinly as possible and place in a bowl. Season with a pinch of salt and squeeze of lemon juice and let it sit for 20 minutes.

Add the quinoa to a small pot, add the water and a pinch of salt, and simmer until tender, 12 to 15 minutes. Strain and let cool in a bowl.

If grilling the asparagus, prepare a hot grill. Snap off the bottom of each stalk of asparagus, which is too woody and fibrous to eat. Take half of the asparagus and toss it with salt, pepper, and just enough olive oil to coat.

Cook the asparagus over high heat on the grill or in a hot cast-iron pan until almost tender, 1 to 2 minutes. Transfer the cooked asparagus to a plate and let it cool while you use a peeler to peel the other half of the asparagus into thin ribbons. Set aside.

Preheat a deep fryer or a few inches of oil in a heavy pot to 350°F on a deep-fat/candy thermometer. Place about 2 tablespoons of cooked quinoa in a small fine-mesh sieve or chinois, lower it into the hot oil, and fry until crispy and golden, 3 to 4 minutes, stirring constantly to prevent clumping. Let the quinoa cool in a bowl before serving. (The leftover un-fried quinoa will keep in the fridge for up to 1 week.)

Halve, pit, and peel the avocados, then slice into 1/4-inch slices and lay them flat over the entire plate or platter. Season with the coarse sea salt, pepper, and a squeeze of lemon juice.

Evenly spread the cooked and shaved asparagus over the avocado. Do the same thing with the marinated fennel, spring onion, and sesame and sunflower seeds. Season with more coarse sea salt, pepper, and lemon juice.

Pour about a 1/2 cup of the dressing evenly over the salad so you will get some with every bite. Sprinkle the pea shoots, fried quinoa, and parsley on top, along with some good finishing olive oil.

FLAXSEED-TAHINI VINAIGRETTE

This dressing can be used on a lot of different things—we love it on beets and even on sirloin.

Makes about 2 cups

1/4 cup soy sauce or gluten-free soy sauce or Bragg's Liquid Aminos

1/4 cup Bragg's apple cider vinegar

5 tablespoons tahini paste

1/4 cup sesame oil

2 tablespoons flaxseed oil

1/4 cup maple syrup

2 tablespoons diced fresh ginger

3 cloves garlic

1 cup coarsely chopped scallion tops

Sea salt

2 tablespoons water

Combine all the ingredients in a blender and blend on high for 1 minute. Taste and adjust the seasoning if necessary. The dressing will keep in a tightly closed jar in the fridge for up to 10 days.

honeycrisp apple and kohlrabi salad
with burnt chile chimichurri

Serves 2 to 4

½ cup good ricotta

Sea salt

Freshly ground
black pepper

Whole milk (optional)

1 Honeycrisp apple,
cored and cut into
irregular-size pieces

⅓ cup peeled and
diced kohlrabi (about
1 small bulb)

⅓ cup seeded
and thinly sliced
cucumber

3 tablespoons toasted
pumpkin seeds

3 tablespoons Burnt
Chile Chimichurri
(recipe follows)

1 lemon wedge
(optional)

COSMO We get our apples from a local celebrity. Susie Differding at Timeless Prairie Orchard in central Illinois has won first place at the Illinois State Fair for Best Overall Apple three years in a row and even won a special award for winning the most blue ribbons—two years in a row. She grows twenty-three different varieties at her farm, which is great for us because we're pretty nuts about apples, too. When they're in season, there's an apple salad on all of our menus, from a more classic version at avec to less traditional versions like this one.

This is the kind of salad you serve with a spoon. It airs on the side of overdressed—we call it "wet"—so the combined juices of the apples, cucumber, and Burnt Chile Chimichurri soak into the ricotta.

The apples we love most are the ones with texture, like Honeycrisps, Mutsu, or any tart green apple that's in season. We like to pair them with kohlrabi because it has an apple-like quality but is firmer and more savory. The key thing for this salad is the ricotta. We get a really special one from Bellwether Farms in Sonoma County, California. Its fat content is through the roof, making it really rich and creamy. It's worth finding the best possible quality you can find—the hand-dipped stuff is really good, and they sell it in most markets now, or you could make your own. If you start off with a really good apple and really good ricotta, then you're going to end up with a really good salad.

Start by making sure the ricotta is seasoned well; taste it and add salt and pepper. If the mixture is stiff, thin it out with a spoonful of milk. It should be really creamy. Set aside.

Combine the apple, kohlrabi, cucumber, and pumpkin seeds in a medium bowl. Toss, season with salt and pepper, and drizzle in the chimichurri. The salad will be almost overdressed. Taste again and decide if you want to add a squeeze of lemon juice as sometimes that's just what this salad needs.

To serve, place the ricotta on the bottom of a plate or bowl and heap the salad over the top. Be sure to serve it with a spoon.

BURNT CHILE CHIMICHURRI

COSMO When I was trying to interpret the recipe for Doug Bigwood's Salmon Frames (page 249), I happened to be reading a bunch of Thai cookbooks. I noticed that they always burn their chiles to make them really dark and fragrant, and I found that blasting 'em in the oven gives them a really nutty character that not only adds heat to a dish but richness, too, without the acrid bitterness that you'd expect. Now we try to use burnt chiles whenever we can, especially to season fish or meat and always in our version of chimichurri.

Makes about 1 cup

8 dried dried chiles de árbol

1 bunch parsley, finely chopped

1 bunch cilantro, finely chopped

3 tablespoons capers, rinsed and chopped

1 teaspoon red pepper flakes

2 cloves garlic, minced

1½ tablespoons red wine vinegar

2 teaspoons fish sauce

Zest and juice of 1 lime

½ cup olive oil

Sea salt

Freshly ground black pepper

Preheat the oven to 450°F and open a kitchen window (because the smoke from the blackening chiles can cause some serious coughing).

Place the chiles on a baking sheet and cook in the oven until they burn and turn black, 4 to 5 minutes. Remove them and let them cool.

Remove the stems and blend them into a powder using a spice grinder. Discard any large pieces that remain.

Combine 1 tablespoon of the chile powder with the parsley, cilantro, capers, pepper flakes, garlic, vinegar, fish sauce, and lime zest and juice in a mortar and pestle. Work the mixture really hard, slowly adding the olive oil as you go. It should come out looking like a thick green salsa. Season with salt and pepper to taste. Store any leftovers in your fridge for up to a couple of days.

plum and dandelion greens salad with urfa pepper vinaigrette

Cosmo's big thing is "You gotta try this; try this; try this." He sometimes comes at me like an electrified dog with a great product, like a sudachi lime or shiro dashi or Blain Farms' pecans. I've been walking down the street and seen Cosmo out of the corner of my eye running across the street with a spoonful of something for me to taste. A lot of times I then say, "Hey, Ryan [Pfeiffer], you gotta get those limes over at Blackbird" or "Perry [Hendrix], let's think about calling those avocado guys at Mud Creek Ranch." (And, of course, they inspire parts of the menu at The Publican, too). In the early days, I fancied myself an ingredient guy—a kind of forager and gardener—and I still do, but I don't have time to go out and find new products. Now Cosmo drives a lot of the product and creativity in our organization. So when he asked me to try one of Penryn Orchard's green gauge plums—which are only in season for, like, a week and are difficult to get outside of California, but they still certainly merit us talking about them—I knew he was on to something really great. Hands-down, they're the best thing ever. The skin is really tart, the flesh is really sweet, and there's no mush to them at all. They're super-meaty and snap like a hot dog when you bite into one. And they're this really beautiful neon green.

It also happens that they're in season when we host the big fund-raiser for Alex's Lemonade Stand to raise money for pediatric cancer research. The first year the event was in town, we wanted to invite some of the participating chefs to have dinner at The Publican the night before. I told Cosmo—who'd been chef de cuisine for about six months at that point—that about ten chefs were coming. Then it was twenty. Then it was basically all of them. We're talking thirty of the greatest chefs—Marc Vetri, Sean Brock, Stu Brioza, Michael Tusk, Jonathon Sawyer, Donald Link, John Besh—coming in. Heavy hitters. No pressure, Cosmo. He did this salad, though, and people went berserk. After dinner, they were taking these plums out of the walk-in and just eating them.

Now the salad's become a staple on the menu, and we keep it really simple—just some pine nuts and a little Urfa pepper, which is a Turkish pepper that's more fruity than spicy with really base, guttural, earthy notes; kind of like Aleppo pepper. It's rich, too, so it makes for a great balance of flavor with the tart plums. And it's also one of the only peppers you can leave kind of coarse, like coffee grounds, for added texture.

Serves 2 to 4

4 Green Gauge or Santa Rosa plums, pitted and cut into bite-size pieces

Sea salt

Juice of 1 lemon

3 tablespoons Pine Nut Relish (recipe follows)

1 shallot, sliced in rings

1 small bunch dandelion greens

1½ tablespoons Urfa Pepper Vinaigrette (recipe follows)

CHOOSING PLUMS

The only thing comparable to a green gauge plum is a Santa Rosa, which is what we call for because the salad will still turn out really well. You could also use a Mirabel, an Italian plum, or even pluots—any good stone fruit, really.

cont'd.

Toss the plums with salt to taste, lemon juice, and the Pine Nut Relish.

In a medium bowl, dress the shallots and greens with the vinaigrette.

To serve, arrange the plums on a platter and top with the greens.

PINE NUT RELISH

This is almost like an *aillade,* which is the French word for a thick nut dressing. You get rich, creamy, crunchy, and tart all in the same relish.

Makes about 3 1/2 cups

1 cup toasted pine nuts	1/3 cup Bragg's apple cider vinegar
1 cup extra-virgin olive oil	Zest and juice of 1 lemon
1/2 cup diced shallots	Sea salt
1 tablespoon Hatch chile powder	

Using a mortar and pestle, mash the pine nuts into a chunky paste. Slowly add the olive oil while still mashing. It's important to add the oil to the nuts while mashing because the nuts will get gummy if mashed without it. Transfer the mixture to a bowl and stir in the shallots, chile powder, vinegar, and lemon zest and juice. Season to taste with salt. Cover tightly and store in the fridge for up to 2 days.

URFA PEPPER VINAIGRETTE

This dressing is really good on meat and fish and great with sweeter veggies, like ripe tomatoes and roasted summer squash.

Makes about 2 cups

1/2 cup diced shallots	Zest and juice of 2 lemons
1/2 tablespoon neonata (see page 28)	1/4 cup fish sauce
2 1/2 tablespoons sugar	2/3 cup extra-virgin olive oil
2 tablespoons Urfa pepper	Sea salt

Mix everything except the salt together in a bowl. Season to taste and store in the fridge for up to 3 days.

Henry Brockman, Henry's Farm

Along with the guys at Nichols and Kinnikinnick farms, Henry Brockman of Henry's Farm, about 2 hours away from Chicago, is one of our core farmers. His vegetables are always the irregular, warty ones—nothing's perfectly shaped because he's using heirloom seeds and not growing industrialized varieties that all look the same and have been sprayed with ten different kinds of pesticides. If you walk into his booth at the Evanston Farmers' Market when lettuce season starts, the experience is like one described in an Alice Waters's book. Sometimes there's even a sign that says, "The Amazing Wall of Lettuce." People assume that all lettuces taste the same, but—when they're grown well—they're just as different as tomatoes or peppers. Plus, he grows stuff that other people don't, like chicories, burdock root, tatsoi, and one of my favorites— agretti, a kind of wispy-looking green that people in Tuscany poach with their pasta and toss with salsa verde. At the restaurant, we never have to say, "Hey, you gotta be the guy to go to the market today." Someone always just goes because they want to buy from Henry. It happened organically, passing from one chef to the next, starting with Brian Wolfe to Dylan Fultineer to Brian Huston and then to Cosmo. Now, every Saturday, Cosmo's like, "Hey, you gotta see what I got from Henry," and it'll be laid out nicely on sheet pans. It's the kind of produce that inspires you to treat it like that.

Product grown in a socially, economically, and environmentally sustainable way has been a heavy-duty credo for us, and it's why we work with the purveyors we do. But Henry goes above and beyond—as a farmer and a parent who cares deeply about the state of the planet he's leaving for his kids. He doesn't just grow without pesticides, he also lets half of his land lay fallow for two years under a cover crop, which means the soil microbes and fungi can re-establish themselves before a new crop-for-sale is farmed. It's better for the plants, it's better for the soil, and it's definitely better for us because it means more flavorful, nutrient-dense vegetables. In the coming years, he plans to scale back his growing so he can focus on using nothing but renewable energy sources—no more gas, no more oil. It might mean fewer vegetables for us, but ultimately we're pretty excited to go along for the ride in what is undoubtedly a journey that lets us do what we do with a clear conscience.

To Bivalves, Mollusks,
and Those Who Shell Before Us

From ocean's depth
  netted, assessed
A bounty aquatic
  by watery largess
Octopus, Squid;
Scallop & Clam
[Neptune's alternative
to Ham or Lamb].
Mussel or Snail
  not bigger than a dime
From "Sea-to-Table":
    A NEW
par—a—digm

The original Publican menu was organized by dishes based on items that had not been manipulated in any way—ingredients whose deliciousness we couldn't take any credit for—to those that we put a lot of ourselves into. The meat column was topped by things like hams and charcuterie, while the opener on the seafood side was oysters. We'd get 'em in, pop 'em, and serve 'em. Maybe with a squeeze of lemon, maybe with a little verjus mignonette, but most important was finding the highest quality oysters, sent directly from the source, and served icy cold. Thanks to Island Creek Oysters, we now have our own proprietary oyster—the Tumblekin (rhymes with Publican)—but more on that in a bit.

This practice of highlighting the ingredient—and being more than happy to not take credit for something that came in tasting as good as it does— is perhaps most apparent in our shellfish and seafood dishes. We aren't waiting around for distributors to send us items that have been sitting in a warehouse for two or three days or that they need to unload because it's the oldest product. We decided from almost Day One—thanks enormously to Erling Wu-Bower, and then Cosmo, whose relationships with people and places like Monterey Bay Fish, Sue Buxton, Peter Stocks at Calendar Island Mussels, Red's Best, Skip Bennett at Island Creek Oyster Company, and Michael Passmore of Passmore Ranch—that we'd much rather take the extra time and energy, cut out the middle man, and go directly to the source. The difference? The only thing between your plate and the water is maybe a few hours with FedEx and a day or two in our walk-in.

We realize that you might not be able to call up Sue in Stonington, Maine, and place your order for halibut. But you *can* ask your fishmonger to order from any of our suppliers. And for God's sake, don't just make these recipes with any old seafood that's laying around in the case. Demand good product. We promise it's worth it.

THE PUBLICAN OYSTER

A few years ago, we were in Miami for the South Beach Wine & Food Festival. We'd wrapped up for the day—I was hanging out with Jonathan Waxman (the two old guys gotta stick together), while Cosmo was running with the cool kids, drinking whiskey and shucking oysters. Later that night, Cosmo told me that these same guys are the ones who run one of our favorite companies we do business with, Island Creek Oysters. I'd never met them in person, and after we were introduced, they told me how much they love us and how they'd "do anything for us." *Anything?* I went home that night and kept thinking about that. *Anything?* Anything. The next morning I asked Chris Sherman, the president of Island Creek, if they'd plant a proprietary oyster for us. And it was on.

We flew out to Duxbury, Massachusetts, to plant thousands of dime-size oyster "seeds." Skip Bennett, Island Creek's founder (an industry trailblazer we talk more about on page 103), transferred the seeds to SEAPA baskets, that he'd learned about from Australian aquaculture techniques. The oysters float on a line and really tumble in the waves, which gives them cleaner flavor and nice, deep cups. Fast-forward to this past spring, when we went out to see the fruits of our labor. The tide had gone out, leaving hundreds of baskets of oysters exposed. There were ours and another variety Skip had planted, called Aunt Dotties, after the aunt who had owned his small cottage on the Saquish sandspit that overlooks the bay. It was about 8 AM, and there we were, standing around in our waders, cracking open oysters, and eating just about the best breakfast you could have. The guys at Island Creek nicknamed our oysters Tumblekins—a nod to their rough and tumble life so far and, of course, The Publican.

BEER FLIGHT

n ——6.40%
wery, Bend, Oregon
ican stout

k ——7.50%
Co., Paso Robles, California
dia pale ale

California

s ——5.50%
bs, Andechs, Germany
zen

Germany

312-733-9555

*the*PUBLICAN

shrimp ceviche with the best homemade crackers

COSMO I got married in Los Barriles, Mexico, a tiny fishing town about an hour north of Cabo San Lucas. The people there for the wedding were just about the only people in town, and for meals we'd take over one of the little restaurants (or open-air thatched-roof huts) on the beach. One day for lunch we ordered ceviche, and they threw a bunch of shrimp into this soupy pico de gallo mixture along with some Saltines. It was the best ceviche I'd ever had—sweet and acidic and spicy—all the flavors I love. And the Saltines made a nice vessel for eating the shrimp, while soaking up all the juices. We pretty much ordered it every day and, because we knew it would take an hour to make, we'd order, go shopping at the market, and come back right when it was ready.

This recipe is our ode to Baja-style ceviche, which has a more tomato-y base than other versions, but it has the same classic, acidic flavor. You almost want to make the dish too acidic because the tomatoes and shrimp are so sweet and the jalapeño is spicy. That's sort of our core motto: When you put in a little too much of everything, it balances perfectly. The liquid is so good that we use it to marinate pretty much every fish we serve as ceviche. You could also leave out the fish sauce and add some tequila for a Bloody Mary base.

We get our fresh shrimp from Indiana. What?! It's because Purdue University got an aquaculture grant to study shrimp farming, and the project was so successful that people from both coasts came to learn from them. The shrimp from Purdue are pretty special. When we can't get Indiana shrimp, we buy American gulf shrimp (if you don't buy American, keep in mind that the shrimp industry in Indonesia is a giant polluter). You could make this dish with any shrimp, but the whole point of ceviche is highlighting how good and fresh the shrimp are, which you can taste when they are just lightly pickled. And while we never buy frozen, you can. Just let the shrimp sit in the marinade a little longer—even as long as overnight—so the acid can cook them all the way through. We like to use head-on shrimp and fry up the heads for added shrimpiness, but if you prefer to skip all that, buy the same amount of 20/30-count shrimp instead.

Make the ceviche liquid: In a large bowl, combine the onion, jalapeño, fish sauce, ketchup, lime zest and juice, vinegar, tomato juice, sugar, and cilantro.

Makes 6 to 8 servings

CEVICHE LIQUID

1 cup diced red onion

1 jalapeño chile, stemmed and slivered (seeds included)

½ cup fish sauce

1¼ cups ketchup

Zest and juice of 4 limes, plus more if desired

½ cup red wine vinegar

1½ cups tomato juice

⅓ cup sugar

½ bunch cilantro, chopped

Sea salt

2 pounds (16/20) fresh shrimp, shelled

1 avocado, pitted and cut into bite-size pieces

2 cups sungold cherry tomatoes, halved

1 serrano chile, stemmed and sliced

Sea salt

Freshly ground black pepper

½ cup extra-virgin olive oil

½ cup cilantro leaves

Best Homemade Crackers (recipe follows)

cont'd.

Season with salt to taste—the finished product should be sweet, spicy, and sour. You can add the juice and zest of another lime if you think it needs more flavor.

Add the shrimp to the ceviche liquid and let them sit for at least 1 hour in the fridge. The shrimp should be opaque and firm.

Transfer the shrimp to a serving plate and top with the avocado, tomatoes, and serrano. Season the ceviche with salt and pepper, then pour the olive oil over it. Set aside.

Sprinkle cilantro over the ceviche and serve with the crackers.

BEST HOMEMADE CRACKERS

I developed this recipe at Blackbird years ago, and it made its way over to The Publican to serve with oysters. They're a thin, herb-y cracker.

Makes about 50 crackers

1 teaspoon active dry yeast

½ teaspoon sugar

1 cup plus 2 tablespoons warm water

3½ cups plus ½ tablespoon all-purpose flour

⅓ cup extra-virgin olive oil

1 teaspoon salt

1 teaspoon minced fresh chives

1 teaspoon tarragon leaves

In a large bowl, dissolve the yeast and sugar in the warm water. Whisk in 1⅓ cups of the flour until fully incorporated, cover loosely with plastic wrap, and set in a warm spot to let rise for 1 hour.

Use your hands to knead in the remaining flour, as well as the olive oil, salt, chives, and tarragon. Cover and set aside to rise for 1 more hour. Oil two baking sheets.

Preheat the oven to 350°F. Liberally oil two baking sheets.

Turn the dough out onto a floured surface and divide in half. Using a rolling pin, roll out one half of the dough as thinly as possible, until almost transparent. Transfer the sheet of dough to one baking sheet. The dough should cover most of the pan. Repeat for the remaining half of the dough. Bake for 15 to 20 minutes, until golden. Remove the pan from the oven and let cool. Break the sheets into cracker-size shards. The crackers will stay crisp in an airtight container for up to 4 days.

PRODUCT MAKETH THE DISH

We don't recommend opening this cookbook—or any other, for that matter—saying, "Oh, I'm going to make mussels for this party," then buying any shellfish you can find. Product should be what inspires you to cook a great-sounding dish—not the other way around. The key ingredient for our mussels, first and foremost, is great mussels. And the same thing goes for just about every other recipe in this book. The great veg/chicken/pork/fish/cheese is what makes our dishes stand out. Don't settle for out-of-season mussels, which have a tendency to be tiny or shriveled like fava beans, flavorless, or stink even when they're fresh. We love our rope-culture mussels from Peter Stocks and his company, Calendar Island, in Maine (page 95). Those mussels have been out of the water for only a day or two before they hit the plate (versus commercial varieties that sit around much longer before they even get to the store). If you can't get your hands on theirs, just be sure to demand the best from your fishmonger. Feel and smell your mussels before you buy them; they should smell like the sea and be heavy—which means they'll be nice and plump and meaty when cooked.

mussels in sour beer

Just after we came up with the idea for The Publican, a few of the chefs started coming over to my house to play around with different dishes, trying them over and over again until we got it right. We probably went through fifty or sixty mussel preparations, riffing on the traditional white wine version but also experimenting with other spirits. The winner was a variation using Gueuze (sounds like *gooze*), a sour Belgian beer that's a little cidery and a little musty and has just the right amount of acidity that we balance with a good amount of butter, garlic, thyme, and chile flakes.

Serves 4

2 tablespoons unsalted butter

1 tablespoon sliced celery

1 tablespoon sliced garlic

1 tablespoon sliced shallot

1 bay leaf

1 teaspoon thyme leaves

½ teaspoon chile flakes

2 pounds mussels

¼ cup Gueuze beer

Sea salt

1 tablespoon freshly squeezed lemon juice

2 tablespoons chopped celery leaves or lovage

Baguette, for serving

In a medium pot—ideally something ceramic or cast-iron that can go right onto the table—heat 1 tablespoon of the butter over high heat. When the butter foams, add the celery, garlic, shallot, bay leaf, thyme, and chile flakes and sweat for 1 minute.

Add the mussels to the pot, flip all the ingredients together, pour in the Gueuze, cover the pot, and cook until the mussels are open, 3 to 5 minutes.

Pull off the lid, stir in the remaining butter, and finish the mussels with a pinch of salt, the lemon juice, and celery leaves.

Serve piping hot with hunks of baguette.

FRIENDS OF THE PUBLICAN
Peter Stocks, Calendar Island Mussel Company

We can honestly say that there are no other mussels like Peter's—and we can say that because we've tried them all. Peter's are hands-down the cleanest, crispest, fattest ones you can find. Let's put it another way: If we can't get mussels from Peter, we're not serving mussels.

Peter's a former corporate lawyer from Boston, who only started farming mussels in Portland, Maine, in 2012. What Peter's doing that sets him apart is rope-culturing his mussels. Most other operations drag them up from the bottom of the ocean, which isn't ecologically sustainable because you dredge up everything else that's down there and that can deplete mussel colonies. Peter grows the mussels on ropes that are suspended from floating rafts. It's efficient because they don't need a hatchery (when the mussels spawn, the seeds naturally want to attach to something and build elastin-like webs to the ropes) and the mussels grow 30 to 50 percent faster; it's cleaner because you don't have to worry about what's on the bottom of the ocean floor; and the mussels are happy because they don't need to worry about predators. (It's such a smart, economical, sustainable operation that now Peter's playing around with rope-cultured scallops—the first grower to in the States to do so.) I could go on and on about Peter's mussels, but the proof is in the 180 pounds of mussels that we order—and sell out of—every week.

the publican fish fry

A friend of mine from Minneapolis came into Blackbird one day with one of his Minnesota fishing buddies. They were talking about "shore lunch"—when fisherman cook their catch on the shore of their favorite lake. There are no real rules for shore lunch, except that it's usually fish, and it's usually fried. Well, this guy said his favorite thing to do was crumble up salt-and-vinegar potato chips and use them to coat the walleye he'd caught. And that's when The Publican Fish Fry was born. We take fish, clams, or oysters; soak 'em in buttermilk; coat 'em with chip dredge—a mix of chips, Wondra flour, and cayenne—and fry 'em. Right now we're loving these Ipswich clams, which we pile high with fried cheese curds, arugula, and a creamy remoulade like a dressed-up version of HoJo's Clam Strips.

Makes 4 servings

2 large bags of salt-and-vinegar chips (we like Cape Cod)

2 cups Wondra flour

Cayenne pepper

Vegetable oil, for frying

4 cups arugula

½ cup slivered red onion

Extra-virgin olive oil

Sea salt

Freshly ground black pepper

2 lemons, cut in half

1 cup buttermilk

2 cups shucked clams or oysters

1 cup Wisconsin cheese curds or halloumi cheese

Fried Caper Remoulade (recipe follows)

Make the chip dredge by adding the chips to a food processor and blending until they're pulverized to small flakes. Pack the flakes into a measuring cup to see how much you have—it should be about 2 cups—and transfer them to a bowl. Add an equal amount of Wondra flour (so for 1 cup of chip flakes, use 1 cup of flour). Season the mixture with cayenne. You can add as much or as little as you want, depending on how spicy you like things. We always go by the color—once there's enough cayenne to give the dredge a light-pink hue, we know it's right.

Preheat a deep fryer or a few inches of oil in a heavy pot to 350°F on a deep-fat/candy thermometer.

Toss together the arugula and sliced onion with enough olive oil to coat. Season with salt, pepper, and lemon juice. Set aside.

In a small bowl, lightly season the buttermilk with salt and pepper. Pop the clams and cheese curds into the buttermilk to get them nice and coated. Strain them from the liquid and toss them in the chip dredge until they're heavily covered.

Line a plate with paper towels. Working in batches, fry the clams and cheese curds until golden brown, 3 to 5 minutes. Using a slotted spoon transfer them from the fryer to the paper towels to drain. Repeat for the rest of the clams and cheese curds. Season with salt, pepper, and a little lemon juice.

To serve, scoop some remoulade onto two plates (about ¼ to ½ cup per serving), put the fried clams and cheese curds on top, and finish it off with the salad. Serve immediately.

FRIED CAPER REMOULADE

A great spicy, citrus-y mayonnaise. We like it with anything fried, and it's particularly awesome with shrimp.

Makes 3¹⁄₂ cups

3 large eggs, at room temperature

1 tablespoon olive oil

¹⁄₃ cup capers, rinsed

1 cup bread-and-butter pickles, chopped

Zest and juice of 1 orange

Zest and juice of 2 lemons

2 cups Garlic Aioli (page 24) or mayonnaise (we like Hellman's/Best Foods)

1 tablespoon Trey's Ashes (page 110)

Start by hard-boiling the eggs. Everyone has a different technique for this, but this is the way Cosmo's been doing it since he first learned to cook: First, fill a large bowl with ice water and set it aside. Then place the eggs in a small pot and add just enough room-temperature water to cover. Bring the pot up to a boil and then turn off the heat. Set a timer for 8 minutes and then plunge the eggs into the ice water and let them cool for about 5 minutes. You should end up with perfectly hard-boiled eggs.

In a small sauté pan, heat the olive oil over medium-high heat. Add the capers and fry just until crispy, about 2 minutes. Using a slotted spoon, transfer the capers to paper towels.

Chop the eggs and add them to a mixing bowl, along with the pickles, capers, orange zest and juice, lemon zest and juice, aioli, and Trey's Ashes. Season to taste. Cover and store in the fridge until ready to use or for up to 1 week.

BUYING CLAMS

We particularly love using the clams we get at The Publican for The Publican Fish Fry. They come from Sue Buxton in Stonington, Maine, where they're dug, shucked, cleaned, then shipped to us overnight every Monday. Buying the freshest clams possible makes all the difference here. And if you can't find fresh clams, lots of different fish—cod, smelt, walleye, perch—would work for this.

Skip Bennett, Island Creek Oysters

I think what I like most about Skip is that he's always done his own thing and made it work. He grew up on the water in Duxbury, Massachusetts, figuring out pretty early that he could make more money digging clams than pumping gas (and not have anyone telling him what to do). He went to school for finance, thinking he'd end up working in the banking industry in New York City (it was the nineties), came back home for one more summer to save up for a new suit and, long story short, ended up becoming the first guy to farm oysters in Duxbury Bay. But then the question was: Who'll buy them? Back in 2000, raw bars weren't the big thing they are now. There were maybe ten places in Boston with oysters on the menu, mainly because there weren't good, reliable sources of quality oysters. (Wild stocks had been decimated by disease, pollution, and overfishing.) So Skip essentially went door-to-door, asking chefs if they'd be interested in buying his product. He bought a book about oysters, and in the back was a directory of all the top seafood restaurants in the country. He couldn't even pronounce the name of the first place he called in New York City. He got the receptionist and asked to speak to somebody in the kitchen, and this guy with a thick French accent picked up. They talked for 45 minutes about their mutual love for oysters, Skip sent a sample, the chef loved them, and the first account was landed. It was Le Bernadin. After that came Grand Central Oyster Bar (also in New York), Michael Cimarusti at Water Grill in Los Angeles, and on and on went the list. He didn't realize it, but by going straight to the restaurants, he was also giving the finger to the traditional seafood distribution system. He knew that if you relied on a distributor to get out your product, they could set their own price to drive demand, hold your product until older stuff got out the door, and basically add three more steps between producer and buyer. So when he said "No, thanks," he pretty much turned the whole industry on its head. But as Skip—who now runs one of the most successful wholesale seafood companies in the country—says, "Well, that worked out."

roasted razor clams with anchovy-pimentón butter

I used to think that eating razor clams raw was my favorite way to have them—and they're still incredible that way, if you're getting them super-fresh—but this preparation is pretty damn hard to beat. We get a pan really, really hot in the oven, throw in the clams, and then hit the pan with butter that we've whipped with honey, lemon, pimentón, shallots, and anchovies. The honey starts to caramelize, the pimentón starts to burn on the outside of the shells, the shallots get tender, and the anchovies perfume the whole thing. Then we add some lemon juice and serve the clams with this sort-of broken pan sauce poured over the top.

Makes 4 to 6 servings

2 razor clams, cleaned (see following note) and bottom shells reserved

1 cup Anchovy-Pimentón Butter (recipe follows)

2 lemons, cut in half

Sea salt

½ cup Bread Crumbs (page 61)

½ cup chopped curly parsley

Preheat the oven to 450°F.

Cut the clams into bite-size pieces. Spoon the chopped clams back into their bottom shells and spread a little Anchovy-Pimentón Butter over each one.

Place a large sauté pan in the oven for 4 to 5 minutes, until it's really hot. Remove the pan, arrange the clams in it, and then put it back in the oven for another 3 to 4 minutes, so the butter melts and the clams roast.

Remove the pan from the oven. Squeeze the juice of 1 lemon over the clams and baste the clams, over medium heat, with the butter that has collected in the pan for 1 to 2 minutes. Season the clams with salt, then transfer them to a serving tray. Sprinkle the bread crumbs and curly parsley over them. Cut the remaining lemon into wedges and serve with the clams.

CLEANING RAZOR CLAMS

Since razor clams can be really sandy, they should first be purged. To purge the clams, place them in a medium bowl and cover them with cold running water for at least 30 minutes to get the sand out.

When cleaning razor clams, you need to be really gentle because they're delicate. Going slowly so you don't tear the clam, run a clam knife around both sides of the shell to loosen the connective tissue and remove the meat from the shell. First, use a knife or scissors to snip off the siphon (the small black tip of the clam's "neck"). Then, along the side of the clam that was once connected to the hinged side of the shell, use your scissors or knife to "fillet" the clam, or separate the two sides of the neck. Now you're basically going to remove anything that isn't white. Snip off the gills, which are on either side of the clam and are dark gray or brown, along with the really dark-brown bit that's called the digger or foot. Lastly, make a small circular incision to remove the stomach, again it'll be a darker color. Now you're ready to cook.

ANCHOVY-PIMENTÓN BUTTER

This is just anchovies, fish sauce, and spicy cayenne plus lemon for brightness and a bit of honey (which also caramelizes in the pan and gives this compound butter a deep, rich flavor) to balance it all out. It's awesome with shellfish, white-flesh fish, such as sea bass and snapper, or just slathered on bread.

Makes 2 cups

1 cup unsalted butter, at room temperature

1 tablespoon plus 1 teaspoon honey

Zest and juice of 1 lemon

2 teaspoons pimentón de la Vera (hot smoked Spanish paprika)

Sea salt

3 tablespoons minced shallots

1 tablespoon fish sauce

3 tablespoons minced brown anchovies, rinsed and patted dry

½ teaspoon cayenne pepper

In a food processor, blend the butter, honey, lemon zest and juice, pimentón, shallots, fish sauce, anchovies, and cayenne until fully incorporated. Season with salt. Store in the refrigerator for up to 2 weeks.

FRIENDS OF THE PUBLICAN
Sue Buxton, Fisherman Whisperer

We knew we'd found the best East Coast seafood connection when we heard about the time Sue Buxton hand-delivered eleven halibut to New York City. It was Memorial Day Weekend, and the fisherman had just missed the FedEx pickup. She never wants to turn a fisherman away with his catch, and she knew there would be no more FedEx deliveries to New York until Tuesday because of the long weekend. So she and her husband, Peter, packed the fish on ice and drove the eight hours from their house in Stonington, Maine, to Manhattan. They pulled up near Central Park, parked illegally, and out came all these chefs in their whites, rolling up with their stainless steel carts to grab the fish.

It's that kind of dedication to the local fisherman and their product—combined with serious hustle—that let us know we'd found the right lady. I mean, she's a Stone Islander whose family was among the first settlers in Stonington in 1798, so the local fisherman might as well be family (and in some cases, actually are family). Five days a week she's fielding calls from the boats—crab, mussels, oyster, halibut, scallops—

then calling her select list of chefs to find homes for everything before it makes its way to her hundred-year-old barn/packing warehouse. Or in some cases, to her van, which she's frantically driving to all the piers with a bunch of ice coolers in the back, trying to make the 3 PM FedEx deadline. We're exhausted just thinking about it, but that kind of commitment to quality is pretty much unparalleled—and makes the world of difference in the food we make.

trey's ashes clam boil

John Besh called me up one day and said, "Hey, I have this kid that I'd like to come work for you." His name was Floyd Harty III, the son of an undertaker. He went by the nickname Trey. I started him off working at The Publican, and he was a good kid. He said maybe five words in an hour, though, so really quiet. But there was one thing he got cocky about, and that was his gumbo. So when we had a gumbo-off at the restaurant because Erling Wu-Bower's dad is Cajun, and in the days leading up to the competition there was all this pumping up and smack talk—I think it was the most we heard out of Floyd the entire year he worked at the restaurant. He didn't end up winning—a huge deal for Erling, who did—but his special Louisiana spice mix, which we call "Trey's Ashes," left a lasting impression.

Now we use it to make a heavily seasoned bath that ultimately becomes the foundation of the clam boil. First we cook our potatoes in it and then use that salty, starchy broth to cook some littleneck clams, corn on the cob, and big chunks of onion and garlic. Then it goes in a bowl, gets a pinch more spice mix, a squeeze of lemon, a healthy amount of butter, some Tabasco, and tons of chopped parsley. We throw everything on a platter with lemon wedges, poblano hot sauce, and grilled bread (see page 286) and let people just have at it.

In a deep stockpot, bring a gallon of water to a boil. Add a generous pinch of salt and all but 2 tablespoons of Trey's Ashes.

Add the onions and garlic to the boiling water and let them cook for about 1 minute. Add the corn, sausage, and clams and cook until the clams just begin to open, 3 to 5 minutes. Add the potatoes and cook for another 2 minutes.

Once all the clams are open and the potatoes have warmed through, strain the boil into a large mixing bowl. Top with a squeeze of lemon, the butter, the reserved 2 tablespoons of Trey's Ashes, and parsley. Mix well so that the butter coats everything evenly.

Serve with your favorite hot sauce and Remoulade.

Makes 5 to 8 servings

1 gallon water

Kosher salt

½ cup Trey's Ashes (recipe follows)

2 cups coarsely chopped onions

¼ cup coarsely chopped garlic

3 corn cobs, shucked and cut into 3 pieces

4 Morteau sausages (page 212)

5 littleneck clams

2 cups "Sarge" Potatoes (page 120)

1 lemon, cut in half

½ cup unsalted butter

¼ cup chopped parsley

1 cup Remoulade #2 (recipe follows)

Hot sauce (we like Poblano Hot Sauce, our new favorite, thanks to Paul's favorite band, Calexico)

cont'd.

TREY'S ASHES

Think of this as an incredible Old Bay–like Cajun spice blend.

Makes about 1 cup

2 tablespoons celery seed

1 tablespoon coriander seed

1 tablespoon whole allspice

1 tablespoon black peppercorns

½ cup pimentón dulce (sweet smoked Spanish paprika)

¼ cup onion powder

2 teaspoons cayenne pepper

In a large, dry pan over low heat, toast the celery seed, coriander, allspice, and peppercorns until fragrant. Grind the spices and transfer them to a small bowl. Stir in the pimentón, onion powder, and cayenne pepper. This spice blend can be stored for 1 month in an airtight container.

REMOULADE # 2

This is great for dipping and on sandwiches.

Makes 4 cups

1¼ cups mayonnaise (we like Hellmann's/Best Foods)

⅓ cup whole-grain mustard

1 tablespoon minced garlic

1 tablespoon freshly squeezed lemon juice

½ teaspoon Tabasco sauce

1 teaspoon Worcestershire sauce

¼ cup minced red onion

Sea salt

In a medium bowl, whisk together all the ingredients and season to taste with salt. Store in the fridge for up to 1 week.

scallops with beef daube, strawberries, and fava beans

When my wife, Mary, was getting her master's degree, she did an externship in Washington, DC. One night we treated ourselves to dinner at the Watergate Hotel, where legendary chef Jean-Louis Palladin commanded the kitchen. I can still tell you everything I ate at that meal, but the standout was the scallop and oxtail dish. The scallops were sweet and dense and held up really well to the unctuous, rich braised meat. I eventually paid homage to this dish at Blackbird with sturgeon and oxtail. It was probably the most memorable dish we ever served in the early days (and it still shows up in one form or another on that menu and its cousin Sturgeon and Brown Butter, made the leap to The Publican.) Oddly enough, Cosmo had also done that dish when he was at the Hungry Cat in Los Angeles because Dylan Fultineer, who was an influential chef at Blackbird, brought it with him.

Now we do another version at The Publican with scallops and daube, which is a really rich, hearty Provençal stew made with beef. One of our secrets—for all braised meats, whether it's short ribs, oxtail, pork belly, or beef stew—is marinating the meat the day before and then basically starting the cooking process as though it were an unseasoned piece of meat. To marinate, we pack the meat with really good quality herbes de Provence, a splash of olive oil, and a couple squirts of Sriracha.

The second secret is throwing traditional braising methods out the window. When you read a cookbook about braising meat or get trained in a kitchen, you're told to never boil your stock or sauce because you don't want to emulsify any fat into the base, or it'll get greasy. But we found that when you take stock, add a little bit of butter along with the fat from braising, and then boil the piss out of a piece of meat until it all cooks down, you can't tell where the braised meat stops and the stock begins. It's just a fluid sauce of braised meat puree.

As for the strawberries, that was something I was hesitant about for a long time. Erling Wu-Bower never met a strawberry he didn't like—strawberries and feta, strawberries and chicken liver pâté, strawberries and strawberries. Cosmo, too, could put strawberries on every dish during strawberry season and be perfectly happy about it. The thing is, when a strawberry is fresh and in season, it's really out of this world—sweet and juicy and perfumed. Don't just go out and buy grocery store strawberries to make this dish. The difference between the ones at the

cont'd.

Makes 6 to 8 servings

BEEF DAUBE

1 pound beef chuck, cut into 2-inch cubes

Sea salt

Freshly ground black pepper

1 tablespoon herbes de Provence

1 tablespoon plus 2 teaspoons Sriracha

2 tablespoons rice bran oil

1 small white onion, diced

1 celery stalk, diced

1 small carrot, diced

2 sprigs thyme

1 bay leaf

1 cup red wine

1 tablespoon fish sauce

2 quarts Chicken Stock (recipe follows, or store bought)

½ cup unsalted butter, at room temperature

25-year-aged sherry vinegar

STRAWBERRY–FAVA BEAN SAUCE

⅔ cup fresh strawberries, hulled and quartered

⅔ cup fresh fava beans, blanched and shucked

½ cup Salsa Verde (page 261)

Sea salt

cont'd.

store and the ones from a farmers' market is the difference between a lump of coal and a diamond.

———————

To make the Beef Daube: Season the beef with salt and pepper and rub the cubes with the herbes de Provence and 1 tablespoon of the Sriracha. Let the beef sit in a covered container in the fridge overnight.

Preheat the oven to 300°F.

Heat the rice bran oil in a large stockpot over high heat. Once the oil is almost smoking, add the beef chuck and sear each side of the cubes evenly, about 1 minute per side. Transfer the beef to a large roasting pan and set aside.

Add the onion, celery, and carrot to the stockpot, decreasing the heat to medium. Cook the vegetables for 5 minutes, until they start to caramelize. Add the thyme and bay leaf. Once the vegetables begin to get tender, after about 5 minutes more, deglaze the pan with the red wine. Add the fish sauce and reduce until about one-fourth of the liquid remains. Pour 1 quart of the stock into the pot and bring to a simmer. Don't season the mixture, since salting braising liquid can dry out the meat.

Pour the braising liquid over the beef. Cover the pan with aluminum foil and transfer it to the oven. Check the meat after 2 hours, at which point it should be fork-tender and easily pulled apart. If not, let the meat cook for another 30 minutes. Once tender, remove the pan from the oven, remove the foil, and set the pan aside to cool.

Remove the meat from the pan and strain the braising liquid, discarding any solids. Transfer the liquid to a large saucepot. Shred the beef with your hands and add it to the pot.

Over medium-high heat, bring the meat and stock to a boil. Add the remaining 1 quart of stock, along with the remaining 2 teaspoons Sriracha and the butter. Bring the mixture to a boil once again, stirring constantly for 10 to 15 minutes, until the liquid has mostly reduced and become a thick and meaty sauce. Season with salt, pepper, and sherry vinegar to taste. Set aside while you make the sauce and scallops.

To make the sauce: In a small bowl, mix together the strawberries, fava beans, and Salsa Verde. Season with salt to taste and set aside.

To prepare the scallops: Season the scallops with salt.

Add the rice bran oil to a large sauté pan over high heat. When the oil is close to smoking, carefully place the scallops in the pan and let them sear for 2 to

scallops with beef daube, strawberries, and fava beans, *continued*

Scallops

10 (U/10) scallops

Sea salt

Rice bran oil

¼ cup unsalted butter, at room temperature

Juice of 2 lemons

6 pea shoots

3 minutes, until they start to caramelize. Flip the scallops and continue cooking for 1 to 2 more minutes.

With the scallops still in the pan, carefully drain off any excess oil from the pan and return the pan to the stove. Add the butter and lemon juice to the pan. As the butter begins to froth, tilt the pan toward you and use a large spoon to continuously baste the scallops for about 1 minute. Remove the scallops from the pan and let them rest for 1 minute.

Spoon the beef daube onto a platter and lay the scallops on top. Spread the strawberry and fava bean sauce over the scallops, garnish with the pea shoots, and serve immediately.

CHICKEN STOCK

We don't use roasted chicken or bones for our chicken stock. We like to keep our chicken stock blond and fairly neutral because we use it as the base for a lot of broths and purees.

Makes 1 *gallon*

10 pounds chicken bones (backs and feet), rinsed

6 tablespoons extra-virgin olive oil

4 yellow onions, large diced

3 carrots, large diced

1 bunch celery, large diced

4 bay leaves

5 sprigs thyme

2 tablespoons black peppercorns

First, blanch the chicken bones: Add the bones to a large pot and submerge in cold water. Bring to a boil and skim the scum from the surface. Boil for 5 to 10 minutes. Strain, reserve the bones, and discard the liquid.

To make the stock: In a second pot, heat the olive oil over medium heat. Add the onions, carrots, celery, bay leaves, thyme, and peppercorns and sweat for 5 minutes, or until fragrant. Add the blanched chicken bones and cold water to cover. Bring to a boil and immediately decrease the heat to a gentle simmer. Simmer for 4 to 6 hours, skimming any scum from the surface every 10 to 15 minutes during the first hour of cooking. Add water as needed to keep the bones submerged. Strain the liquid through a fine-mesh strainer and transfer to the fridge to chill until cold.

Strain any congealed fat off the surface. Refrigerate the stock for up to 1 week or freeze for up to 2 months.

pan-roasted soft-shell crab in green chile sauce

There are two things I want to say about soft-shell crabs: 1) My first marquee moment as a chef was cooking them for Alice Waters at Rick Bayless's Topolobampo here in Chicago. There were eight orders that came in, with two crabs per order, so I had two big pans going—one in each hand. The thing about cooking these guys is that they pop when they hit the hot oil, and one of them popped right in my face. I literally dropped to my knees, but I didn't drop the pans. Apparently I impressed Rick with that move. 2) Soft-shell crab really is the most incredible thing you've ever had. Anyone who has ever eaten soft-shell crab at Topolobambo when I was cooking got a one-claw crab—because I took the angel's share. The Paul share.

As for pan-roasting versus deep-frying them, there's an ongoing battle. So many guys who have worked for me want to deep-fry them, so we compare them side-by-side. Pan-roasting might not look as pretty, but texture-wise it's always the hands-down winner for us. Cosmo and I are both just pan-roasting guys. First we pull the apron off the back of the crab, take the guts out (unless they're super-impeccable they can taste like fishy scrambled eggs), squeeze out all the funky gunk, dredge the crab in rice flour (which is every bit as good as Wondra but has no gluten), then add them to a super-hot pan with just a little more oil than you'd normally use but not so much you take the class out of it. Then we serve 'em with Cosmo's famous Green Chile Sauce. Honestly, for any seafood dish in this book, you could easily sub out this sauce for whatever sauce we call for. Mackerel with Green Chile Sauce, whole-roasted trout with Green Chile Sauce, roasted razor clams with Green Chile Sauce— they would all be so good.

First, clean the crabs. Use sharp scissors to cut the "face" off the crab and remove the lungs and gills, as well as the guts. Some people like the fishy-tasting guts, but we think it takes away from the delicate flavor of the crab. Pat the crabs dry and season them with salt and pepper.

Dredge the crabs in the flour until they are completely coated. Shake off any excess flour.

Line a baking sheet with paper towels. Add the rice bran oil to a large sauté pan over high heat. There should be enough oil to create a thin layer across the bottom of the pan. Once the oil starts to smoke, carefully add 4 crabs to the pan. (Fresh crabs are full of water, so when they hit the pan they like to

Serves 4

4 fresh soft-shell crabs (fresh is ideal but frozen is okay)

Sea salt

Freshly ground black pepper

¼ cup rice flour or Wondra flour

3 tablespoons rice bran oil

1 cup Green Chile Sauce (recipe follows)

Cilantro sprigs

Parmesan

cont'd.

spit hot oil everywhere.) Cook for 2 to 4 minutes, until the first side is golden brown. Flip the crabs and repeat. Transfer the crabs to the paper towels and blot any excess oil.

Arrange the crabs on a serving tray and spoon the chile sauce evenly over the crab. Garnish with the cilantro and grate about ¼ cup Parmesan over the top. Serve immediately.

GREEN CHILE SAUCE

COSMO This is another inspiration from when I got married in Mexico. One night, a bunch of us went to a restaurant where they pulled out a giant molcajete—a mortar and pestle made from volcanic rock—and blended up some cucumbers and avocado with green chiles and lime juice to make this really bright aguachile sauce that was perfect for a ceviche. For some reason, it made me think about Green Goddess dressing, which has the same kind of flavors. So when I got back to the restaurant, I started working on a version that sort of fused the two to make this Green Chile Sauce. It's really good just spooned over these soft-shell crabs or any other kind of seafood.

Makes 4 cups

1 English cucumber	¼ cup chopped cilantro
1 serrano chile	¼ cup chopped parsley
2 scallions	3 tablespoons shiro dashi
¼ cup sugar	2 tablespoons lemon vinegar
⅓ cup water	3 tablespoons fish sauce
1 avocado, pitted and scooped out	⅓ cup diced white onion
Zest and juice of 6 limes	Sea salt

Combine the cucumber, serrano pepper, scallions, sugar, and water in a blender. Blend on high until the mixture is a thick pulp. Strain through a fine-mesh strainer and reserve the liquid. Discard the solids.

Wash out the blender and add the liquid back to the blender along with the avocado. Blend on high until the mixture is a smooth puree. Transfer the mixture to a medium mixing bowl and whisk in the lime zest and juice, cilantro, parsley, shiro dashi, vinegar, fish sauce, and onion. Season with salt to taste. Store tightly covered in the fridge for up to 3 days.

CHOOSE YOUR
OWN SPICY

Unless your serranos are on the spicy side, the Green Chile Sauce may not be hot enough for you. We want it to have just a little kick, but if you'd rather have more spice, you can thinly slice another pepper or two, stir additional pepper into the sauce, and let it sit an hour before serving.

dungeness crab and curried potatoes

This is one of those dishes that people come in to eat again and again and again. It goes back to Erling Wu-Bower bringing in seafood that really wasn't on menus here in Chicago. Dungeness crab was one of his earliest contributions. He grew up eating Dungeness, and people in San Francisco knew about 'em, but I—along with most people here—had never eaten one, much less seen one. We ordered them from a guy in Washington whose business is called "Happy Crab." They came in this big fish box with a cooler inside and right away I picked one up. Of course this six-inch-long creature just clamped down on my finger and started going to town. I had to fling it against the wall to get it off and back into the box. (Don't worry; unharmed.) Crab that's still fighting to get out of the box . . . it doesn't get any fresher than that in Chicago!

Anyway, what we do with our Dungeness crabs is par-cook them first, then we dip them in a rich, relatively mild massaman curry. You shake off the excess and the crab goes right into a pan, so you kind of burn the curry into the outside of the shell. All that's left to do is get in there with your hands and tear the meat out of the shells. We serve this dish with only a spoon, a crab cracker, and of course, plenty of napkins.

Serves 4

1 tablespoon high smoking-point oil, such as rice bran, sunflower, grapeseed, or peanut

2 tablespoons massaman curry

1 Dungeness crab, steamed and cleaned

⅓ cup Fish Stock (recipe follows)

2 cups "Sarge" Potatoes (recipe follows)

2 tablespoons unsalted butter

Sea salt

½ lemon

3 sprigs cilantro

Add the oil to a large sauté pan over medium heat. Stir in the curry as the oil heats and let it toast for 1 to 2 minutes. Add the crab and half of the fish stock. Cover and let the crab steam for 2 minutes. Add the potatoes and the remaining stock, stirring until the potatoes begin to warm through, 2 to 4 minutes. By now the oil, curry, and stock should have begun to form a sauce that coats the crab and potatoes.

Mix in the butter and continue to stir until it has melted and the sauce has the consistency of a light gravy. Taste and season with salt, if desired. It's not always necessary, depending on the saltiness of the crab. Squeeze lemon over the pan and transfer the whole mess to a serving platter. Garnish with the cilantro and serve.

TOASTING CURRY PASTE

You always want to toast curry paste before cooking with it because otherwise it can give your dish a bitter flavor.

FISH STOCK

We keep our fish stock pretty simple. It's light and bright and great a base to build on—sometimes we fortify it by adding kombu and mackerel to the stock, or we add grapefruit juice and fish sauce to a cupful and spoon it over seafood.

Makes 1 gallon

6 tablespoons extra-virgin olive oil

3 yellow onions, diced

1 bunch celery, diced

2 fennel bulbs, diced

4 bay leaves

4 sprigs thyme

2 cups white wine

1 cup pernod

Zest and juice of 4 lemons, zest peeled in strips

10 pounds flat fish bones (halibut and turbot work well), rinsed and removed of any skin

In a large pot, heat the olive oil over medium heat. Add the onions, celery, fennel, bay leaves, and thyme. Sweat for 5 minutes, or until the onions start to become translucent. Add the wine, pernod, and lemon juice and cook for an additional 2 minutes. Add the fish bones to the pot and cover in cold water. Bring to a boil and immediately decrease the heat to a gentle simmer. Simmer for 30 minutes, then add the lemon zest. Simmer for 5 minutes more.

Strain the liquid through fine-mesh strainer and chill. Strain any congealed fat off the surface. Refrigerate the stock for up to 3 days or freeze for up to 2 months.

IF YOU CAN FIND FRESH AND RAW CRAB

Most crab you're going to buy outside of the Pacific Northwest is going to be pre-cooked. But if you can find fresh and raw, here's how to prep them for this recipe: In a large heavy pot, add 2 chopped onions, 1 cup chopped carrots, 1 cup chopped celery, 1 bay leaf, and 2 chiles de árbol. Pour in 3 cups of water and bring to a boil. Add 1 cup of white wine. Place a basket steamer inside the pot. Add 2 live crabs and cover the pot. Set a timer for 9 minutes. Once it goes off, remove the crabs and plunge them into ice water. Let them cool, 4 to 5 minutes. Remove the tail flap from the crab, then peel off the head and remove the guts and lungs. Serve the crab that day.

cont'd.

"SARGE" POTATOES

This recipe is named after James "Sarge" Lehmann, a line cook-turned-server who has worked at The Publican for about seven years. He introduced us to this method for cooking potatoes, which employs his philosophy that the cooking water should be, "so highly seasoned it's gross to taste." We've been cooking potatoes his way ever since.

Makes 2 cups

½ cup kosher salt

2 tablespoons sugar

2 tablespoons red pepper flakes

5 fresh bay leaves

8 sprigs thyme

6 cups water

3 cups fingerling or small red or white potatoes, cut into bite-size (about 1-inch) pieces

Add the salt, sugar, red pepper flakes, bay leaves, and thyme to a stockpot and pour in the water. Bring to a boil over high heat.

Once the water boils, taste it. It should be aggressively salty and spicy. Strain the solids from the water and discard. Return the seasoned water to high heat and add the potatoes. Cook for 5 to 6 minutes or until the potatoes are fork-tender but not mushy. Strain and transfer to a baking sheet to cool. Once potatoes are dry and cool, they can be stored covered in the fridge for 2 to 3 days.

sardinian seafood stew

Our business partner, Eddie Seitan, is the mastermind behind our beverage program at The Publican—along with a few of our other restaurants. In addition to making sure we always have new and interesting offerings on our menus, he also organizes dinners to champion some of the lesser-known wine regions. We've done everything from a central Illinois wine dinner to a Croatian wine dinner. Then he told me that he'd met with a couple Sardinians, Fabio and Francesco Pibiri, a father-son operation that imports wine and all kinds of ingredients from Sardinia, such as bottarga and fregula sarda, which are like little toasted pearls of pasta. Eddie knew I'd get really excited about their products, so he introduced us. Fabio and Francesco were two of the most beautiful, sweet people, and Eddie was right—their products were incredible. I was especially excited about the different varieties of pecorino they were importing. These cheeses are so good that every time you taste one you're like sick to you stomach because you know you can't serve them—they're way too expensive. But they're pretty spectacular.

So we did a Sardinian wine dinner, and Cosmo came up with the idea to do a traditional Sardinian fish stew. He did some research and found a traditional version with sea urchin puree (or store-bought uni paste), fregula sarda, estratto (Sicilian sundried tomato paste), and chickpeas. But because it's typically really heavy and intense, he made more of a broth with the urchin plus fish and pork stock. Then he added clams, mussels, braised octopus—borrowed from our ribollita recipe—and fava beans. It was insane.

Braise the octopus as you would for the Braised Octopus "Ribollita" (page 136). Cut into bite-size pieces and set aside.

Heat the olive oil in a large stockpot over medium heat. Add the onion, garlic, estratto, bay leaves, thyme, jalapeño, and fennel and stir to combine. Stir every minute or so for 7 to 10 minutes, until the vegetables start to become tender and translucent. Increase the heat to medium-high and add the white wine, fish sauce, and shiro dashi. Let the liquid reduce by two-thirds before adding the fish and pork stocks.

Makes 8 *to* 10 *servings*

2 pounds octopus

½ cup olive oil

1 white onion, thinly sliced

10 cloves garlic, thinly sliced

3 tablespoons estratto (Sicilian sundried tomato paste) or tomato paste

2 bay leaves, toasted (see page 65)

2 tablespoons thyme leaves

1 jalapeño, stemmed, seeded, and thinly sliced

1 fennel bulb, very thinly sliced

1½ cups white wine (preferably Sardinian)

¼ cup fish sauce

2 tablespoons shiro dashi

1½ quarts Fish Stock (page 119, or store-bought)

2 cups Pork Stock (page 65, or store-bought) or Chicken Stock (page 114, or store-bought)

1½ cups fregola sarda

1 cup store-bought uni paste or pureed uni tongues

2 pounds clams

2 pounds mussels

1½ cups fava beans, blanched and shucked

cont'd.

Sea salt

**Freshly ground
black pepper**

Juice of 1 lemon

**3 tablespoons 12-year-
aged moscatel vinegar**

**3 tablespoons
chopped parsley**

**2 tablespoons
red pepper flakes**

**1 tablespoon chopped
tarragon leaves**

Decrease the heat to medium-low. Add the fregola sarda and cook until just tender, 6 to 7 minutes. Whisk in the uni paste and stir in the clams. Cover the pot with a lid and let the clams steam for 3 to 4 minutes, until they open. Add the mussels and cover the pot once again, steaming until all of the shellfish have opened, 3 to 5 minutes. Cover for 1 or 2 more minutes if the shellfish need more time to open, but discard any that haven't opened beyond that.

Add the fava beans and octopus and season with salt and pepper to taste. Add the lemon juice and vinegar and cook for 1 to 2 more minutes. Finish the stew by whisking in the parsley, chile, and tarragon. Spoon into bowls and serve.

To Noble Creatures of the Sea and the Much Maligned

Who,
From under Ocean
Who,
From under Lake
Who,
With Line and Net
We,
Take and Take
From,
Sea-to-Town
Scaled, De-Boned,
Grill,
Skin-Side-Down.

People are often surprised how much seafood we offer on our menu. And not just seafood, *fresh* seafood—crudos, escabeche, and simply grilled sardines, trout, and sturgeon. That's namely because The Publican has become a place where we feel comfortable doing anything, so long as it's product-driven and delicious. A little while ago, Cosmo was working on this Brazilian fish stew, called moqueca, with roasted tomatoes and coconut milk, and I was thinking, *You can't make that here.* But then I tried it and was like, "If you told me a week ago we'd be serving something with coconut milk, I'd say you were nuts." Do we do pasta? Occasionally. Pasta dishes are not a mainstay, but we do great pastas just because they're tasty. At brunch we sometimes do a version of bibimbap, and at first there was a little bit of a culture shock, but at the end of the day, do people come in and order that and a beer at 10 AM and make the whole idea of The Publican work? Absolutely. It's bigger than the rules.

So when Erling Wu-Bower joined our starting lineup and brought with him his relationships with West Coast fisherman (thanks in part to his mom Olivia Wu's *San Francisco Chronicle* column, "Seafood by the Seasons," plus the time he spent hanging around the Monterey Fish Market in Berkeley and a passion for fishing), it only made sense to give a good chunk of real estate to great seafood dishes on the menu. We were getting pristine product straight from the source, which you didn't see around here at the time. And when Cosmo started working with us, he took things even further, making connections with other incredible operations like McFarland Springs Trout Farm, Mount Lassen Trout, Water 2 Table, Passmore Ranch, Red's Best, and TwoXSea. These are all businesses run by people who—just like any other grower or producer we work with—take the utmost care with their product and are as interested in building relationships as they are sending invoices. They send us the best seafood money can buy and, in turn, we do our best not to totally muck it up with unnecessary fuss.

tuna crudo with preserved mushrooms

COSMO We get most of our tuna from the Tsujiki market in Tokyo (where it's called *hagatsuo*), or in the fall, when the albacore run along the West Coast for a few weeks. But you could use pretty much any other sushi-grade fish. Slice the fish really thin, lay it on a chilled plate, and sprinkle on some coarse salt and lemon (or in this case, lemon vinegar because it works so well with the mushrooms). Mushrooms *sott'olio*—which are mushrooms that are pickled and then plunged in olive oil—is an Italian preservation method that's used for all kinds of vegetables, like those jars of artichoke hearts that you see at the grocery store. We like putting these mushrooms on lots of stuff, but they're particularly great with fish.

Serves 3 to 4

1 (6-ounce) albacore tuna fillet

Coarse sea salt

2 teaspoons lemon vinegar

2 teaspoons toasted sunflower seeds

1 scallion, white and green parts, sliced on the diagonal

3 tablespoons Preserved Mushrooms (recipe follows)

Chill your serving plate in the fridge for at least 30 minutes.

Using a very sharp knife, cut the fish into sashimi-size slices (about ¼ inch thick) and arrange them on the chilled plate. Sprinkle them with the salt and lemon vinegar, then scatter the sunflower seeds, scallion, and mushrooms over the top. Serve immediately.

PRESERVED MUSHROOMS

The mushrooms get tender and tart from hot pickling, but you're still preserving their texture, so they retain that great subtle firmness.

Makes about 2 cups

2 cups extra-virgin olive oil

2 bunches maitake or chanterelle mushrooms

1 cup champagne vinegar

1 cup water

½ cup granulated sugar

1 teaspoon red pepper flakes

3 sprigs thyme

1 bay leaf

1 teaspoon sea salt

Put the olive oil in a bowl and place in the freezer to chill while you clean and pickle the mushrooms.

Brush any dirt off the mushrooms with a damp paper towel or pastry brush (there shouldn't be much dirt since these mushrooms are almost always farmed and not wild). Trim the bottom ¼ inch off the stems (it's woody and fibrous), then tear the mushrooms into small pieces with your fingers.

Combine the vinegar, water, sugar, red pepper flakes, thyme, bay leaf, and salt in a small sauce pot and bring to a boil. Add the mushrooms and cook until they're tender and have a nice pickled flavor, 2 to 3 minutes.

Remove the oil from the freezer and, using a slotted spoon, transfer the mushrooms to the cold oil, making sure they're fully submerged. Let them cool and transfer to the fridge. They should keep for about 6 months.

yellowtail escabeche with apricots

COSMO Escabeche is basically fish that has been cooked in vinaigrette and then chilled, so it's almost pickled. Then we take that escabeche liquid—which has a really bright flavor from orange and lemon juice, champagne vinegar, and sherry wine plus toasted coriander—and toss it with apricots (or any good stone fruit) as a kind-of overdressed salad, and pour it all over the fish to serve.

You only need about half of the fish called for here to serve the dish, but because escabeche will keep in the fridge for 5 to 6 days, we recommend saving the rest, especially for seafood sandwiches on crusty bread.

Makes 3 to 4 servings

1 (1-pound) yellowtail fillet

Sea salt

Freshly ground black pepper

2 cups extra-virgin olive oil

1 yellow onion, halved and thinly sliced

Cloves from 1 head of garlic, thinly sliced

¼ cup toasted and cracked coriander

½ cup sherry wine

1 cup champagne vinegar

¼ cup honey

2 tablespoons Sriracha

Zest and juice of 2 lemons

Zest and juice of 2 oranges

3 apricots, halved, pitted, and cut into ¼-inch slices

Coarse sea salt

4 or 5 sprigs cilantro

Start by getting your grill hot and seasoning the fish with salt and pepper. Place the fish on the grill and cook on each side for 10 to 15 seconds. Set aside and let cool.

Heat a heavy saucepan over medium heat and add the oil. When the oil starts to shimmer, add the onion, garlic, and coriander, stirring constantly as they cook. When they start to get tender, after 3 to 5 minutes, add the sherry wine and champagne vinegar. Cook for another 3 to 5 minutes, until the sharpness starts to subside. Stir in the honey, Sriracha, orange and lemon juice and zest. Cook for 3 to 4 more minutes so all the flavors meld together, then season with salt and pepper. It should be a little on the salty side because when you serve it cold the flavors won't be as bright as they are when hot. Remove from the heat and let cool to 132°F (use an instant-read thermometer for this—it makes a difference to get it exact).

Pour the mixture over the grilled fish. Let everything cool until room temperature and then transfer it to the fridge to chill, about 30 minutes minimum or overnight. You could make this part ahead and store it for up to 5 days. Put a serving plate in the fridge to chill for 30 minutes, too.

In a small bowl, toss the apricots with ¼ cup of the escabeche liquid and season with salt and pepper. Set aside.

Using a very sharp knife, slice the yellowtail into slices that are ¾ inch thick. (Use a sharp knife, or you'll tear the fish. Seriously.) Arrange the slices on the chilled plate and sprinkle the fish with sea salt. Add the apricot salad on top along with any extra escabeche liquid that has collected in the bottom of the bowl. Garnish with cilantro sprigs and serve immediately.

squid and blood sausage

COSMO I'm always the guy trying to do surf and turf, which is a long-time family tradition at The Publican. This recipe uses our favorite squid from Monterey Bay—which is really small, tender, and sweet—and pairs it with earthy blood sausage. The squid gets a simple marinade of olive oil with garlic, red pepper flakes, thyme, and lemon zest and then is grilled along with the sausage, giving them both a little smokiness. Then we add a lemon aioli that you caramelize with a kitchen torch, which is my nod to the torched mayonnaise you get in a sushi restaurant. If you don't have a hand-held butane torch, you can use a broiler, but you'll need to get the dish really close to the flame and keep it there for about a minute.

Add the squid to the marinade and let it sit for at least 2 hours; overnight is ideal.

Prepare a hot grill.

Lay the squid and sausage on the grill. Let the squid cook for about 1 minute per side, or until the flesh turns a creamy white color. Set it aside. Cook the sausage for 3 to 4 minutes or until cooked through. Cut the sausage into bite-size pieces and set aside with the squid.

Add the clarified butter to a large sauté pan over medium heat. Throw in the Waxman Potatoes and move them around the pan for 2 to 3 minutes, making sure they're crispy all over. Add the peppers and cook until they start to blister, about 2 minutes. Toss in the corn and season with salt. Once the corn starts to get tender, after 1 to 2 minutes, add the squid and sausage to the pan. Taste the mixture and season again with salt. Squeeze a little lemon juice over the pan and give the contents a shake.

If using a hand-held torch, transfer the mixture to a serving platter. If using the broiler, transfer to a baking sheet and preheat the broiler. Drizzle with the Lemon Aioli. Using a blowtorch or the broiler, blaze the top of the aioli until it starts to caramelize. Transfer the fish from the baking sheet to a serving platter. Sprinkle the dish with the parsley and serve.

Makes 6 to 8 servings

3 cups squid, cleaned (we likes ones from Monterey Bay)

Roasted Garlic Marinade (page 246)

3 Blood Sausages or Boudin Noir (page 215, or store bought)

Clarified butter or ghee

4 cups Waxman Potatoes (recipe follows)

6 cups shishito peppers (seems like a lot, but they cook down to about 2 cups)

2 cups fresh corn kernels (from 2 to 3 ears)

Sea salt

½ lemon

1 cup Lemon Aioli (recipe follows)

¼ cup parsley leaves

cont'd.

WAXMAN POTATOES

Jonathan Waxman, a culinary hero of almost everyone I know, has a way of preparing potatoes that we're kind of nuts about. The potatoes are steamed, smashed, fried, and cooled before getting crisped back up in clarified butter. I mean, crazy good. We like to give credit where credit is due, so whenever we put these on the menu, we call them Waxman Potatoes.

Makes 4 cups

2 pounds Yukon Gold C-size potatoes
(a bit larger than a golf ball)

Vegetable oil, for frying

1 tablespoon clarified butter or ghee

Sea salt

Place a steamer basket in a stockpot and add water up to the bottom of the basket. Add the potatoes, cover with the lid, and bring the water to a boil over medium-high heat. Cook the potatoes until they're creamy all the way through, 12 to 15 minutes. Transfer them to a cutting board and give them a good smash—the back of a pan works well for this.

Line a baking sheet with paper towels. Preheat a deep fryer or large pot filled with oil to 350°F on a deep-fat/candy thermometer. Add the potatoes and cook for 3 to 5 minutes, until golden brown. Using a slotted spoon, transfer the potatoes to the paper towels, season with salt, and let cool.

When you're ready to serve—if you're eating them on their own or with something other than the squid dish—heat a large pan over medium heat and add the clarified butter. Toss the potatoes in the pan and move them around for 3 to 5 minutes, until they're crispy on all sides. Season with salt, then serve.

LEMON AIOLI

Bright and tangy yet rich, you could pair this aioli with any seafood or roasted pork for a nice tart punch. If you're not going to be caramelizing it with a blowtorch or broiler, use half the egg yolks.

You might break the emulsion the first couple times you make this and will need to start over. Sometimes you make it too quickly, and it's loose. Don't worry, we've been doing it for years and we still break it sometimes.

Makes 4 cups

4 egg yolks, at room temperature

¼ cup sugar

Zest and juice of 3 lemons

1 garlic clove, grated

3 cups grapeseed oil

Sea salt

In a large bowl, combine the yolks, sugar, lemon juice and zest, and garlic. Whisk vigorously. Once everything is well incorporated, continue whisking as you slowly stream the oil into the bowl. The mixture will start to thicken. If it starts to get too thick, add 1 to 3 tablespoons of water. Continue to add the oil until it's all completely emulsified. The consistency should be a little looser than store-bought mayonnaise. Season the aioli to taste with salt and store in a sealed container in the fridge for up to 10 days.

braised octopus "ribolitta"

Makes 4 to 6 servings

BRAISED OCTOPUS

¼ cup extra-virgin olive oil

1 large yellow onion, diced

6 stalks celery, diced

1 fennel bulb, cored and diced

6 cloves garlic, smashed

2 bay leaves, toasted (page 65)

3 dried chiles de árbol

5 sprigs thyme

2½ cups white wine

¼ cup sugar

2½ cups champagne vinegar

12 cups water

2 lemons, cut in half

¾ cups sea salt, plus more as needed

1 (3- to 4-pound) octopus, beaks and eyes removed (ask your fishmonger to do this)

This is a soup that's always on the menu at Publican Quality Meats and goes back to Brian Huston, who made a great ribollita. The story behind it is, back in the day in Tuscany, if you couldn't afford meat for your stew, you would take leftover bread—the sad, stale bread that nobody wanted—and throw it in to make this hearty porridge. So we take our sourdough, cut off the crusts, saturate it with olive oil, and grill it until the outsides are almost burnt. Then we rub it with garlic, pick it into pieces, and let it sit for a few hours to get extra stale, so it acts like a sponge once it hits the broth. We mix together some tomato sauce, some beans, and some leafy greens with a little stock, bring it to a simmer, and then in goes the bread to soak everything up. The stew gets so thick that when you put it on the plate, it doesn't run all over. Then we top it with big grilled octopus arms and our Salsa Verde.

To braise the octopus: Add the olive oil to a large stockpot over medium heat and heat for 1 minute. Stir in the onion, celery, fennel, and garlic. Cook, stirring occasionally, for about 2 minutes, then add the bay leaves, chiles, and thyme. Sauté until the onion just starts to become translucent, 3 to 5 minutes. Stir in the white wine, bring to a boil, and decrease the heat until it is at a rapid simmer. Cook until only half of the liquid remains, about 5 minutes. Add the sugar, vinegar, and the water and bring the liquid to a simmer. Squeeze the juice of the lemon halves into the pot before throwing in the rinds as well.

Season the liquid to taste with salt. It should be tart and salty like the sea. Bring the liquid to a simmer once again. Decrease the heat to medium-low, so it's barely bubbling. Add the octopus, making sure it's completely submerged. If it bobs to the top, place a smaller pot lid inside the pot to weigh it down. Cook for 1 hour. Note that if the braising liquid reaches more than a simmer, the octopus' skin might start to come off as it cooks. It won't affect the overall taste of the dish, but it doesn't look as nice. Just try to keep an eye on the liquid as it cooks.

The octopus should be tender enough at the thickest part of the leg to pierce the flesh by squeezing it with tongs. If it's not quite there, submerge and cook the octopus in 15-minute installments until it is tender. Remove the octopus from the liquid and let cool, discarding the liquid. Set the octopus aside while you prepare the rest of the dish or refrigerate it for up to 4 days.

cont'd.

To make the Ribollita: Add the olive oil to a medium saucepot over medium heat. Add the garlic and cook for about 3 minutes, or until the garlic is very fragrant. Stir in the tomatoes, red pepper flakes, black pepper, and the water. Let the liquid come to a simmer, but not a boil. Continue cooking for 30 to 40 minutes, until about 4 cups of liquid remain. Add the basil and cook for another 3 to 4 minutes. Season with salt to taste. It should be sweet and slightly spicy. If not sufficiently sweet, add a little sugar to taste.

Add the spigarello and half of the chicken stock and stir for about 2 minutes, or until the greens have started to wilt. Add the croutons and stir constantly. Once the bread has started to fully absorb the moisture, add the remaining ½ cup of chicken stock. The mixture should be slightly wet and chunky like porridge. Finish by adding the sherry vinegar and butter. Season with salt and pepper to taste. Set aside while you grill the octopus.

Coat the braised octopus with olive oil and season with salt and pepper.

Lay the octopus on a hot grill and char on all sides, flipping constantly, for 5 to 7 minutes total. The outside should be crisp, while the inside should be hot, tender, and moist. Cut up the octopus into bite-size pieces.

Spoon the stew onto a high-sided serving platter and squeeze the lemons over it. Arrange the octopus on top, drizzle with the salsa, and serve.

GRILLED CROUTONS

Use a nice loaf of sourdough for this, preferably something long fermented with a high hydration (like the one in this book). It's how our bakery makes bread—really moist, strong sourdough—and it's amazing to work with. This crouton recipe is great for panzanellas. Or if using the croutons the same day you make them, they're nice in a fresh salad.

1 loaf Spence Sourdough (page 282, or store-bought)

½ cup olive oil

Sea salt

1 garlic clove

Slice off the crust from all sides of the loaf and slather the bread with a good amount of olive oil. Season with salt. Grill on all sides until evenly charred, almost burnt. Rub the bread with the garlic and let it cool. Tear the loaf into 1-inch chunks. Let the croutons sit for a few hours before using, ideally uncovered overnight to allow them to get a little stale.

RIBOLLITA

½ cup extra-virgin olive oil

5 cloves garlic

1 (28-ounce) can of tomatoes (we like Bianco DiNapoli)

1½ tablespoons red pepper flakes

2 teaspoons freshly ground black pepper

3 cups water

⅓ cup basil leaves

Sea salt

Sugar (optional)

2 cups spigarello, kale, or hearty mustard greens, rinsed and cut into 2-inch pieces

1 cup Chicken Stock (page 114, or store-bought)

Grilled Croutons (recipe follows)

1½ tablespoons 25-year-aged sherry vinegar

1 tablespoon unsalted butter

Sea salt

Freshly ground black pepper

Olive oil

2 lemons, cut in half

⅓ cup Salsa Verde (page 261)

swordfish and butternut squash in acqua pazza

Makes 4 servings

**PAN-ROASTED
BUTTERNUT SQUASH**

**2 tablespoons high
smoking-point oil,
such as rice bran,
sunflower, grapeseed,
or peanut**

**2½ cups butternut
squash, peeled and cut
into ½-inch pieces**

Sea salt

**1 tablespoon chopped
fresh thyme**

**1 tablespoon
minced garlic**

**1 teaspoon
red pepper flakes**

**2 tablespoons
maple syrup**

**2 tablespoons
unsalted butter**

ACQUA PAZZA

**3 tablespoons
extra-virgin olive oil**

**1 cup thinly sliced
red bell pepper**

**1 jalapeño, stemmed
and sliced into thin
rings (with seeds)**

**3 cloves garlic,
thinly sliced**

**½ cup thinly sliced
fennel**

**1 cup thinly sliced
white onion**

**1 bay leaf, toasted
(page 65)**

3 dried chiles de árbol

½ cup white wine

¾ cup vermouth

COSMO When our patio closes for winter, we know it's time to make this dish. *Acqua pazza* means "crazy water" or a spicy seafood broth in Italian. But unlike a totally traditional version that's essentially just poached fish, we make ours more like a stew, layering up pan-roasted butternut squash, swordfish, and clams. Then we top it off with our favorite herbed Bread Crumbs and Calabrian Chile Aioli.

———————

To make the squash: Heat the rice bran oil in a large sauté pan over medium heat. Place about half of the squash in a single layer on the bottom of the pan and sauté until all sides start to caramelize, about 3 minutes. Season with salt. Evenly coat the squash with half of the thyme and garlic. The squash should just be starting to get tender at this point. Add half of the red pepper flakes to the pan and cook for 1 minute before adding half of the maple syrup and butter. Taste the squash once the butter is melted and the syrup has evenly coated it. It should be tender but not mushy. Transfer to a plate to cool. Wipe out the pan with a wet towel and repeat with the second half of the squash and seasonings. Let the squash cool completely. You may store it in the fridge for up to 2 days, if you want to make this ahead.

To make the Acqua Pazza: Heat the olive oil in a large saucepot over medium heat. Add the pepper, jalapeño, garlic, fennel, onion, bay leaf, and chiles and stir to combine. Cook and stir every 30 seconds for 6 to 8 minutes, until the onions start to caramelize and become tender. Stream in the white wine and decrease the heat to medium-low. Cook until almost all of the liquid has evaporated, 1 to 2 minutes. Add the vermouth and cook for 4 to 5 minutes, or until the liquid is reduced by half.

Stir in the fish and chicken stocks, fish sauce, and neonata. Bring the liquid to a simmer and season with salt to taste. Continue cooking for 10 to 15 more minutes, until about 2 quarts of liquid remain.

Add the sugar, lemon juice, and vinegar and cook for 3 to 5 minutes to neutralize some of the acidity and tartness of the lemon and vinegar. Adjust the seasoning to taste before removing the pot from the heat. Set aside at room temperature while you finish the dish, or let the broth cool completely and store in the fridge for up to 5 days.

cont'd.

2½ cups Fish Stock
(page 119, or store-
bought)

2½ cups Chicken
Stock (page 114,
or store-bought)

3 tablespoons
fish sauce

2 tablespoons neonata
(see page 28; optional)

Sea salt

2 tablespoons sugar

Juice of 1 lemon

1½ tablespoons rice
wine vinegar

4 (4- to 5-ounce)
swordfish fillets

Sea salt

Freshly ground
black pepper

Rice bran or other
high smoking-point
oil, such as sunflower,
grapeseed, or peanut

12 littleneck clams

2 cups Pork Stock
(page 65, or store-
bought) or water

1 tablespoon
unsalted butter

2 tablespoons fines
herbes (see page 69)

¼ cup flat-leaf
parsley leaves

Juice of 1 lemon

2 tablespoons 12-year-
aged moscatel vinegar

¼ cup Calabrian
Chile Aioli (page 309)

¼ cup Bread Crumbs
(page 61)

To assemble the dish, season the swordfish with salt and pepper. Heat the rice bran oil in a large pot over medium heat. Place the swordfish in the pan and cook for 2 to 3 minutes, until the first side is golden brown. Flip the fish over and add the clams and pork stock to the pan. Cover the pan with a lid. Once some of the clams start to open, after 3 to 5 minutes, add the Acqua Pazza broth (it should be about 6 cups) and bring to a simmer, about 2 minutes. Add the squash and butter. Season with salt to taste.

Stir in the fines herbes, parsley, lemon juice, and the moscatel vinegar and let the stew cook for 1 to 2 more minutes. At this point, the clams should be open (discard any that aren't), and the swordfish should be cooked through. If the fillets are less than 1 to 1½ inches thick, remove them from the pan a little earlier so they don't overcook.

Divide the stew among the serving bowls and spread each with an even layer of aioli and bread crumbs and serve.

grilled sardines

Three years ago, the greatest meal I had that year was in summer when the sardines we were getting from Monterey Bay were giant, and we had the wood-burning oven going in the kitchen at The Publican, which a couple of the guys reconfigured so there was a grill grate inside to get more flavor from the fire. I was starving when I got over to the restaurant, so we just put this big, fat sardine on the grill with lemon and olive oil. I sat on the back stoop and tore it apart with my hands, juice and oil running down my arms.

COSMO This recipe is a total homage to Delfina in San Francisco, though it's also a tribute to all things Californian. The sardines get butterflied completely—the bigger the sardine, the better—so there are no bones left. We lightly salt them, rub them in olive oil, and coat them in Parmesan bread crumbs, which is how they sit until orders come in. Then they get more oil and more bread crumbs and are roasted right over the hot embers.

It is crucial that the sardines are really fresh. We have them overnighted from Monterey Bay Fish Market because even if the best sardines in the world are a few days old, they can get very fishy. The best thing to do is to ask your fishmonger to ship them in and butcher them for you, or, if you feel confident, butcher them yourself. We have our sous chef Melba Ortiz do it—she's the fillet knife ninja (see page 147).

Lightly salt the sardines and set them aside. Prepare a hot grill.

In a small bowl, mix the bread crumbs with a little less than ¼ cup of the Parmesan. Coat the sardines with olive oil, roll them in the bread crumb mixture, and repeat until each sardine is nicely coated.

Fold each sardine in half along the spine so they resemble a whole fish again. Place the fish on the grill over medium heat and let them cook for about 2 minutes per side, or until the bread crumbs are golden brown and the sardines are fully cooked. Transfer the sardines to a serving platter and squeeze the juice of one of the lemons over them. Drizzle the Oregano Dressing over the fish.

Cut the other lemon in half and place it flesh-side down on the grill. Garnish the sardines with the grilled lemon and some mint. Evenly sprinkle the rest of the Parmesan over the sardines and serve.

Makes 4 servings

Sea salt

4 sardines, boneless and butterflied, heads removed

1 cup panko bread crumbs

⅓ cup grated Parmesan cheese

½ cup olive oil

2 lemons

¼ cup Oregano Dressing (recipe follows)

¼ cup torn mint leaves

cont'd.

OREGANO DRESSING

In addition to fish, we love using this dressing on gamey meats, like lamb or venison, or game birds like guinea hen.

Makes ¹/₂ cup

¼ cup olive oil

1 tablespoon lemon zest

2 tablespoons lemon juice

1 teaspoon minced garlic

2 teaspoons minced parsley

1 tablespoon capers, rinsed and minced

1 tablespoon minced shallot

1 teaspoon red pepper flakes

1 teaspoon minced oregano

1 teaspoon granulated sugar

Sea salt

In a small bowl, mix together the olive oil, lemon zest and juice, garlic, parsley, capers, shallot, red pepper flakes, oregano, and sugar. Season with salt to taste. This will last for up to 1 week in the fridge.

Melba Ortiz, Kitchen Ninja

Melba is one of the sous chefs at The Publican and has been at the restaurant since day one, starting out as a prep cook making the oyster crackers. She does all the fish butchering, and she's just a machine—breaking down fish twice her size in seriously no time. It's like she passes everything she needs to do through her special Melba system and comes up with a way to do things that's fifty times better and faster than the original. She has this method for cleaning sardines in which she doesn't even need to gut 'em—just butterflies them with the heads on. It is genius and takes a fraction of the time. I asked her why she did it that way, and she just said, "I don't like touching the guts." And she's like a living, breathing record of everything we do in the restaurant because she needs to see something made only once to know how to do it perfectly. One morning there was no seafood in yet, so she started making the cultured butter because she saw me do it *once*. She has to go over to Publican Quality Meats every year to re-teach those guys how to make the Pork Pie, because sometimes it starts to drift from the original version that Brian Huston and I made. Every time she takes a stretch of time off to go back to Ecuador with her family, it takes two to three people to do her job. She's pretty paramount to the success of the restaurant.

sand dabs with tangerine butter

COSMO Sand dabs are a small flatfish you find in the Pacific. They're sweet, firm, and pretty much the flakiest fish of all time. It's funny because in California, you see them everywhere, and growing up, my mom would use them for fish tacos. I remember suggesting that to The Publican's original chef de cuisine, Brian Huston, and his reaction. *"What?!"* Because they're not easy to come by here, they're treated like more of a delicacy. But we ended up getting our hands on some, and when we did, we wanted to keep the preparation really simple. Okay, maybe not lemon wedge-and-curly-parsley-simple (which Brian was always telling Paul he wanted to do because it's the ultimate in simplicity), but just a step further. We quickly sear the fish—dredge it in Wondra flour so it gets crispy and doesn't stick to the pan—and then add Tangerine Butter, a compound butter flavored with tangerine juice, honey, fish sauce, and pimentón. The honey starts caramelizing in the pan and grabbing the fish, which stays crispy and supple. Then, because we're purists at heart, we hit it with a little lemon and serve it with curly parsley.

Truth is, it's hard to find sand dabs outside of California. And there's no great substitute for them. But they're so good that we had to put this recipe in this book. So if you can find them, go for it.

Serves 4

4 sand dabs, tail, head, and guts removed

Sea salt

Freshly ground black pepper

½ cup Wondra flour

1 tablespoon rice bran oil, or other high smoking-point oil such as sunflower, grapeseed, or peanut

3 tablespoons Tangerine Butter (recipe follows)

½ cup tangerine segments

2 tablespoons water

1 lemon, cut in half

Curly parsley

Pat the sand dabs dry with a paper towel. Season them with salt and pepper and dredge them in the Wondra flour. Heat a sauté pan over high heat and add the oil.

Once the oil is on the verge of smoking, shake off any excess flour on the sand dabs, place the fish in the pan, and decrease the heat to medium. Cook the fish for 2 to 3 minutes per side, until cooked all the way through. The edges of the fish will start to shrink toward the bone, and the flesh should be hot in the center. Add the Tangerine Butter to the pan and, using a large spoon, baste the fish for about 30 seconds.

Leave the pan over the heat but transfer the fish from the pan to a serving plate. Add the tangerine segments to the pan and cook for about 30 seconds. Add the water, squeeze the lemon over, and stir, turning the tangerines and butter into a sauce. Taste the pan sauce, season to taste, and pour over the fish. Garnish with the parsley and serve immediately. To eat, just run a fork or dinner knife down either side of the fillet, and the meat will detach from the bones.

TANGERINE BUTTER

This is super easy to make and great on white-fleshed flaky fish or warm bread.

Makes about 1 cup

½ cup unsalted butter, at room temperature

Zest and juice of 1 lemon

Zest and juice of 2 tangerines

2 tablespoons honey

2 tablespoons fish sauce

2 teaspoons red pepper flakes, ground into powder

2 tablespoons minced shallot

2 teaspoons pimentón de la Vera (hot smoked Spanish paprika)

Whisk everything together until well combined. Store in the fridge for up to 2 weeks.

mackerel and mayo with grilled chicories

One of my favorite people to cook with is Michael Cimarusti, out in Los Angeles—arguably one of the best seafood cooks in America. He's my chef crush. This one time he was making black bass, and before he put it on a rippin' hot grill, he brushed both the skin and flesh with mayonnaise, which is traditionally done in Mexico. It creates an extra-caramelized, charred flavor that is just ridiculously good. So we put our Publican spin on it, swapping out the bass for mackerel—one of the lesser-appreciated oily varieties that we like to give their due—and using our own mayo and seasoning it with salt and our favorite stand-by, piment d'Espelette.

Rub the mackerel with the aioli or mayonnaise and season with salt and pepper.

Build a fire on one side of a grill and let it burn down to embers. Cook the fish over a medium-hot area of the grill for roughly 2 to 3 minutes. You can tell the fish is done by pressing your finger right behind the top of the gill plate. If the flesh starts to release from the bones, the fish should be fully cooked.

Remove the fish from the grill and cover with the Hazelnut Aillade.

Toss together the Treviso, figs, and red onion; add enough olive oil just to coat; and season with salt, pepper, and a squeeze of lemon juice. Taste, adjust the seasoning if necessary, pile over the fish, and serve.

Makes 8 servings

2 whole Boston mackerel

¼ cup Garlic Aioli (page 24) or prepared mayonnaise (we like Hellman's/Best Foods)

Sea salt

Freshly ground black pepper

⅓ cup Hazelnut Aillade (recipe follows)

1 small head Treviso, just washed and raw or grilled, cut or torn into bite-size pieces

5 black mission figs, quartered

¼ red onion, very thinly sliced

Extra-virgin olive oil

1 lemon, cut in half

GRILLED CHICORIES

We love to grill chicories—Treviso, radicchio, dandelion greens, puntarelle—anything we can find at the market. We marinate them with a little balsamic vinegar and olive oil, char them on the grill, then put them back in the marinade with a little salt and pepper and a squeeze of lemon. It's just as delicious with mackerel and mayo as it is on its own.

cont'd.

HAZELNUT AILLADE

Aillade is traditionally a garlic and walnut puree, but we sub in hazelnuts since we get such incredible ones from a guy named Ted Lang at Truffelburt Farm in Oregon, the only place the variety we like is grown. Every time I use them at an event, chefs are always saying how they're the best they've ever tasted. They're bigger, creamier, and have a lot more flavor than the kind you find at the store. We keep them in the refrigerator, along with our pistachios and pecans, so they stay fresher longer. What can I say? We're nuts for nuts.

Instead of making this into a smooth sauce, we make it more like a chunky dressing. It's usually paired with chicken, but it's awesome on vegetables—especially beets—and would be great on seafood.

Makes about 2 cups

Sea salt

1½ cups hazelnuts, toasted

Freshly ground black pepper

1½ cups extra-virgin olive oil

1 small garlic clove, finely grated using a Microplane, or finely minced

Zest of ½ lemon

Zest of ¼ grapefruit

Juice of 1½ lemons

1 tablespoon honey

2 drops orange blossom water

Using a mortar and pestle and working in batches with a pinch of salt, pound a ½ cup of the hazelnuts until very fine and the natural oils begin to release. Transfer to a mixing bowl. Coarsely pound the rest of the nuts until they're broken into small pieces. Add to them to the mixing bowl. Drizzle in the olive oil while whisking (important or the sauce will be gummy), and then the garlic, lemon zest, grapefruit zest, and lemon juice, honey, and orange blossom water. Adjust the seasoning with salt and pepper. The aillade is best the day it is made but will keep in an airtight container in the fridge for up to 2 days.

dover sole with caper berries and moscatel vinegar

I fell in love with Dover sole because of John Hogan, a Chicago chef who, while tremendously respected, is still an unsung hero. He was a classic charcuterie and French technique guy and had a restaurant called Savarin, where the food was incredible. I remember eating there shortly after I became a chef and was just starting to understand flavors and food. It was the first time I'd ever had sole *meuniere*—a classic French preparation where the fish is dredged in flour, pan-fried in butter, and served with a brown-butter pan sauce with parsley and lemon. That's essentially what this dish is, just with some revved-up ingredients.

Sole is really rich, but not rich and oily like turbot. It's firm like sand dabs but more supple. The meat just slides off the bones and has so much flavor—it's crazy good. We get ours at auction in Holland so we can get it wild and fresh, not frozen or farm-raised, like about 98 percent of restaurants serve. There's just no contest between the two. And we want to share that quality with our customers, which is why we usually just charge what we're paying for it. It's a gimme, but it's part of the experience.

To make this at home, try to find the freshest local flatfish you can find—lemon sole, blackback flounder, sand dabs, even skate wing. If something's caught that day, it's going to be a lot tastier than frozen.

COSMO Someone once asked me to describe the food at The Publican and how the flavors worked. I ultimately came up with it being as if you put too much sweetness, too much salt, and too much acid together and then tried to shove them all through a small hole, the combination somehow becomes really balanced even though each element has a ton of different flavors. This dish is a great example because you have the moscatel vinegar—one of the first pantry items we sourced at The Publican because it's sweeter and lighter than other vinegars—plus lemon, herbs, capers, and butter. Together it becomes this composed buttery, acidic, lemony, sweet-sour mixture that still doesn't mask the super-richness of the Dover sole. We cook the fish skinned and whole. We'll walk you through how to remove the skin yourself, but it's definitely easier if you can ask your fishmonger to do it for you.

First, here's how to remove the skin if your fishmonger hasn't already done it for you: Dip the tail of the fish in boiling water for just a few seconds until the skin starts to release. Use tweezers to peel the skin off the top and bottom of the fish and discard.

Makes 2 to 4 servings

1 pound Dover sole

1 tablespoon high smoking-point oil, such as rice bran, sunflower, grapeseed, or peanut

Sea salt

Freshly ground black pepper

3 tablespoons unsalted butter

2 tablespoons caper berries

1 grapefruit, segmented

2 tablespoons 12-year-aged moscatel vinegar

2 tablespoons water

1 tablespoon chopped parsley

cont'd.

Heat a large sauté pan—big enough to fit the whole fish—over high heat. Add the oil and let it get almost to the point of smoking. Season the fish on both sides with salt and pepper and carefully place it in the pan, top-side down. Cook for 2 to 3 minutes, until golden brown, agitating the pan constantly so the fish doesn't stick. At this point the fish should almost be fully cooked. Pour off any excess oil and add the butter to the pan; within 30 seconds it should start to foam. Tilt the pan slightly toward you and using a large spoon, baste the fish with the frothing butter. Once the butter starts to brown, after about 1 to 2 minutes, remove the fish and transfer it to a serving dish.

Add the caper berries and grapefruit segments to the pan and cook for about 1 minute. Add the vinegar and water and reduce by about half, another 1 to 2 minutes. Taste the pan sauce and season to taste with salt and pepper. Sprinkle in the parsley and pour the sauce over the fish.

To serve, you have two options: You can carefully take the fish off the bones before serving or bring it out whole and let your guests pick the meat off the bones themselves. At the restaurant, we have our staff fillet the fish at the table (pretty fancy).

grilled sturgeon and brown butter

COSMO Farmed fish can get a bad rap, but there are well-managed sustainable farms that produce really high-quality product. We get our sturgeon from Michael Passmore of Passmore Ranch in the Northern California foothills. When you talk to Michael on the phone, you'd think he's a rancher out in Texas with his deep, raspy pack-a-day drawl, like the Marlboro Man or something, not a fish farmer in the Golden State. His fish is incredible—when you hold a fillet at room temperature, the fat just drips down your hand.

In a way, sturgeon is like the meat of the fish family. It holds up really well to grilling. So we wanted to pair it with something that wouldn't overwhelm the richness of the fish, like a bunch of fresh herbs and our Brown Butter Vinaigrette.

In a small saucepot over medium heat, bring the currants and verjus to a simmer. Remove the pot from the heat and let cool. The currants should be plumped, juicy, and a little tart from being reconstituted in the verjus. Strain and discard any excess liquid. Set aside ¼ cup of the currants and store the rest in the fridge for up to 10 days. (Toss them into any salad; they are especially good with bitter greens, like chicories.)

Prepare a hot grill.

Season the sturgeon with salt and drizzle with a very light coating of olive oil.

Place the fillets on the grill directly over medium heat. Flip the fish after 2 to 3 minutes and grill for another 5 to 6 minutes, until the fish is cooked medium-well. Transfer the sturgeon to a serving platter and squeeze the juice of 1 lemon evenly over the fillets. Set aside.

Add a thin layer of olive oil to the bottom of a large sauté pan over medium-high heat.

Add the cauliflower and move it around in the pan for 6 to 7 minutes, until the outside is caramelized and the inside has started to become tender when pierced with the tip of a knife. Add the Brown Butter Vinaigrette and season with salt and pepper to taste. Remove the pan from the heat after 30 to 60 seconds, or when the butter stops frothing, and pour the cauliflower and brown butter mixture over the fish.

In a small bowl, toss together the plumped currants, fennel, pine nuts, mint, and parsley. Season the salad with salt and drizzle with olive oil. Squeeze the juice of the second lemon over the salad, spread it over the sturgeon, and serve.

Makes 4 servings

½ cup dried currants

½ cup verjus

4 (4- to 5-ounce) sturgeon fillets

Sea salt

Extra-virgin olive oil

2 lemons, cut in half

3 cups bite-size Romanesco or cauliflower florets

½ cup Brown Butter Vinaigrette (recipe follows)

½ cup shaved fennel

¼ cup pine nuts, toasted

2 tablespoons minced mint

2 tablespoons minced parsley

cont'd.

BROWN BUTTER VINAIGRETTE

This vinaigrette is rich but has great acidity from the reduced orange juice. It's great on seafood and roasted fall veggies, such as delicata squash and broccolini.

Makes 1 cup

⅓ cup thinly sliced shallots

Sea salt

1 cup freshly squeezed orange juice

⅓ cup unsalted butter, at room temperature

1 tablespoon ground Aleppo pepper

2 whole cloves

3 allspice berries

1½ tablespoons champagne vinegar

In a small bowl, season the shallots with a pinch of salt.

In a small saucepan over medium heat, bring the orange juice to a simmer. Once the liquid has reduced by two-thirds, pour it into the bowl with the shallots. Set aside to cool.

In a sauté pan over low heat, add the butter, Aleppo pepper, cloves, and allspice. Once the butter is completely liquid, increase the heat to medium-high. As the butter starts to bubble, stir with a wooden spoon, scraping the bottom of the pan to keep the butter from sticking and burning. The butter should start to brown and give off a sweet, caramel-like aroma after 2 to 3 minutes of simmering.

Remove the butter from the heat and pass through a fine-mesh strainer into the bowl with the shallots and orange juice. Discard the spices.

Taste and add the vinegar. Season with salt and taste again. Let cool and transfer to a tightly covered container to refrigerate. This will keep in the fridge for up to 5 days. Serve warm on top of seafood or salads. To reheat, gently warm the vinaigrette for a few seconds in the microwave or in a water bath. Shake to re-emulsify.

tokyo-style trout with publican spice

We get sustainably farmed trout from Mt. Lassen Trout farm in the Sierrra Nevada mountains of California. We got connected with them by Water2Table Fish Co. in San Francisco, which is an awesome company that buys hook-and-line-caught fish directly from local fisherman, essentially connecting chefs directly to the boats their fish are coming from. Mt. Lassen trout is just amazing. We always say it's the best freshwater fish in the world, but it's actually the best *fish* in the world. Their ponds are fed from spring water that flows from the base of Mt. Lassen, and the fish are delivered live to the processing plant within three hours of harvest. The taste, as you can imagine, is just as pristine as their operation.

Like all our great products, we didn't want to clobber the trout with tons of other ingredients. We started off serving it plain, but then we realized that was a little *too* simple. So now we rub it with our Publican Spice Blend (page 32) and salt, then just kiss it, skin-side down, with a white-hot grill. We take it off while it's still rare and cool and then serve it with a lemon wedge and maybe a simple shaved baby fennel salad. But that's it.

If you don't live in a place where you can get your hands on Mt. Lassen trout, you can substitute ocean trout or arctic char.

Get the grill as hot as you can. When the grates start to turn white—that's the perfect heat.

Season the fish with the salt and Publican Spice, then rub just enough olive oil into the skin side to coat. Reserve any leftover oil.

Place the fish, skin-side down, on the part of the grill that's starting to get white. Let it cook for 30 seconds to 1 minute, until the skin is crispy and starting to char heavily but the flesh is still raw. Remove from the grill and lay it skin-side down on a cutting board. Squeeze half the lemon over the fish.

Toss the baby fennel with salt, a little lemon juice, and any leftover olive oil that hasn't been rubbed on the fish. Mound it on top of the trout and serve. Or, skip the fennel salad and just serve the fish with a couple lemon wedges and call it a day.

Makes 4 to 5 servings

2 (7-ounce) Mt. Lassen trout, ocean trout, or arctic char fillets

Sea salt

1½ tablespoons Publican Spice (page 32)

2 to 3 tablespoons extra-virgin olive oil

1 lemon, cut in half

2 heads baby fennel, shaved (optional)

To the Swine, Bovine, and Particularly Fowl

The chicken, the hen,
The pheasant and fowl—
    Pluck'd, behead'd
    Then disembowel'd.
A bit severe, yes, indeed:
    "The ANIMALS giveth
    what the CHEF guarantees."
'Tis our chosen lot
    as EP-I-CUR-E-ANS;
for those too squeamish,
    try VEG-E-TAR-I-AN.

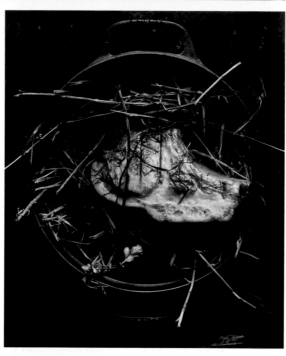

When it comes to any of our product—animal, vegetable, mineral—we're gonna go with the best when it comes to flavor and quality. We're not going to try to save twenty cents to cut corners (apologies to our partners). And we're definitely not going to sacrifice working with people whose livelihood it is to make sure they're getting us that quality week after week. Our meat is a great example of that. We get most of our product—beef, pork, poultry—from Louis John Slagel of Slagel Family Farm, just outside Chicago. I remember the first day he came to the city, looking for restaurant accounts. He was a smart kid—no more than twenty-one at the time—who wanted to change the course of his family's farm, which at that point was keeping afloat by selling their hogs to Tyson and Cargill for next to nothing. He'd picked up a copy of *Chicago* magazine, read restaurant reviews, and researched who was known for their butchering, and he came to Blackbird with a ribeye and a New York strip for us to cook and sample. They were delicious. He was persistent, eager to make actual relationships with people, and best of all, his product was unbelievably tasty—not to mention allowed to live cage-free, eat a varied diet, and skip getting injected with hormones. I realized it would never work if he was bringing just me a little bit of product every week, so I gave him a whole list of other chefs to talk to. Fast-forward to now, when we write him pretty big checks every week for his meat—along with almost every major restaurant in the city.

Then there's Kim Snyder of Faith's Farm in Bonfield, Illinois, who walks the line between pig farmer and animal lover. She left the corporate world twelve years ago—she was an operations manager for American Express—to focus on raising her daughter, Abigail Faith, and maybe ranch like her aunt had. She fell in love with an endangered heritage breed of pigs called Gloucestershire Old Spots—"laid-back, hippy pigs," as Kim says. You pet them, and they just roll over so you can rub their bellies. A whole bunch of rabbits, some cows, chickens, and guard-donkeys later, and she has built an operation where the animals' well-being comes first. Her sows are given about a year to rest between litters (until they get big and fat again—unlike many farmers, who will push up to three litters a year) and aren't forced to wean; and her hogs aren't castrated (she swears that makes a huge difference in the meat). The pigs eat a hand-made mix of corn, oats, and wheat that Kim grinds herself, plus things like beet pulp, eggs, diatomaceous earth, and holistic supplements. They rotate to new pasture every two to three months, and they're given fourteen to sixteen months to get to market weight (as opposed to the norm, which is closer to six to seven months). And the pork? Pretty much the best thing ever. The meat is bright red and sweet, and the fat has the feel of butter—it's not greasy. There's no way we could settle for only getting twelve to sixteen whole animals a year—so we asked Kim if she would breed one of her hogs with one of Louis's sows.

So Louis heads down to Kim's farm to pick up her hog, and Erling Wu-Bower gets a call from Kim. She said she doesn't know if she feels comfortable with the arrangement. The hog would have to be quarantined for thirty days and pigs are really social creatures. "I don't know if you know this," she said, "but pigs can die from loneliness." She told him that the only way she'd agree to the arrangement would be if Louis also took a hog "friend" to go with and keep him company. Done and done. We ended up with a special Publican breed—a Berkshire-Duroc-Hampshire cross—and when the friend was big enough to slaughter, Louis brought him down, too. We labeled all his goods as "Faith's Friend." It was such a cool example of two of our favorite farmers getting together and doing something great.

Through Kim we met Roger Marcotte. He's Kim's neighbor, and she told us that he had a small-scale beef operation and that the meat was really good. She dropped off some frozen ribeyes—these thin little things—and they pretty much got tossed aside in the walk-in. As Cosmo tells it, it was super-late one night when someone pulled them out and cooked 'em, and they were like zombies eating them, they were so delicious. We found out that Roger raises about twelve steers a year. Now he slaughters one a month to sell to us. He saves only one for himself to take to the county fair. His steers don't have the show-off marble-y look that will sell well in the butcher case, but the meat is sweet and mild and has the most incredible texture—perfect for recipes like Flap Steak with Strawberries, Mint, and Feta (page 202).

Both Roger and Kim's meats are what we love to highlight, the same way we'd show off perfectly ripe tomatoes or just-flown-in-today sardines. They definitely get the special tartare/carpaccio/cured-meat treatment. It's safe to say though, that all of our meat purveyors get us product that's worth going a little nuts about—and, believe me, we do.

publican chicken

This is the most famous Publican dish, if there is such a thing. It's what I'm eating when I'm in the restaurant, and it's what I'm making at home, whether people are coming over or it's just me and my wife. It has its roots in a Portuguese restaurant in Montreal (that Donnie and I read about in *Gourmet*), where this guy was grilling spiced and spatchcocked chicken over a charcoal grill—while smoking a cigarette—and then served it over a bed of French fries. We ate that chicken and looked at each other like *Eureka!* The Publican wasn't even a twinkle in my eye, but I knew we had to serve this in some restaurant, some day.

Our interpretation of the dish includes cooking the chicken over wood, which adds a lot of flavor, and seasoning it with Espelette pepper (of course) and Mexican oregano, which I love for its almost minty flavor. But the real secret, aside from a squeeze of lemon at the end, is pre-salting and then marinating the chicken. It's a technique I borrowed from Judy Rodgers, the late chef-founder of San Francisco's Zuni Café, via Brian Huston—who worked for her before he came to The Publican. We salt the bird an entire day before it marinates, which allows the flavor to permeate and makes the flesh really tender, juicy, and zingy. It's crazy good.

First, clean the chicken. Rinse the bird under cold water, and dry with a paper towel.

Now butterfly the chicken, which means taking out all but the drumstick and wing bones so the chicken will lay flat as it cooks. Start by removing the wing tips at the first joint. Then turn the chicken vertically so its head (or at least where its head used to be) is on your cutting board. Holding on to the tail, run a sharp boning knife down the right side of the spine, from top to bottom. Repeat on the other side and remove the backbone.

With the bird flat on the table, breast-side down and legs pointing away from you, make a small vertical cut in the white cartilage that runs over the breastbone. Bend both halves of the chicken backward at the cut, which will make the breastbone pop right through. Run your thumbs or index fingers down both sides of the breastbone, pull to separate it from the meat, and then pull the bone out. If it doesn't come out easily, use your knife to loosen any remaining bone or cartilage.

Finally, with the tip of your knife, make a slit along each thighbone to the knee joint. Use your fingers to move the flesh away from the bone and pull the bone out.

Makes 2 to 4 servings

1 whole chicken (about 3 pounds)

Sea salt

cont'd.

MARINADE

2½ tablespoons freshly squeezed lemon juice

½ cup extra-virgin olive oil

1 tablespoon piment d'Espelette

1 tablespoon dried oregano

1½ tablespoons brown sugar

2 cloves garlic, sliced

½ teaspoon salt

¼ teaspoon freshly ground black pepper

1 lemon, cut in half

Season the chicken on both sides, slightly less than you'd normally season if you were cooking right away. Put the chicken on a plate, cover it with plastic, and let it sit in the fridge overnight.

The next morning, combine all the marinade ingredients in a large mixing bowl. Toss the chicken in there and gently rub the marinade into both the skin and the flesh. Let it sit for at least 1 hour and as many as 12 hours. (Put it back in the fridge if it's going to sit for more than an hour and remove it from the fridge about an hour or two before you want to cook it.)

If grilling the chicken, build a fire on one side of a charcoal grill and let it burn down to embers. Alternatively, preheat your oven to 450°F.

To grill the chicken: Cook the chicken skin-side down over indirect heat and positioned so the legs are just touching the direct heat. Cover the grill with the air holes open so you get good high heat. Cook for 6 minutes, then turn the chicken so the breasts are over the direct heat. Cook for another 6 minutes. Flip the bird over and do it again (another 6 minutes with the legs over direct heat, another 6 minutes with the breasts over direct heat).

To tell if the chicken's done, you can put a sharp paring knife in the breast and thigh (the thickest parts of the bird), hold it for a few seconds, then touch it to your arm. If it's hot, it's done. People will tell you that you shouldn't be poking and prodding your meat to tell if it's done, but I'm telling you that there's no human being on this planet who can tell you if a whole chicken is done just by touching it. There's nothing wrong with poking and prodding. Really. You could just use an instant-read meat thermometer instead; the chicken's done at 160°F. Let the chicken rest for 5 minutes.

To roast the chicken in the oven: Add enough olive oil to coat the bottom of a big ovenproof skillet and heat over high heat until it smokes; then put the chicken, skin-side down, in the pan and cook over medium heat until a nice golden crust forms, about 5 minutes. Transfer the pan to the oven, without flipping the chicken over, and cook for 10 more minutes. Flip the chicken and cook for 8 minutes for a total of 23-ish minutes. Let the chicken rest for 5 minutes in the pan.

Put the chicken on a carving board and hack it up. Or more specifically: Transfer the chicken to a carving board and cut it into 8 pieces. Start by cutting it in half from the neck to the tail. Next, remove each breast from the leg and thigh, then cut through each breast on the diagonal, dividing it into two pieces. Then cut the thighs from the legs at the knee joint.

Squeeze lemon juice over the whole thing on the cutting board and be sure to save all the juices—it's important to pour them over the chicken just before you serve it, especially if it's over a mound of Frites (page 42).

dry-aged duck breast with pumpkin seed vinaigrette

The entire idea with duck is buying the whole animal and getting all that great stuff—the fat, the legs, the thighs, the breasts. This recipe and the cassoulet (page 173) put all those bits to work. The thing about duck is that if you just break down the breasts from the bone, score 'em, season 'em, and roast 'em, they're really chewy and the flavor is a little washed out. One solution is to cook them closer to medium than medium-rare, but then they can start to taste a little livery. We learned from Mike Sheerin—one of the chefs at Blackbird who learned this method working at Jean-Georges—that dry-aging is the perfect solution. As with dry-aging any meat, there's an enzyme that starts to break down the muscle fiber. So the meat loses some of its wateriness, the flavor gets more concentrated, and the skin forms a pellicle, or film, just like it would if you had smoked it, so that when you sear it, the meat gets denser and crispier. You can cook the breast to a true medium-rare, and it's like butter-tender. That means we can just cut it into three big slabs and serve it like giant duck steaks.

Makes 4 servings

¼ cup rice bran or olive oil

4 (6- to 7-ounce) dry-aged duck breasts

Sea salt

Freshly ground black pepper

½ cup verjus

¼ cup unsalted butter

2 cups sunchokes

Sugar

1 cup Sunchoke Puree (recipe follows)

1 cup Pumpkin Seed Vinaigrette (recipe follows)

2 small handfuls arugula or other greens, for garnish

1 cup Sunchoke Chips (recipe follows)

Heat 2 tablespoons of the oil in a large sauté pan over low heat. Season the duck breasts with salt and pepper and place them, skin-side down, in the pan. Cook for 5 to 10 minutes, then increase the heat to medium. Cook for 2 to 3 minutes, then turn them over. Increase the heat to medium-high and carefully pour out any excess fat that has collected in the pan (save this and use it for frying potatoes). After 1 minute, increase the heat to high. Add the verjus and butter to the pan and use a spoon to start basting the duck as the liquid reduces until it's thick and tacky (reduced by half). Remove the duck from the pan and let it rest on a wire cooling rack.

Pour the remaining tablespoon of oil in a second large pan over medium-high heat. Add the sunchokes and sauté until they're golden brown and creamy all the way through and there's no resistance when pierced with the tip of a knife, 4 to 6 minutes. (Undercooked sunchokes are not tasty!) Season with salt and a sprinkle of sugar. (We like to finish all of our root vegetables with sugar as well as salt because they can be slightly bitter and the sugar rounds them out.) Set aside.

Cut each duck breast into ½-inch slices. Set aside.

To assemble the dish, spread the Sunchoke Puree on a serving platter. Top with the sautéed sunchokes and then the slices of duck. Pour over the verjus pan sauce and then spoon the Pumpkin Seed Vinaigrette over the top. Garnish with arugula or greens of your choice and serve with Sunchoke Chips.

SUNCHOKE PUREE

We use *maguro shuto*, or fermented tuna stomach, to give this puree a rich, almost foie gras–like flavor. You can buy it online, but it's completely optional; this puree will still be awesome without it. It is great with duck (obviously), and we also love it with fish, particularly lean ones like halibut and yellowtail.

Makes 2 cups

½ **cup unsalted butter**

⅓ **cup sliced onion**

1 **clove garlic slivered**

1 **cup sunchokes, rinsed and cut into bite-size pieces**

Sea salt

1 **quart water**

1½ **tablespoons maguro shuto (optional)**

In a heavy stockpot, melt the butter over medium-high heat. Add the onion and garlic. Stir constantly for 3 to 4 minutes, until the onion starts to caramelize. Stir in the sunchokes and season the mixture with salt. Cook for another 2 to 3 minutes and add the water. Bring the pot to a boil and cook until the water has evaporated, 10 to 12 minutes.

Remove the pot from the heat and transfer the mixture to a blender. As you slowly increase the speed to high, incorporate the maguro shuto. Blend for 60 seconds, until the puree is nice and smooth. Season to taste. Store leftover puree in an airtight container in the fridge for up to 5 days.

IF YOU'RE FEELING AMBITIOUS

We normally suggest asking your butcher to age the ducks for you, but if you're feeling ambitious, you might give the butchering a crack at home. It's fairly simple: Tell your butcher that you need duck breasts still on the carcass (or cage)—essentially a whole duck sans legs and neck. Take it home and place it, uncovered, in your fridge for ten days. (We swab ours with a little brandy and keep it very cold so it doesn't grow surface bacteria or get too funky.) Then you can remove the breasts, using a sharp knife.

cont'd.

PUMPKIN SEED VINAIGRETTE

We're obsessed with the depth of flavor that green chile powder has, so we threw some in some of that, too. We use this on all kinds of stuff, from seafood to grilled summer fruit, like peaches.

Makes 2 cups

½ cup pumpkin seeds, fried in oil until golden brown

⅔ cup olive oil

½ cup minced shallots

Zest and juice of 1 lemon

2 tablespoons sugar

2 teaspoons green Hatch chile powder

½ teaspoon jalapeño powder

3 tablespoons champagne vinegar

Sea salt

With a mortar and pestle, grind the pumpkin seeds into a paste. Drizzle in the olive oil while continuing to mix until well combined. (This will help keep the seeds from getting too chewy.) Transfer the mixture to a medium bowl and whisk in the shallots, lemon zest and juice, sugar, chile powders, and vinegar. Season with salt to taste. This keeps in an airtight container in the fridge for up to 4 days.

SUNCHOKE CHIPS

These are so tasty and crunchy. You'll need a mandoline or sharp knife and a deep fryer.

Makes 1½ cups

½ pound sunchokes, skin on

Vegetable oil, for frying

pulverized salt (see page 40)

Rinse the sunchokes and scrub them well. Fill a mixing bowl with water. Thinly slice the sunchokes (about ¹⁄₁₀-inch thick) into the bowl of water to prevent them from oxidizing.

Preheat a deep-fryer or large pot of oil to 300°F on a deep-fat/candy thermometer.

Shake any excess water from the sunchoke slices and pat them dry with a paper towel. Fry the sunchokes for 3 to 4 minutes, until golden brown. Transfer the chips to a paper towel and season with pulverized salt. Allow them to cool completely before packing them into an airtight container. These will keep for 1 to 2 days if the air is dry.

ode to chef david cassoulet

I have this friend, David, who owns a restaurant in Castelnaudary, France. It's part of the "cassoulet belt," or the region in Southwest France that's known for its traditional slow-cooked, extremely rich, duck fat–soaked casserole. Every town has its own version, so the saying is that Castelnaudary is the Father to Carcassone's Son and Toulouse's Holy Ghost, each one different, but each one honoring age-old custom.

I was introduced to David by Mike Miller, an old-school rock-and-roll guy who owns Delilah's in Chicago, the greatest whiskey bar on Earth. He and his wife decided to take a trip to France to find out who made the best cassoulet in the world. They did a bunch of research and read about this tiny place in Castelnaudary that serves about twenty-six people a day in the summer and thirteen in the winter. They walk in, and there's punk rock music playing—which is a little peculiar. Then they had the cassoulet, and it blew their minds. David, the chef, came out—all long hair and piercings—and told them about how his father taught him how to make the dish. Mike invited him to come out to Chicago, and then bugged me to meet him for lunch. I didn't really know what to say except, "Hey, let's do some cassoulet dinners."

I had a preconceived notion about what cassoulet was—and it wasn't exactly close to the real thing, which David was happy to correct. It's not a dish that you mess with; everything has to be followed to a T. When I asked David about putting bread crumbs in the crust, he almost fainted. Then I figured we'd serve the cassoulet in some copper pots or buy some clay this or that, but David was adamant that he would ship us his *cassoles,* or proper ceramic terrines (which of course all broke in transit and cost us an arm and a leg). The beans had to be from that year's harvest in his town, so those had to be sent, too. Then we went about sourcing a great pig (from Slagel Farms) and great ducks (from Au Bon Canard, up in Caledonia, Minnesota). When David got to Chicago a few days before the event, all the conversations—every hour of every day—were about setting up the cassoulets. But it was all worth it. Those cassoulets—were so good. Like sickeningly good.

This dish is all about the fat. The beans are cooked with salt pork and spices and tons of garlic so when they come to room temperature, the cooking liquid forms this kind of gelatin. Then there are the pork sausages, duck legs and thighs, and pork ribs that have all been partially cooked in duck fat. Everything gets layered inside these large clay pots—along with some pork skin—and cooked for hours. The top forms a

cont'd.

chewy, crunchy, salty crust (sans bread crumbs) that you punch through to get to the creamy beans and buttery meat. It's pretty much the saltiest, fattiest thing you'll ever have. It's like a Quaalude—you need a nap after just a small bowlful. But it changes your whole outlook on life, and it's something you have to have at least once. This is our loyal interpretation of the original dish, and while it's a project, it's fun to do.

Makes 10 *to* 12 *servings*

4 cups dry cannellini or tepary white beans

2 pork trotters

2 pounds pork skin

2 cloves garlic

½ cup pork fatback

Kosher salt

Freshly ground black pepper

4 teaspoons sea salt

¼ cup duck fat

Olive oil

6 Confit Duck Legs and Ribs (recipe follows), thigh bone removed

6 toulouse or other mild, uncooked pork sausages, cut in half

1 rack pork ribs, cut into single ribs

Freshly ground black pepper

In a stockpot large enough to hold the beans as they expand by 20 percent during soaking, soak the beans in water to cover for 6 hours, or until they stop expanding, checking to make sure they are submerged in water the whole time and adding more water as needed. Do not drain the beans.

While the beans are soaking, start the cooking stock: Add the trotters and skin to a large stockpot of water over medium-high heat, and bring to a rolling boil. Continue to boil for 2 hours until the trotters are beginning to fall apart. Strain the stock, setting it aside, and pick the meat from the trotters, discarding the fat, bones, and skin. Reserve the picked trotter meat.

Place the garlic and fatback in a food processor and pulse it into a paste. Transfer to an airtight container, season generously with salt and pepper. Store in the refrigerator for up to 1 week.

Bring the pot of beans and soaking water to a boil over medium-high heat. Drain the beans in a colander and discard the water. Transfer the beans to a heavy-bottom pot. Add the garlic-fat back paste and enough stock to just cover the beans. Season with the salt and, over medium-high heat, bring the liquid to a boil. Turn off the heat. The beans should be just tender, but not fully cooked or falling apart. (Adding the salt at this stage prevents the beans from getting too creamy and falling apart later.)

Now you are ready to build the cassoulet. Preheat the oven to 350°F. Rub the inside of a large casserole pot or high-sided ceramic baking dish with the duck fat and a thin film of olive oil. Add a scoop of beans and a ladleful of stock. Then layer in about one-third of the trotter meat, duck legs and ribs, sausage, and pork rib bones, distributing them north-south across the baking dish— this will make the cassoulet easier to serve at the table. Top the meat with another scoop of beans, just enough stock to just cover the beans, and a second layer of meats. Add another scoop of beans, stock to cover, and the remainder of the meats. Top with the remaining beans and stock to not-quite-cover, reserving about 1½ to 2 quarts of stock to add while the cassoulet cooks.

Place the dish, uncovered, in the oven with a baking sheet underneath to catch any liquid that bubbles over. Cook for 4½ hours, ladling in stock every

30 minutes just to barely cover the beans. After each addition of stock, press down the crust with the back of a spoon. After a few hours of cooking, a crust will start to form on the top from the proteins that are starting to caramelize; just ladle stock over the crust and around the edges. The cassoulet is done when the tip of a knife can be inserted from crust to the bottom of the baking dish without any resistance.

Let the cassoulet cool for 30 minutes before serving. Finish the dish by grinding pepper over the top. Use a knife to cut through the crust and a large spoon to scoop it out, making sure each person gets a little bit of everything.

Leftover cassoulet is amazing. When completely cool, cover and store in the refrigerator for up to 3 days. To reheat, gently warm, uncovered, at 300° for 20 to 30 minutes, until warmed through.

CONFIT DUCK LEGS AND RIBS

For cassoulet, we confit the legs and ribs only about two-thirds done because they finish cooking in the cassoulet. To completely confit, simply cook 1 hour longer.

Makes 6

9 tablespoons sea salt

3 tablespoons freshly ground black pepper

½ cup herbs de provence

2 cloves garlic

6 duck legs and ribs

5 cups liquefied duck fat

1 bay leaf

In a small bowl, combine salt, pepper, and herbs de provence. Spread the spice mixture evenly over the duck legs and ribs. Rub the meat with the garlic. Cover, and let rest in the fridge for 2 days.

Preheat the oven to 300°. Add 1 tablespoon of duck fat to a large skillet over medium-high heat and sear the duck legs and ribs until golden brown on all sides. Place the duck in a small baking dish with high sides and cover with the remaining duck fat. Seal with foil and cook for about 1½ hours, until the meat on the legs just begins to pull away from the bone when prodded with a fork. To finish the confit, cook for 1 hour more.

Remove the foil and let cool completely in the fat, about 2 hours. Whether partially or fully confited, the duck will keep in the fridge, completely covered in the fat, for up to 3 weeks.

pork country ribs with watermelon and sungold salad

Serves 4 to 6

1 tablespoon sambal

½ cup grated
palm sugar

4 sprigs cilantro

½ yellow onion, sliced

1 (2-inch) piece
of ginger, minced

6 cloves garlic,
minced

½ cup soy sauce

3 scallions,
thinly sliced

¼ cup rice
wine vinegar

1 teaspoon freshly
ground black pepper

1 tablespoon
sesame oil

3 pounds pork ribs,
with or without ribs
(you want a good mix
of meat and fat)

2 tablespoons Chinese
mustard

Watermelon and
Sungold Salad (recipe
follows)

My wife and I used to throw these giant barbecues for the staff of Blackbird—and then Blackbird and avec, and then Blackbird, avec, and The Publican. That's when we stopped because there would be about six hundred people at my house, and my wife, her parents, and I would be up all night beforehand pulling about twenty pork shoulders. And while the parties were always raging (often until the sun came up), they got to be just too much work. But the thing I miss the most—besides the soft-shell crab sandwiches and pulled pork we always did—were the country ribs my buddy Jason Monroe and his wife Diana would bring. Every year, they'd show up with ziplock bags full, and we'd just throw them on the grill. I remember being a few drinks in and gnawing on these ribs, and thinking how delicious they were. I sent them an e-mail—which I still have—that said, "Guys, if you give me this recipe, it will be at The Publican always, and you can forever eat in our restaurant for free." They said yes, and the rest is history.

Jason taught me that the trick to making the perfect country rib is first to char them really well. They're excessively fatty by nature, so you want them to be charred to the point where you don't know whether you're eating meat or fat. The other secret is the Triple Dip: you get a char on the ribs, put them back in the marinade, and then back on the grill—three times over. We modified the original recipe to include a sort-of Asian-style marinade and sauce—ok, very Asian-style—with things like palm sugar, soy sauce, ginger, garlic, and scallions, but you don't eat these ribs and think, "Wow, this tastes like Asian food." You just think they're sweet and a little spicy and incredibly delicious. A lot of chefs who eat at the restaurant ask for this recipe, and we give it to them—we're not secretive about these things. Eat them hot or room temperature, but definitely pair them with the Watermelon and Sungold Salad. The combination is by far one of the best recipes in this book

COSMO Everyone who has ever worked at The Publican can tell you that we push acid and salt almost to the point of too salty or too acidic. We like salt, and we like vinegar, and we like fat, and the combination of the three—when they're balanced—is pretty hard to beat. The combination of the Pork Country Ribs with Watermelon and Sungold Salad is the perfect example of our Holy Trinity.

Combine the sambal, palm sugar, cilantro, onion, ginger, garlic, soy sauce, scallions, vinegar, pepper, and sesame oil. Put two-thirds of the marinade into a resealable plastic bag and reserve the remaining one-third in a separate container.

Slather the ribs in the mustard, then submerge them in the marinade in the resealable bag. Let them marinate in the fridge for at least 6 hours, or as long as overnight.

Build a fire on one side of a charcoal grill and let it burn down to embers.

Start the ribs on the hot part of the grill—you're really trying to get a char, so you want to brown and even burn any fat on there. Cook for about 1½ minutes, flip, then dip the ribs back in the marinade. Put them back on the grill and repeat three more times, so the ribs cook for about 12 minutes total.

Serve with the Watermelon and Sungold Salad and sharp knives.

KEEP THE GUTS

If you're planning to make the Chicken Liver Pâté (page 227)—our twist on the classic that includes Asian-flavored ingredients—be sure to reserve the rib "guts," which is what we call the leftover onions, garlic, and ginger that have been marinated along with the ribs.

cont'd.

WATERMELON AND SUNGOLD SALAD

We offered this salad with the pork ribs on the first menu we ever did—and it really is the best thing you ever had in your life. It's a cold salad, which goes against the whole traditional French cooking thing of hot accompaniment with hot dish, cold accompaniment with cold. But we don't care.

1 large shallot	2½ tablespoons honey
Sea salt	1 cup olive oil
Freshly ground black pepper	1½ cups watermelon, or any other seasonal melon, cut into 1-inch cubes
2 tablespoons green coriander seeds	1½ cups sungold tomatoes, halved
⅓ cup champagne vinegar	Chopped cilantro

Mince the shallot and work in the salt and pepper to make ¼ cup haché. Add the green coriander seeds to the haché shallot and run your knife through it a couple more times. Transfer the paste to a bowl and whisk in the champagne vinegar, followed by the honey. Slowly drizzle in the olive oil while you whisk until you get the right acidity and the dressing is emulsified. Taste and adjust the seasoning with more vinegar, honey, salt, or pepper if necessary

In a large bowl, season the watermelon and tomatoes with salt and pepper and dress with about 3 tablespoons of the vinaigrette, making sure you scoop out some of the solids (the shallot and coriander seeds) and add them, too. Taste, adjust the seasoning if necessary or add more vinaigrette, then dump the lot over the ribs and garnish with cilantro.

HACHÉ

Haché is the French word for "minced," and it refers to a technique that we use for all our vinaigrettes. It's when you mince a shallot, add a pinch of salt and pepper, run your knife back through it, then use the side of your knife to mash it all into a paste. This not only ensures that your shallot will be minced really well, but it's also extra insurance that your salad will be well seasoned, since salt added after a vinaigrette is made doesn't always dissolve.

pork loin en tonnato

COSMO *We're always poaching albacore tuna for brunch, seasoning it first before breaking it into chunks and cooking it really slowly in olive oil. Then one day Erling Wu-Bower got the idea to brine pork loin and cook it the same way. It was insanely good—unctuous, tender, and delicious. So we came up with a riff on Vitello Tonnato, a traditional Italian dish that's poached cold veal served with tuna mayonnaise and capers. We serve the pork with some oil-poached tuna (you can skip making it and use high-quality canned white tuna instead if you want) that has been whipped with mayonnaise and then we add Italian-made truffled peach olives, which are immature peaches that have been cured like olives. (Order them. They make the dish.) This is also a great mayo replacement for BLTs and ham sandwiches. We made this for an event that Cleveland native Jonathan Sawyer organized to celebrate the hundreth anniversary of the Central Market there. All these amazing chefs came in for it, and Sawyer's super-competitive, so he was walking around checking out what everyone else was doing. When he came over to our table to watch us put out the food, he just nodded at me and said, "You won, dude." We've also put these ingredients together as a sandwich we named "Tonnato Cubano," down in Miami for the South Beach Food & Wine Festival. People went crazy for it.*

To brine and poach the pork loin: In a medium pot over medium heat, combine the salt, sugar, curing salt, and water. Bring the mixture to a simmer and continue heating until all of the salt and sugar have dissolved, about 4 minutes. Let the brine cool completely, transfer it to a large nonreactive container, and submerge the pork in the brine. Cover and refrigerate for 4 days.

Remove the pork from the brine and rinse under cold water. Pat the meat dry with paper towels. Tightly wrap the pork loin with cheesecloth and fasten with butcher's twine. Continue with the cooking or store the brined pork in the fridge for up to 6 days.

In a large saucepot over low heat, combine the olive oil, thyme, bay leaf, chile, and lemon peel and heat until the oil reaches 165°F on a deep-fat/candy thermometer, 10 to 12 minutes. Add the pork loin and cook until the internal temperature is between 133°F and 135°F, 12 to 15 minutes. Remove the meat from the poaching liquid and let it cool to room temperature. When room temperature, you can store the loin in the fridge, covered and unsliced, for up to 6 days. Bring it back to room temperature, by leaving it out on the counter for about 1 hour, before serving.

Makes 4 to 6 servings

PORK LOIN

½ cup plus 2 teaspoons salt

½ cup granulated sugar

½ teaspoon curing salt #1 (see page 208)

8 cups water

2 pounds boneless pork loin

3 cups olive oil

1 sprig thyme

1 bay leaf

1 chile de árbol

Peel of ½ lemon

POACHED TUNA

½ pound high-quality tuna (such as albacore, yellowfin, bigeye), cleaned and bloodline removed, and cut into 2-inch cubes

Pinch of sugar

Pinch of salt

Zest of 1 lemon, peeled in strips

2 sprigs thyme

1 chile de árbol

1 cup olive oil

cont'd.

Tonnato

**2 tablespoons freshly
squeezed lemon juice**

2 large egg yolks

**1 cup reserved
poaching oil or
grapeseed oil, plus
more as needed**

**2 teaspoons
lemon zest**

**2 diced sautéed
scallions**

**2 teaspoons
chopped chives**

**1 teaspoon
Worcestershire sauce**

**¼ cup Poached Tuna
or canned white tuna,
drained**

Sea salt

**Freshly ground
black pepper**

Sea salt

**Freshly ground
black pepper**

Olive oil

**¼ cup sliced truffled
peach olives**

2 cups arugula

**2 large pinches thinly
sliced red onions**

Juice of 1 lemon

To poach the tuna (if not using canned): Lightly rub the fish with the sugar and salt.

Combine the tuna, lemon zest, thyme, chile de árbol, and olive oil in a small but deep saucepot over the lowest possible flame. Flip the fish in the oil every 3 to 5 minutes, until the fish has lost almost all of its pink color, 20 to 30 minutes total. Remove the pot from the heat and let the fish cool in the oil for 20 to 30 minutes. Set aside.

To make the Tonnato: In a medium bowl, whisk together the lemon juice and egg yolks. While whisking, slowly stream in the oil. The mixture will start to thicken as you add the oil. You're looking for aioli-like consistency, so if it starts getting too thick, whisk in 1 tablespoon of water. Once almost all of the oil is added, whisk in the lemon zest, scallions, chives, and Worcestershire. Using your hands, break up the tuna as finely as you can and whisk it into the bowl. Whisk in the remaining oil. Aside from the chunks of scallions and chives, the sauce should have the consistency of aioli. If it seems a little loose, whisk in a drizzle of poaching oil to thicken. Season with salt and pepper to taste. Use immediately or store in the fridge, covered, for up to 5 days.

To assemble: Cut the cold pork loin into ⅛-inch-thick slices. Lay the slices on a serving platter. Season with salt and pepper, drizzle with olive oil, and top with ⅓ cup of the Tonnato. Flake the remaining 1 cup of poached tuna over the top.

In a medium bowl, combine the peach olives, arugula, and onions and season with salt and pepper. Dress the salad with the lemon juice and olive oil. Layer over the top of the pork and serve

pork belly with calabrian chile glaze

We're putting this recipe in here under protest. Is it a really solid recipe? Absolutely. Have people come in and asked for it every day since we put it on the menu seven years ago? You bet. But are we really still talking about pork belly? I was cooking pork belly like a hundred years ago, when no one was into it. Now everyone is cooking it. So, there, that's my grumpy old man rant.

This is my old-school belly braise recipe. A few days before, we brine them. Then, we score 'em and sear 'em to render off some of the fat. Then we rub the bellies with a garlic and fennel paste and braise them in white wine. It's the best recipe I've found for tender, unctuous belly. We finish it with a sweet, spicy Calabrian Chile Glaze that's great for pretty much anything you want to be really caramel-y. Douse some roast chicken in it or dunk some quail in it and then grill it—super-good.

To brine the belly: In a medium pot over medium-high heat, combine the water, salt, sugar, and curing salt #1 or blend of celery salt and cherry power. Bring to a simmer, making sure all the salt and sugar have dissolved. Let cool and then transfer to a nonreactive container.

Crosshatch the fatty side of the belly, making ¼-inch-deep cuts 1 inch apart. Submerge the pork in the brine and refrigerate for 2 days.

Remove the belly from the brine and rinse under cold water. Let dry overnight, uncovered, in the fridge.

In a large sauté pan over low heat, heat a thin layer of rice bran oil and place the belly into the pan, fatty side-down. Render the fat for 12 to 15 minutes, until a good amount of the fat has collected in the pan and has taken on a golden brown color. Flip the meat and let the lean side cook for 3 to 5 minutes, until golden brown. Let the meat rest until cool enough to touch.

To make the rub: Combine the garlic cloves, confit oil, rosemary, porcini powder, ground fennel, red pepper flakes, Sriracha, and sugar in a blender. Blend until the mixture forms a paste. Use your hands to rub it evenly over the meat. Place the belly in a roasting pan.

To braise the belly: Preheat the oven to 300°F. Heat about a tablespoon of the oil in a large saucepot over medium heat. Add the onion, carrot, celery, and fennel and sauté for about 3 minutes, stirring occasionally with a wooden spoon. Stir in the thyme, chiles, and bay leaf. Squeeze in the juice from the orange halves and then throw in the rinds. Cook for 5 to 6 minutes, until the

Makes 10 *to* 12 *servings*

BRINE
1 gallon water

⅓ cup kosher salt

⅓ cup sugar

¾ ounce curing salt #1 (see page 208) or ½ ounce celery salt mixed with ½ ounce cherry powder (for an all-natural alternative)

1 (5-pound) boneless, skinless pork belly

Rice bran or other high smoking-point oil, such as sunflower, grapeseed, or peanut

RUB
3 cloves of Garlic Confit (page 28)

1 tablespoon oil from Garlic Confit (page 28)

¼ cup fresh rosemary leaves

1 teaspoon porcini powder

¼ teaspoon fennel seeds, ground

¼ teaspoon red pepper flakes

½ teaspoon Sriracha

1 teaspoon sugar

cont'd.

BRAISING LIQUID

Rice bran or other high smoking-point oil, such as sunflower, grapeseed, or peanut

1 white onion, medium diced

1 carrot, diced

2 ribs celery, medium diced

1 fennel bulb, cored and diced

2 sprigs thyme

2 dried chiles de árbol

1 bay leaf

1 orange, halved

1 cup white wine

1 gallon Pork Stock (page 65, or store-bought) or Chicken Stock (page 114, or store-bought)

GLAZE

¾ cup sherry vinegar

¼ cup maple syrup

1 oil-packed Calabrian chile

Rice bran or other high smoking-point oil, such as sunflower, grapeseed, or peanut

¼ cup unsalted butter

onion starts to become translucent. Add the white wine and simmer for 4 to 5 minutes, until the liquid has reduced by three-quarters. Pour in the pork stock and simmer for 4 to 5 minutes, or until the liquid has reduced by three-quarters.

Pour the braising liquid over the belly and cover with foil. Transfer the pan to the oven and cook for 3 hours. The belly should be tender; pierce the meat with the tip of a knife to test it. If it is not tender, re-cover and return the pan to the oven, checking the belly every 15 minutes until it is.

Let the belly cool completely in the liquid at room temperature, about 2 hours. If not serving immediately, you can refrigerate the meat, separate from the braising liquid, in a covered container for up to 6 days. Once refrigerated, return the belly to room temperature before serving. Strain the braising liquid, cover, and store in the fridge for up to 1 week or in the freezer for up to 1 month. You can use it as a fortified seasoned stock for braises, sauces, or soups.

To make the glaze: Combine the vinegar, syrup, and chile in a blender and blend until smooth. Set aside.

To assemble, heat a thin layer of rice bran oil in a large saucepan over medium-high heat. Add the belly to the pan and sear on both sides until golden brown, about 3 minutes per side. Drain off any excess oil and top the meat with the glaze and butter. Let the mixture reduce in the pan while basting the belly with a spoon. Once the mixture becomes nice and tacky and is reduced by about three-quarters, and the belly looks nice and glazed, remove the belly from the pan, slice, and serve.

porchetta with chicories

I once went to Dario Cecchini's butcher shop in Tuscany, where he roasts a porchetta every day. It sits on a giant butcher block and he just cuts chunks off it as people come in. Several people have told me it's the best porchetta they've ever had . . . but I think ours is better. I mean, I kind of have to think that, but seriously, people who come into Publican Quality Meats when they've just pulled a fresh one out of oven and are serving it warm on sandwiches, they see it my way. I love rolling in around noon, cutting a crispy bit off the end, and stuffing it down my gullet.

At The Publican, this dish was one of our original "big box" items—like Ham Chop in Hay, it's a dish to share. When making porchetta, a lot of people take just the belly and the loin and wrap them around each other, but we always want to use the whole animal. We take the entire middle of the pig, trim out the ribs and the tenderloin, then roll that up. We've tweaked the recipe over the years, but the part that's never changed since we started serving it is the marinade. It's an homage to Alice Waters with rosemary, thyme, red pepper flakes, and olive oil. We make a coarse paste, slather it all over the meat, let it marinate, and then roast it. In fact, if you decided you didn't want to go through the process of breaking down the middle of a pig, you could just as easily bring your butcher a container of the marinade, show him or her our recipe, and wind up with a perfectly acceptable ready-to-roast porchetta.

One thing to keep in mind is that porchetta is never as good as it is right after you roast it and it's still warm. Once it cools down, the fat congeals and you lose that supple caramelization. It's definitely the kind of dish you want to cook, let sit for just a quick moment, and then eat.

COSMO We like serving porchetta with our Chicories with Pecorino and Creamy Anchovy Vinaigrette (page 68). You could substitute any chicory besides escarole, like puntarelle, or something a little more mellow, like endive or frisée, which are basically like chicory gateway lettuces.

cont'd.

Makes 14 to 18 servings

¼ cup salt

1 (12- to 14-pound) boneless pork middle section

1¼ cups chopped rosemary leaves

1 tablespoon fresh thyme leaves

3 brown anchovy fillets, rinsed, patted dry, and minced

¼ cup garlic cloves

1 tablespoon freshly ground black pepper

1 tablespoon minced cilantro leaves

1 tablespoon fennel seeds

½ cup extra-virgin olive oil

Spread the salt evenly over the meat and let sit, uncovered, in the fridge overnight.

Combine the rosemary, thyme, anchovies, garlic, pepper, cilantro, and fennel seeds in a blender. Blend on low, slowly bringing it up to medium-high speed. Slowly add the olive oil as the blender is running. Blend until emulsified and smooth, 1 to 2 minutes, using the blender's tamper tool to help, or stopping periodically to scrape down the sides with a spatula.

Slather the flavored oil evenly over the pork. Carefully and tightly roll up the pork so that the belly is wrapped around the loin. Tie the porchetta crosswise with kitchen twine at 1-inch intervals. This will help it keep its shape as it cooks.

Transfer the porchetta to the fridge, uncovered, to sit overnight.

Remove the porchetta from the fridge 1 hour before cooking.

Preheat the oven to 300°F.

Place the pork on a roasting rack set inside a roasting pan. Cover the pan with aluminum foil and transfer it to the oven. Roast for 90 minutes, then check the meat's temperature, and re-check it every 15 minutes thereafter, until the internal temperature reaches 100°F on an instant-read thermometer. Remove the foil and increase the oven temperature to 450°F. Once the internal temperature of the meat reaches 112°F to 115°F, remove the porchetta from the oven and let it cool for about 15 minutes before serving.

Remove the twine and slice thinly. Serve immediately.

BUYING YOUR MEAT

Ask your butcher for a 20- to 25-pound piece of "pork middle," which is essentially the loin attached to the belly. And depending on the section you get, it may also have some of the tenderloin in it. Ask the butcher to remove the bones, glands, and sinuses, at which point the meat will only weigh 12 to 14 pounds. Keep the bones so you can use them to make stock.

pork shoulder and white grits

This recipe 100 percent came from Suzanne Goin. We have differing stories, Suzanne and I, but basically we did a farm dinner in Chicago with Gabrielle Hamilton, Wylie Dufresne, and Michael Schlow and Suzanne made this dish, which she has continued to make. She confited a whole suckling pig in duck fat, picked out the meat, and packed it back together into a patty with residual duck fat. Then she cut squares of the pig skin and put them on top of the patties, so it was like a burger, served them with Tuscan kale cooked with shallots and pancetta, and finished it with a simple salsa verde. My first thought was, *Oh my God.* My second thought was, *I'm stealing that.* And my third thought was, *If I ever write a cookbook, there will be a whole homage to Suzanne* (see page 22). We've interpreted the dish a little differently, but it's got that same fatty, hyper-meaty flavor with tons of texture.

COSMO At the restaurant, we take the picked meat; throw it in a hot pan to crisp it up; deglaze the pan with jus, stock, and a little knob of butter; and cook it down until maybe a touch of juice is left but most of it has gotten to that lip-smacky-tacky place. There's the crunchiness from what got crisped up and the supple meat and the glaze that it's all coated in—it's crazy.

For home-making purposes, we made it a little simpler though—don't get us wrong—it's still a time-consuming project. Don't worry; it just takes time, space, patience, and some help from your local butcher. Instead of cooking an entire suckling pig, you can confit the shoulder—or cook it low and slow in a bunch of lard—then finish it off on the grill with a shellac of tart-sweet verjus glaze, and mound it on a platter with a dandelion green salad and a hot pot of grits. It's a great recipe for having people over. Oh, and don't get fancy when it comes to buying grapes. No local, special variety farmers' market grapes will ever be as good as the ones you get from the grocery store. They might be awesome the first hour after you buy them, but then they get all mushy and don't keep that great grape crunch. We did a taste test; it's true.

To make the confit, start with the spice rub: In a small sauté pan over medium heat, toast the fennel seeds, annatto seeds, and peppercorns for 1 minute, or until the oils start to release and the spices become aromatic. Transfer the spices to a spice grinder or blender. Add the pimentón and red pepper flakes and blend into a fine powder.

cont'd.

Makes 10 to 15 servings

CONFIT

1 tablespoon fennel seeds

2 teaspoons annatto seeds

1½ teaspoons black peppercorns

1½ teaspoons pimentón de la Vera (hot smoked Spanish paprika)

1½ teaspoons red pepper flakes

½ cup firmly packed light brown sugar

½ cup salt

1 (10- to 12-pound) pork shoulder, cut into 4 equal pieces by your butcher

6 pounds lard

VERJUS GLAZE

1 cup honey

1 bay leaf

3 sprigs thyme

2 teaspoons red pepper flakes

1½ quarts verjus

1 quart Pork Stock (page 65, or store-bought) or Chicken Stock (page 114, or store-bought)

SALAD

2 heads Belgian endive, separated into spears, rinsed, and dried

2 cups shelled pistachios, toasted

4 cups red table grapes, halved

Juice of 2 lemons

Olive oil

Sea salt

Freshly ground black pepper

¼ cup saba

White Grits (recipe follows), hot

In a small bowl, mix the spice powder with the sugar and salt. Spread the rub evenly over the pork shoulder pieces, then transfer the pork to a covered container and refrigerate for 5 days.

When ready to confit the pork, rinse the meat under cold water until the rub is removed. Pat dry with paper towels.

Preheat the oven to 300°F.

Add the pork to a large, ovenproof stockpot and add enough lard to just cover the pork. Cook over medium-low heat until the lard is hot and melted.

Cover the stockpot and transfer it to the oven. Cook for 2½ hours. The meat should be just tender enough to be pulled apart. If necessary, cook for an additional 30 minutes. Remove the shoulder from the oven and let it cool in the lard. Transfer the meat and lard to a covered container and refrigerate for up to 1 week. Remove the pork confit from the lard the day before you plan to cook it. Let the shoulder pieces sit at room temperature for about 1 hour prior to cooking. Wipe off as much fat as possible.

Meanwhile, make the verjus glaze: In a large saucepot over medium heat, combine the honey, bay leaf, thyme, and red pepper flakes and bring to a simmer. Add the verjus and stock and reduce until 3 cups of liquid remain. The mixture should be slightly thick, tacky, and still pretty tart from the verjus. Set aside 2 cups for cooking the pork and save the remaining cup in the fridge. The glaze will last for up to 1 week and is great with just about any type of pork or richer meats.

Prepare a medium-hot grill.

Place the pork confit over direct heat. Once you start to get nice char on the first side, flip the pieces and start to brush on the verjus glaze. Continuously flip and glaze the meat for a total cooking time of 15 to 18 minutes, until the outside of the meat is charred and the inside is hot. Remove the pork from the grill and set on a serving platter.

Make the salad: In a large bowl, combine the endive, pistachios, and grapes. Dress the salad with lemon juice and olive oil; season with salt and pepper to taste.

Mound the salad on top of the pork and drizzle saba over everything.

Serve with the pot of White Grits, along with carving knives, forks, and tongs, so everyone can pick at the meat.

WHITE GRITS

We learned how to cook grits from local chef Paul Virant: Use a 4-1 ratio of milk to grits, cook them over super-low heat, and add a shit-ton of butter, salt, and pepper and a squeeze of lemon and maybe a hit of Tabasco.

We get our grits from Geechie Boy Mill in South Carolina—hands-down the best and easily ordered online. If you use another kind, just make sure to check their recommended ratio of liquid to grits.

Serves 8

2 quarts whole milk

1 pint white grits
(we like Geechie Boy Mill)

½ cup unsalted butter, cubed

Juice of 1 lemon

Sea salt

Freshly ground black pepper

Tabasco sauce (optional)

In a large saucepot over medium-low heat, bring the milk to a simmer. Stream in the grits while whisking and then reduce the heat to low. Slowly cook the grits, stirring every few minutes, for about 30 minutes, or until the grits are tender. Stir in the butter and lemon juice and season with salt and pepper to taste. Add a dash of Tabasco, if you want.

Serve the grits immediately, or cool them and save for later. Reheat the grits over very low heat in a wide, shallow pan, stirring in 1 to 3 tablespoons milk to loosen and keep them from burning.

ham chop in hay

To come up with the food that would define The Publican, I looked to what peasants were eating in nineteenth-century Europe. I wanted to offer dishes that were not only rustic and old-timey but also that evoked that kind of over-the-top revelry of a feast or last supper. I ended up pulling a lot of inspiration from old English cookbooks, where I found farmers' recipes for things like mutton and game birds roasted in hay. I had to see for myself if you could taste the grassiness from the hay, so I tried it various ways, sometimes using the kind they sell at pet stores for guinea pigs if my farmer friends didn't have any (though I wouldn't recommend that option—try to find hay from a local farm and make sure it hasn't been sprayed with any chemicals). I found that there's a real richness that comes from the smoke and butter and hay. Sure, it's a complicated recipe, but it's one that pays off big time. I made this dish for a chef event after The Publican first opened, and one table full of chefs, including Tom Colicchio, Jonathan Waxman, Marc Vetri—all these big name guys—started chanting, "Ham Chop in Hay, Ham Chop in Hay." When it's done right, it's the best pork chop you've ever tasted. We serve it with whatever is in season, like grilled fruit and chicories, but it's just as delicious with nothing as it is with a lot of stuff.

COSMO At the restaurant, we hot-smoke the ham chops for four hours and then vacuum-seal them with butter, herbs, and hay before cooking them in the oven. We're not suggesting you try to do that at home, but you can recreate the flavor by throwing everything into a Dutch oven and roasting in the oven.

Makes 2 to 3 servings

BRINE

1½ cups kosher salt

2 cups firmly packed brown sugar

1½ ounces Insta Cure #1

1 gallon plus 1 quart water

1 (20- to 25-ounce) double-bone pork chop

To make the brine: Combine the salt, brown sugar, and Insta Cure #1 in a large pot along with the water. Heat over medium-high heat and cook until the pot comes to a simmer or the sugar and salt have dissolved. Let cool.

Add the pork chop to the brine and let sit in the fridge for 3 days.

Remove the chop from the brine and let it dry, uncovered, in the fridge overnight.

Take the chop out of the fridge 1 hour before cooking. Preheat the oven to 375°F.

cont'd.

1 large handful of hay (enough to cover the chop on all sides)

3 sprigs thyme

1 fresh bay leaf, toasted (see page 65) or 2 dry bay leaves

1/2 bunch dandelion greens, washed and torn into 2-inch-long pieces

2 plums or 1 large peach (about 3/4 cup of fruit), pits removed and cut into wedges

1 recipe Poppy-Seed Vinaigrette (recipe follows)

Put the chop in a Dutch oven with the hay, thyme, and bay leaf. Cook until its internal temperature reaches 140°F on an instant-read thermometer. Remove from the oven and let rest 10 minutes before serving.

Toss together the dandelion greens and plums or peach and dress with Poppyseed Vinaigrette.

Cut the chop off the bone into 1/2 inch-thick slices. Lay the slices on your serving platter, top with the dressed greens and plums, and serve.

POPPY-SEED VINAIGRETTE

This vinaigrette is creamy and savory, with just a little bit of sweetness from the mayonnaise. Tossing fruit in it is a great way to accentuate the natural sweetness of the produce. Tropea onions are a sweet Italian variety, ovoid in shape; find them at farmers' markets.

Makes about 2 cups

1 cup buttermilk

2 tablespoons heavy cream

1/2 cup mayonnaise (we like Hellman's/Best Foods)

1 1/2 tablespoons 12-year-aged moscatel vinegar

Zest and juice of 2 lemons

1/3 cup tropea or red onions, sliced into thin rings

2 1/2 tablespoons poppy seeds

Sea salt

Freshly ground black pepper

Whisk everything together and taste. Adjust the salt and pepper if needed. Leftovers will keep in an airtight container in the fridge for up to 1 week.

lamb leg "ham steaks" with shelling beans

COSMO Lamb sinew can be really tough; tougher than pork or some cuts of beef, and stringy. So doing anything other than roasting a leg whole can be a huge pain because you need to take out all the bones and dig out all the silver skin. But we discovered an old Italian dry-aging method—from Joseph Mussillami, whose family owned a lamb-only butcher shop in Chicago—for which you salt the leg, wrap it in newspaper, and just leave it in your fridge for a month. When you unwrap it, the sinew will have broken down, so you can cut the lamb into "ham steaks," or cross-section slices where you see the bone in the middle. And when you grill it, the meat is tender and juicy. We've changed the method slightly, though we're still letting the lamb dry-age.

You can ask your butcher to age the lamb for you. If choosing the latter, lightly salt the lamb when you get home, let it sit in your fridge wrapped in newspaper for two weeks to one month, then take it back to your butcher to have him remove the shank, aitchbone, and anything that looks a little funky from the aging process. You can also have him cut the leg into ½-inch-thick steaks. It's normal for the steaks to range in size and weight from a few ounces to about a pound.

The Charred Herb Vinaigrette is borrowed from the Argentine chef Francis Mallmann, who is pretty much a fire-cooking wizard. We bundle together herbs like sage and parsley and aromatics like scallions and leeks, dunk them in verjus or vinegar, and roll the bundle on the grill. We keep dunking and rolling, dunking and rolling, until the herbs are charred and tender. Then we chop everything up, so it's almost like a cross between a vinaigrette and a relish. Add that to the beans and their cooking liquid plus the lamb? So good.

———————

Prepare a hot grill.

Season the lamb steaks with salt and pepper and place them on a hot grill. Cook for about 2 minutes on each side and then dunk them in the Sumac Glaze. Place the glazed meat back on the grill and cook for another 1 minute per side, or until the glaze starts to char. Remove from the grill.

While the steaks are cooking, slowly warm the Shelling Beans up in a pot. Once hot, taste and, if needed, season again with a splash of sherry vinegar.

Makes 12 to 16 servings

1 (8- to 12-pound) leg of lamb, cut into ½-inch-thick steaks

Sea salt

Freshly ground black pepper

3 cups Sumac Glaze (recipe follows)

2 quarts Shelling Beans (recipe follows)

Sherry vinegar

2 cups Charred Herb Vinaigrette (recipe follows)

Freshly squeezed lemon juice

Olive oil

½ cup mint leaves

½ cup parsley leaves

½ cup dill fronds

cont'd.

Arrange the lamb steaks on a serving platter and spoon the beans over the top. Drizzle everything with the Charred Herb Vinaigrette and give it all a sprinkle of salt, lemon juice, and olive oil.

In a small bowl, combine the mint, parsley, and dill. Spread the herb mixture on top of the lamb leg and serve. The meat should be tender enough to eat with just a fork, but you may want to serve it with a knife, just in case.

SUMAC GLAZE

The sugars in this glaze start to caramelize as the meat cooks, giving everything a nice sweet 'n' sour char with a little bit of heat. It's great with any red meat; just be careful not to use too much or your dish will get too sweet.

Makes 3 cups

1 tablespoon olive oil

5 garlic cloves, sliced

2 tablespoons sumac

2 tablespoons Aleppo pepper

2 tablespoons pomegranate molasses

2 cups firmly packed brown sugar

2 tablespoons champagne or white wine vinegar

2 tablespoons salt

3 tablespoons water

Peel of 1 lemon

In a medium saucepot, heat the olive oil over medium heat. Sweat the garlic for about 1 minute. Add in the sumac and Aleppo pepper and toast them in the oil for 30 to 60 seconds, until fragrant. Pour in the molasses, sugar, vinegar, salt, and water, and bring the liquid to a simmer. Throw in the lemon peel and turn off the heat. Let the mixture steep for 30 minutes. Strain the sauce. The glaze will keep in a closed container in the fridge for up to 1 week. Remove the glaze from the fridge for at least 1 hour before using, as it can be very thick when cold.

cont'd.

SHELLING BEANS

We cook our shelling beans using the classic Chez Panisse method in a wide skillet over low heat with water, olive oil, onion, garlic, and thyme—like a stovetop braise. We've also found that because drying beans makes them more acidic as measured by their pH level, if we throw a couple Brussels sprouts or cabbage leaves into the pot, the beans will cook twice as fast and get nice and creamy. Just remember not to add salt or anything acidic like vinegar or lemon until the very end, or the beans will get tough.

It's important to use good-quality dried beans—the shells shouldn't be flaking off, and the beans shouldn't be cracked. They're typically more expensive because it means they've been properly dried and well cared for, but it makes a huge difference in their flavor and consistency.

Makes about 8 cups

⅓ cup olive oil

1 fresh bay leaf, toasted (see page 65)

1 sprig rosemary

3 dried chiles de árbol

1 tablespoon chopped thyme

1 white onion, sliced

1 head garlic, cloves slivered

6 cups fresh shelling beans (preferably fresh cranberry beans, but rehydrated dried beans will work too)

2 quarts Chicken Stock (page 114, or store-bought), another type of stock, or water

1 Brussels sprout or 2 cabbage leaves (optional)

Sea salt

Freshly ground black pepper

3 tablespoons 25-year-aged sherry vinegar

In a large saucepot, heat the olive oil over medium heat. Add the bay leaf, rosemary, chiles, and thyme. Stir them in the oil for about 1 minute before adding the onion and garlic. Continuously stir the mixture until the onion is tender and translucent, 5 to 7 minutes, then add the beans, stock, and Brussels sprout or cabbage. Allow the liquid to come to a simmer and then decrease the heat so it's just under a simmer. Let the beans cook for about 45 minutes, stirring occasionally and making sure the pot does not simmer or boil in order to prevent the beans from overcooking or breaking up.

Once the beans are tender and creamy all the way through, remove them from the stove and season them with salt and sherry vinegar. (Don't be tempted to do this sooner—it can make the beans tough.)

CHARRED HERB VINAIGRETTE

We first saw a version of a charred herb salsa in Francis Mallmann's book *Mallmann on Fire*. We loved the idea, maybe because we like grilling stuff so much, or maybe because we're all jealous of cooking over a campfire in Patagonia. Either way, we have been using versions of Mallman's salsa ever since. The wine in this recipe adds an almost floral note, with a little spice on the back from the Marash pepper (a Turkish spice). We love this on fish, meat, or vegetables—particularly anything grilled.

Makes 4 cups

Dipping Liquid

Zest and juice of 2 lemons	2 cups extra-virgin olive oil
½ cup rice wine vinegar	1 tablespoon Marash pepper flakes
1½ cups dry white wine	2 tablespoons granulated sugar

Herb Mix

1 bunch parsley	1 bunch mint
1 bunch thyme	1 bunch cilantro
1 bunch dill	1 bunch scallions
1 bunch basil	

Vinaigrette

1 cup champagne vinegar	1 tablespoon Marash pepper flakes
1 cup olive oil	2 tablespoons fish sauce
¼ cup honey	1½ tablespoons minced garlic

To make the dipping liquid: In a medium bowl, combine the lemon zest and lemon juice. Add the vinegar, wine, oil, pepper flakes, and sugar and stir to combine. Set aside.

To make the herb mix: Remove any larger stems from the herbs. Use butchers twine to bundle the herbs together with the scallions. Place the herb mix on a grill over medium heat and let it char. Every few minutes, dunk the herbs in the dipping liquid, then return the bundle to the grill. Once all the herbs are charred and the scallions have become tender, remove them from the grill. Untie the herb bundle and cut off and discard all the stems. Chop the herbs and transfer them to a medium bowl.

Make the vinaigrette: In a small bowl, whisk together all the ingredients.

Mix in any remaining dipping liquid and the herb mix. Season with salt to taste. Transfer to an airtight container and store in the fridge for up to 5 days.

flap steak with strawberries, mint, and feta

Makes 4 servings

MARINADE

6 tablespoons star anise

2 tablespoons black peppercorns

2 teaspoons red pepper flakes

4 teaspoons minced garlic

1 teaspoon minced fresh ginger

¼ cup rice wine vinegar

1½ cups mirin

1 cup soy sauce

2 cups extra-virgin olive oil

1 pound flap steak (or hanger or sirloin)

STRAWBERRY, FETA, AND MINT SALAD

1½ cups strawberries, stemmed and cut into bite-size pieces

1 lemon, cut in half

Sea salt

Extra-virgin olive oil

½ cup crumbled French feta (see note, opposite)

2 tablespoons chopped wild mint

2 tablespoons saba or aged balsamic, plus more for garnish (see note, opposite)

1 handful arugula

Flap steak—or bavette—is hands-down our favorite cut of meat, and it's one that not too many people know about. It's got deep, rich flavor and great marbling like hanger steak, in addition to nice mouthfeel and chew, almost like a flank or skirt steak would have. We tell everyone who comes into Publican Quality Meats, "You gotta try it; you don't like it, come back, and we'll get you a New York." We've never had to take one back and now people keep coming in and ordering it. If you can't find flap, you can substitute hanger or sirloin.

Flap steak needs a marinade to help break it down, so we use a star anise marinade that comes from a guy named Ken Minami. Ken is one of my cooking mentors—I started as a prep cook in a little kitchen at a local place called Metropolis Café, and we'd make stuff fresh, like cannelonis and casseroles, every day for the deli case. Ken just has this amazing finesse, and one of the tools in his satchel is this star anise recipe. It's coarsely ground star anise pods, black pepper, mirin, soy sauce, and lots of red pepper flakes. You don't eat a piece of meat that's been marinated in it and think, *Oh, star anise*. Something just trips the delicious receptor in your brain, and you know that it's really, really good. And once you've marinated the meat in this, it doesn't need any extra salt when cooking— maybe only a little before you serve it. As for strawberries and feta—right out of the box it's really 1980s, but in-season strawberries and creamy French feta? You can't deny the combo. It's really good.

To make the marinade: Add all the anise, peppercorns, pepper flakes, garlic, ginger, vinegar, mirin, and soy cause to a blender and blend. Keep the blender running as you slowly add the oil until all the oil has been incorporated. Pour the marinade into a shallow container big enough to fit the steak and fully submerge the meat. Cover and let sit in the fridge overnight.

Transfer the steak directly from the marinade to a hot grill and cook until there's a nice char on both sides and the inside is medium-rare (130°F, if you're using an instant-read meat thermometer), about 5 to 7 minutes total. If you want it a little more done, just cook a little bit longer. Transfer the steak to a plate to rest for 5 to 10 minutes.

While the steak is resting, make the salad: Place the strawberries in a bowl, season with a squeeze of lemon juice, a pinch of salt, and a drizzle of olive oil (just enough just to coat). Add the feta and mint and gently toss to combine.

Slice the steak against the grain. Taste a corner piece, and season with salt if needed. Arrange the pieces on a serving platter and top with the strawberry, feta, and mint salad. Squeeze a little lemon over the steak, garnish with the arugula, and lastly, drizzle a little saba over everything and serve.

A FEW RECOMMENDATIONS

This recipe is best made on the grill, so make sure you get your grill nice and hot before cooking the steak.

Resting the steak is key. If you cut into it right away, the proteins won't have time to relax, all the juices will run out, and your steak will be tough and dry. Resting it for 5 to 10 minutes will result in a nice pink, juicy steak.

We like French feta better than Greek—it's creamier and less salty. We use the Valbreso brand.

If you can find saba—a syrupy Italian vinegar that tastes like the best balsamic and is made from cooking down grape must, sometimes with pear or apple in there, too— we really like it for this dish. You can substitute aged balsamic, but it doesn't have the same bitter notes.

To the Mad Butcher:
Charcuterie and Sausages

Here's to the MAD BUTCHER:
    Who, with Blades that Blur
        —through tendon, I'm sure—
    Carves the Barnyard's Fetid Flavor
    Into Rare Meats
    We Graciously Cook
    And Respectfully Savor.

We knew when we opened The Publican that we'd make our own charcuterie. And not just dry-cured salumi but terrines and headcheese and pork pies— all those old-school, old-world classics that utilize every inch of an animal. We had super-lofty goals for what we could produce, and we had all the talent to drive it (namely Brian Huston, Erling Wu-Bower, and Cosmo, who were really passionate about taking on the charcuterie program). So we did what we could in the space that we had. But we were basically doing the impossible—trying to stuff everything that we were sourcing and curing into a very small walk-in. We tried out different locations for our stash—a storage room in an undisclosed location (Erling's parents' basement)—but we needed more space. That's when the idea for the butcher shop, Publican Quality Meats, came about.

Our style of sausage making was sort of born out of a lot of failure. A lot of our sausages were breaking—the fat and meat were separating when you cooked them—and they didn't have the firm hot-dog snap that we love. Honestly, a lot of times when you order house-made sausage in a restaurant, it's broken. It might taste good, but it'll be crumbly and oily. Or when you're grilling at home, if the sausage is sort of spitting fat at you, that's a sign that it's probably broken. So we were losing a big batch of sausage just about every week after Publican Quality Meats opened, which lead Erling to develop our now-signature method: Keep everything super-cold (we partially freeze the meat before we grind it, in addition to the mixing bowl, paddle, and meat-grinder parts), then we paddle the crap out of it with a mixer. It's like making mayonnaise—you're creating a bond with the water and fat around the proteins. The same thing applies to sausages. We like to joke that the sausage at The Publican is so tight you could bounce a quarter off it. That nice, taut bind gives the sausage great snap and texture. Don't get discouraged if yours don't come out perfect the first couple times. Keep at it. It has taken us years to become mediocre at it.

COSMO We've broken down our charcuterie into four basic categories. You got your sausages (Mettwurst, Morteau, Toulouse, Boudin Noir), your bacons (Publican Bacon and Pancetta), your whole-muscle salamis (Spicy Coppa and Lonza), and your terrines (Pork and Duck Rillettes, Chicken Liver Pâté, Harissa Pâté, Headcheese, and Pork Pies). But first, a tutorial on making cured meats:

OTHER STUFF YOU'LL NEED

Hog casings (28- to 32-millimeter size)

Beef middles or casings (we use 14-inch pre-tied beef middles that we get from a natural casing company in Wisconsin, see page 316)

Stand mixer with a paddle attachment

Meat grinder or stand mixer attachment

Sausage stuffer or stand mixer attachment

Sausage pricker

Sharp boning knife

Butcher's twine

Cheesecloth

Terrine mold

To Make Cured Meats, You Need These Five Things

1. Salt

Salt (specially curing salt #1 and curing salt #2, which you can buy in specialty stores and online) is the most important ingredient in curing meat. It not only enhances the flavor of the meat, but it also increases the speed at which the meat dehydrates, which is a good thing because it limits the amount of water available for certain bacteria to grow and spoil the meat. The amount of salt in cured meat affects its texture, flavor, moisture, and ability to slice by reacting with the salt-soluble proteins in the meat.

2. Water

Water or other liquid of some sort (for example, wine) is not necessarily required but can help with the flavor and the ability to mix and emulsify the meat.

3. Nitrate or Nitrite

Nitrates are converted into nitrites during the curing process. Without them, we wouldn't be able to cure meat because nitrites keep bacteria from growing, especially botulism. They also keep the flavor fresh-tasting and the meat from oxidizing and turning brown. They're the reason the meat is nice and red when you cut into a salami.

4. Sugar

Sugar is used for flavor and is also what lactic acid feeds off of in fermented sausage (which is a good thing). Sugars converted into lactic acid directly result in the sourness or tang of the salami. You can use granulated sugar, but refined sugars, such as dextrose, are more commonly used, and that's what we use.

5. Spices

Although spices aren't necessarily important to the curing process, they're crucial for the final flavor of the meat. Without spices, cured meat, such as prosciutto or Serrano ham, would taste like the pure animal it came from. When making salami, though, you want to enhance the off-cuts you're using and produce a unique flavor.

The Process

1. Selecting the Meat

This is the crucial first step for making great cured meat. If you use poor-quality meat, you end up with a poor-quality product. We use heritage Shlagel, LaPryor, and Becker Lane pork because these high-quality meats have better flavor. This is particularly important when you're curing the whole muscle (as for prosciutto, coppa, and lonza) because you can't hide the meat behind a bunch of seasoning—the point is to taste the pure richness of the pork.

2. Mixing

This is when a sound recipe is your friend. You're combining your ground meat with spices, curing salts, water or wine, sugar, and nitrates.

3. Fermenting

This is the process of putting the meats at a slightly higher-than-desirable temperature and humidity, ideally 65°F to 70°F and 80 to 90 percent relative humidity. Fermenting is important because it helps lower the acidity or pH level of the meat, which makes for a safer product. It also helps kick-start lactic acid formation, which plays a big role in the final flavor.

4. Drying

The final step of the process is drying the meat. Ideally the meat would sit in a temperature and humidity-controlled room (between 52°F and 57°F and 75 to 80 percent relative humidity). In your home, your basement or garage can work, so long as you're keeping a close eye on a temperature/humidity sensor and there's no chance of bugs or pests getting into your meat. It usually takes 6 to 8 weeks for a normal-size salami to dry and can be longer with larger products.

mettwurst

This is inspired by a great ring bologna that I get at Brandon Meats and Sausage in Brandon, Wisconsin, on the way to ice fishing every year. Brian Huston and I started tasting ring bolognas and testing recipes. We realized that the best ring bolognas are all about massive amounts of salt and fat.

Makes 5
[1-pound] sausages

1½ tablespoons mustard seeds

½ tablespoon coriander seeds

1 teaspoon caraway seeds

1 allspice berry

1½ teaspoons celery seeds

1½ teaspoons black peppercorns

1 teaspoon freshly grated nutmeg

3 rounded tablespoons kosher salt

1 teaspoon curing salt #1 or 1¼ teaspoons celery salt

1 teaspoon garlic granules

3½ tablespoons dextrose

2½ pounds pork shoulder, cut into 1- to 2-inch cubes

2½ pounds beef chuck

5 (14-inch-long) beef casings

Over medium heat in a small skillet, toast the mustard seeds until fragrant, 30 seconds to 1 minute. Set aside. Return the skillet to the heat and add the coriander seeds, caraway seeds, allspice, celery seeds, and peppercorns. Transfer the toasted spices, except the mustard seeds, to a spice grinder. In a large bowl, combine the toasted and ground spices with the nutmeg, kosher salt, curing salt #1 or celery salt, garlic granules, and dextrose. Add the meat and toss until it's well coated. Cover and transfer to the fridge to marinate overnight.

Fit a grinder with the smallest die and grind the meat. Lay the ground meat on a baking sheet and transfer it to the freezer for 1 hour, or until the edges start to freeze and get crispy. If there's room, put the paddle attachment and mixer bowl in there, too.

Preheat the oven to 350°F.

Add the meat to the chilled mixer bowl and, using the chilled paddle attachment, mix until fully emulsified, 3 to 4 minutes. Test the mixture to see if it is well mixed: form a golf ball–size round and set it in a small pan. Place the pan in the oven and bake for 3 to 5 minutes, until cooked through. If the ball stays firm, doesn't crumble, and doesn't leak any (or very much) fat, then it's emulsified, and the sausage mixture is ready to stuff into the casings. If the mixture isn't ready, mix for 1 more minute.

Stuff one-fifth of the sausage into the beef casing. Poke the filled casing with a sausage pricker, and then tie as tightly as you can. Repeat until you have 5 sausages. Hang the sausage links from the top rack in the fridge overnight.

Prepare a smoker, using hickory or applewood chips. Smoke the sausages until they are fully cooked or their internal temperature reaches 155°F on an instant-read meat thermometer. Cool and serve. The sausage will keep in the fridge for up to 2 weeks or vacuum sealed in the freezer for up to 4 months.

morteau

Morteau is a traditional smoked sausage from the Morteau region in eastern France, where they take their sausage very seriously. We learned this the hard way when the French government sent us a "Cease and Desist," saying we aren't allowed to call it Morteau if it isn't made in Morteau. We tried re-naming it Freedom Sausage, but that just didn't have the same ring to it . . . Basically, it's the godfather of andouille sausage.

Makes 15
[6- to 7-inch] links

3 allspice berries

½ teaspoon whole cloves

½ teaspoon ground mace

6 juniper berries

2½ tablespoons kosher salt

1 teaspoon curing salt #1

1 teaspoon dry mustard powder

2½ teaspoons granulated garlic

2½ teaspoons piment d'Espelette

1½ teaspoons onion granules

1½ teaspoons thyme leaves

2½ teaspoons ground cayenne pepper

1 (6-pound) pork shoulder, cut into 1- to 2-inch cubes

1 hank hog casings

Toast and grind the allspice, cloves, mace, and juniper. Combine the toasted spices with the kosher salt, curing salt #1, dry mustard powder, granulated garlic, piment d'Espelette, onion granules, thyme, and cayenne in a large bowl and mix well. Add the pork and coat completely with the seasoning. Cover the bowl and place in the fridge to marinate overnight.

Fit a grinder with the ³⁄₁₆-inch die and grind the meat. Lay the ground meat flat on a baking sheet and transfer it to the freezer for 1 hour or until the edges start to freeze and get crispy. If there's room, put the paddle attachment and mixer bowl in the freezer, too.

Preheat the oven to 350°F.

Add the meat to the chilled mixer bowl and, using the chilled paddle attachment, mix until fully emulsified, 3 to 4 minutes.

Test the mixture to see if it is well mixed: form a golf ball–size round and set it in a small pan. Place the pan in the oven and cook for 3 to 5 minutes, until cooked through. If the ball stays firm, doesn't crumble, and doesn't leak any (or very much) fat, then it's emulsified, and the sausage mixture is ready to stuff into the casings. If the mixture isn't ready, mix for 1 more minute.

Stuff the sausage into the hog casing, filling 6 to 7 inches. Poke the filled casing with a sausage pricker and then tie as tightly as you can. Repeat until you have 15 sausages. Set the sausages on a baking sheet or platter and let rest in the fridge overnight.

Prepare a smoker, using hickory or applewood chips.

Smoke the sausages until they're fully cooked or their internal temperature reaches 155°F on an instant-read meat thermometer. Cool and serve. The sausage will keep in the fridge for up to 2 weeks or, vacuum-sealed, up to 1 month in the freezer.

toulouse sausage

This is a white wine–garlic sausage, like a French-style Brat. It's our fancy hotdog.

3 tablespoons kosher salt

1 teaspoon curing salt #1

2 teaspoons granulated garlic

1 tablespoon thyme leaves

1 (5-pound) pork shoulder, cut into 1- to 2-inch cubes

½ cup white wine, chilled

1 hank hog casings

Combine the kosher salt, curing salt #1, granulated garlic, and thyme in a large bowl and mix well. Add the pork and coat completely with the seasoning ingredients. Cover and transfer to the fridge to marinate overnight.

Fit a grinder with the 3/16-inch die and grind the meat. Lay the ground meat flat on a sheet pan and transfer to the freezer for 1 hour or until the edges start to freeze and get crispy. If there's room, put the paddle and bowl from your mixer in the freezer, too.

Add the meat and white wine to the chilled bowl and, using the chilled paddle attachment, mix until fully emulsified, 3 to 4 minutes. Test the mixture to see if it is well mixed: form a golf ball–size round and set it in a small pan. Place the pan in the oven and cook for 3 to 5 minutes, until cooked through. If the ball stays firm, doesn't crumble, and doesn't leak any (or very much) fat, then it's emulsified, and the sausage mixture is ready to stuff into the casings. If the mixture isn't ready, mix for 1 more minute.

Stuff the sausage into hog casing, filling 6 to 7 inches. Poke the filled casing with a sausage pricker and then tie as tightly as you can. Repeat until you have 15 sausages. Set the sausages on a baking sheet or platter and let rest in the fridge overnight.

Bring a large pot of water to a boil. Line a baking sheet with paper towels and set out a cooling rack. Decrease the heat so the boiling water is 180°F to 190°F on an instant-read thermometer. Poach the first 5 sausages until their internal temperature reaches 155°F on the thermometer. Transfer the poached sausages to the paper towels to drain, and then to the cooling rack to cool. Repeat for the remaining 10 sausages.

The poached sausages will keep in the fridge for up to 2 weeks, in the freezer for up to 1 month, or for as long as 4 months in the freezer if vacuum-sealed. Alternatively, you may skip the poaching step, in which case the sausages will keep for 4 to 5 days in the fridge before you grill or pan-fry them.

boudin noir [blood sausage]

COSMO There are some styles of boudin noir that are composed completely of blood, and then there are those that are mostly meat and just flavored with blood. This one is half and half. It has a nice heat to it and great sort of floral flavor. You can find beef blood at almost any Asian market or you can ask your butcher.

Combine the kosher salt, curing salt #1, granulated garlic, coriander seeds, anise seeds, pimentón, piment d'Espelette, thyme, oregano, parsley, cooked onions, sherry, and white wine in a large bowl and mix well. Add the fat back and pork and coat completely. Cover and transfer to the fridge to marinate overnight.

Fit a grinder with the smallest die and grind the meat. Lay the meat flat on a baking sheet and transfer to the freezer for 1 hour or until the edges start to freeze and get crispy. If there's room, put the paddle and bowl from your mixer in there, too.

Add the beef blood to a heavy pot over low heat, stirring constantly until the blood starts to thicken, 5 to 10 minutes. It should almost have the look of black whipped cream when it's ready.

Preheat the oven to 350°F.

Add the meat, cooked blood, buttermilk, and chives to the chilled bowl and, using the chilled paddle attachment, mix until fully emulsified, 3 to 4 minutes. Test the mixture to see if it is well mixed: form a golf ball–size round and set it in a small pan. Place the pan in the oven and cook for 3 to 5 minutes, until cooked through. If the ball stays firm, doesn't crumble, and doesn't leak any (or very much) fat, then it's emulsified and the sausage mixture is ready to stuff into the casings. If the mixture isn't ready, mix for 1 more minute.

Stuff the sausage into hog casing, filling 6 to 7 inches. Poke the filled casing with a sausage pricker and then tie as tightly as you can. Repeat until you have 15 sausages. Set the sausages on a baking sheet or platter and let rest in the fridge overnight.

Bring a large pot of water to a boil. Decrease the heat so the boiling water is 180°F to 190°F on an instant-read thermometer. Poach the sausage until its internal temperature reaches 155°F on the thermometer. Transfer the poached sausages to the paper towels to drain, and then to the cooling rack to cool. Repeat for the remaining 10 sausages.

The poached sausages will keep in the fridge for up to 2 weeks, in the freezer for up to 1 month, or for as long as 4 months in the freezer if vacuum-sealed. Or you can skip the poaching step and the sausages will keep for 4 to 5 days.

Makes 15
[6- to 7-inch] links

2 tablespoons kosher salt

1 teaspoon curing salt #1

1½ teaspoons granulated garlic

1½ teaspoons coriander seeds

1½ teaspoons anise seeds

1 teaspoon pimentón de la Vera (hot smoked Spanish paprika)

1½ teaspoons piment d'Espelette

1 teaspoon fresh thyme leaves

1 teaspoon dried Mexican oregano

1½ teaspoons chopped parsley

1 onion, thinly sliced, sautéed, and cooled

3 tablespoons sherry

3 tablespoons white wine

1¼ pounds pork fatback

4¾ pounds pork shoulder, cut into 1- to 2-inch cubes

3½ cups beef blood

1½ teaspoons buttermilk

1½ teaspoons minced chives

1 hank hog casings

publican bacon

Since our goal at The Publican was to do over-the-top oysters, pork, and beer—and because people are crazy about bacon—we decided to do our own ridiculous version. We cure pork bellies in maple syrup, hot smoke them, and then cut them into super-thick slices that are more like blocks. I'm a huge fan of when you have pancakes with bacon or sausage on the side and the syrup gets on the meat—this is just like that, a little salty, a little smoky, and a little sweet. To serve it, we get it as crispy as we can, baste it with a little more maple syrup, and that's the story. Like any other recipe of ours, it's about the quality of the ingredients, so start with great pork and great maple syrup.

Makes 5 pounds

5-pound slab pork belly

1 gallon Pork Stock (page 65, or store-bought) or water

½ cup B-grade maple syrup plus more for drizzling

1 tablespoon rice bran oil

Preheat the oven to 350°.

Place the pork belly, pork stock or water, and maple syrup in a braising pan over medium heat and bring to a simmer. Cover tightly with plastic wrap and foil. Braise in the oven for 2½ hours, until the tip of a knife easily slides through the thickest part. Set aside to cool in the liquid, about 1 hour.

When completely cool, cut the slab in half and then cut each half into ¾-inch slices. The bacon is very rich, so cut 1 or 2 slices per person.

Heat the oil in a saute pan over medium-high heat. Sear the slices on both sides, working in batches. Transfer the slices to a serving platter and drizzle each slice with 1 teaspoon of maple syrup.

Leftover bacon slab keeps in the fridge, tightly wrapped, for up to 3 weeks.

pancetta

COSMO Pancetta is often referred to as "Italian bacon." Unlike bacon, however, it's not smoked and is much more herbaceous and spicy (from a ton of black pepper).

————————

In a large bowl, combine all the ingredients except the pork and the pepper. Mix well. Rub the mixture evenly over the belly, transfer the pork to an airtight container, and store in the fridge for 7 days. Flip the belly every other day.

Rinse and dry the belly. Rub the lean side of the meat with the black pepper. Roll up the belly into a cylinder as tight as you can so the seasoned side is on the inside. Use butcher's twine to tie the cylinder as tightly as you can so it keeps its shape. Transfer to the fridge to dry for 2 weeks, hanging from the top rack if possible. Make sure to remove the strings before eating. The pancetta will last for about 1 month in the fridge.

Makes 5 pounds

4 cloves garlic, minced

2 teaspoons curing salt #1

¼ cup kosher salt

2 tablespoons dark brown sugar

2 tablespoons whole black peppercorns

2 tablespoons juniper berries

4 bay leaves

1 teaspoon freshly grated nutmeg

8 sprigs thyme

5 pounds pork belly

2 tablespoons freshly ground black pepper

guanciale

COSMO Guanciale (pronounced gwan-chee-AHL-ay) is like bacon, except instead of being made from pork belly, it's made from pork jowls, which are essentially pure fat. The wine adds a nice tang and fruitiness, combined with Christmas spices, like allspice and cloves, and then some chile for well-rounded heat.

We use guanciale for a lot of things—making other charcuterie, including pâtés and sausages, to add rich meatiness to various dishes (especially beans and pasta), and also as the fat in warm vinaigrettes. It is probably most famous for being a main ingredient in Amatriciana sauce. We can't tell you how many times someone has come into the butcher shop and completely butchered the word "guanciale," but we just smile and say, "Yep. Making pasta Amatriciana?"

Makes 5 pounds

½ cup plus
1 tablespoon whole
black peppercorns

½ teaspoon
whole cloves

½ teaspoon
whole allspice

2 teaspoons freshly
grated nutmeg

2 tablespoons
plus 1 teaspoon
red pepper flakes

1 teaspoon juniper
berries

3½ cups sugar

3½ cups salt

1⅓ cups chopped
fresh garlic

2 cups red wine

5 pounds cleaned
pork jowls

In a small skillet over medium heat, toast the peppercorns, cloves, allspice, nutmeg, red pepper flakes, and juniper berries until fragrant. Transfer the mixture to a spice grinder and grind them into a coarse powder. We use a mortar and pestle at the restaurant, but a coffee grinder will also work. Transfer the ground spices to a large bowl and stir in the sugar, salt, garlic, and wine. Rub the mixture evenly over the pork.

Transfer the pork to a nonreactive container with a fitted lid and cure in the fridge for 7 days. Flip the guanciale every day, unlike pancetta and bacon, which you turn only every other day.

Rinse the jowls and let them dry on a rack, uncovered, in the fridge overnight. Wrap the jowls in cheesecloth so they are completely covered and tie with butcher's twine. Hang the meat from the top rack in the fridge for a minimum of 2 weeks before using. The outside should be completely dry. At that point, it'll keep for 3 months.

spicy coppa salami

COSMO A note before getting started: When making salume of any kind, it's critical to be exact. That's why we give the measurements in grams for this recipe and the Lonza (page 224) and suggest you invest in a scale if you're going to make them. Wash your hands, work clean, and be smart because there are many more opportunities for harmful bacteria to grow in salume than in cooked sausage.

We do our salume a little old-school—we ferment them naturally instead of using a starter culture, which can mute the funkiness of the cured meat and lead to a salami that's a little one-note. We like to think of our products as "barnyardy" in the best possible way. Starter cultures can also affect the texture of a salami, giving it a rubbery mouth-feel.

The process is the same for making both the Spicy Coppa and Lonza; the only thing that differs is the rub. It's essential for both that you buy the best possible pork you can find that has never been processed or vacuum packed. It should be fresh off the whole animal. And while we let our salume age for about 3 months in a temperature- and humidity-controlled room, we realize that's most likely not possible for you. We've compensated by adding a step: wrapping the meat in cheesecloth before hanging it in your fridge to age. The cheesecloth wrap retains any excess moisture and prevents the outside of the muscle from hardening too quickly before the inside dries out.

Makes 1
[5 to 5 ¹/₂-pound] salami

4.5 ounces kosher salt

1.3 ounces dextrose

1.28 ounces curing salt #2

8 pounds coppa or fat-on pork loin (roughly 2 coppas or pork loins), cut into 1- to 2-inch cubes

Combine the kosher salt, dextrose, and curing salt. Set aside.

Pat the meat as dry as possible with a clean towel. Look for any flaps where bacteria can grow underneath and trim with a sharp knife. Rub the meat as evenly as possible with the salt-dextrose mixture. Let the pork sit at room temperature for 10 minutes. The meat will begin to sweat as the protein reacts to the salt.

To make the rub, combine the pimentón, cayenne, pepper flakes, and fennel in a small bowl. Divide the rub in half; store half in an airtight container. Coat the pork as evenly as possible with the other half of the rub and place the pork in a clean nonreactive container. A large resealable bag works best. Let the pork sit in the fridge for 10 days, flipping the meat every other day.

On the tenth day, remove the pork from the bag, rinse the meat, and pat it dry with paper towels. Recoat the meat again with the remaining rub. Don't pack it too hard onto the pork; just discard whatever falls off.

Using a large piece of cheesecloth, roll up the coppa as tightly as possible and secure the ends with the butchers' twine. You want it to keep its compact, straight shape. (Look for a roast-tying tutorial on YouTube for the visual—this technique also comes in handy for pancetta, porchetta, and anything else rolled.)

Hang the salami from the top rack in your fridge and then play the waiting game. It will take about 3 to 4 months to age in your fridge.

The cheesecloth may develop mold on its surface. The mold should either be white, or a little blue-green. Both molds are harmless and actually help the aging process. (Both strains are similar to what's found in penicillin.) The amount and color of your mold will depend on the environment in your fridge. Red mold is no good and means you need to throw out the meat. If the meat develops a strong, sour odor, that also means it's no good.

After 4 months test your salami for doneness. There are all kinds of gadgets and gizmos you can buy to help you know when the salami is ready, but we do it the old-world way—we just cut into one side of it. It should be firm on the outside without too much give to it. Old-school Italians like their salami really firm and hard, but we prefer it a little softer and more supple.

When the salami is ready to eat, combine the water and vinegar in a large mixing bowl. Swab the salami with the solution. Pat the salami dry with paper towels and set it on a cooling rack to dry completely. Slice and serve. Once cut into, the salami will keep in the fridge for up to 6 months.

SPICY COPPA RUB

130 grams pimentón de la Vera (hot smoked Spanish paprika)

40 grams ground cayenne pepper

40 grams red pepper flakes

30 grams fennel seeds

½ cup water

½ cup distilled white vinegar

lonza salami

Lonza's rub is mellow and herbaceous, resulting in a salami that tastes a little like speck (except that it's not smoked).

_____

Combine the kosher salt, dextrose, and curing salt. Set aside.

Pat the meat as dry as possible with a clean towel. Look for any little flaps where bacteria can grow underneath and trim with a sharp knife. Rub the meat as evenly as possible with the salt-dextrose mixture. Let the pork sit at room temperature for 10 minutes.

To make the rub, combine the fennel, oregano, pepper flakes, and pepper in a small bowl. Coat the pork as evenly as possible with the other half of the rub and place the pork in a clean nonreactive container. A large resealable bag works best. Let the pork sit in the fridge for 10 days, flipping the meat every other day.

On the tenth day, remove the meat from the bag, rinse it, and pat it dry with paper towels.

Using a large piece of cheesecloth, roll the pork as tightly as possible with the cheesecloth. You want it to keep its compact, straight shape. (Look for a roast-tying tutorial on YouTube—it'll also come in handy for pancetta, porchetta, or anything else rolled.)

Hang the salami from the top rack in your fridge and then play the waiting game. It will take about 3 to 4 months to age in your fridge.

The cheesecloth may develop mold on its surface. The mold should either be white or slightly blue-green. Both molds are harmless and actually help the aging process. (Both strains are similar to what's found in penicillin.) The amount and color of your mold will depend on the environment in your fridge. Red mold is no good and means you need to throw out the meat. If the meat develops a strong, sour odor, that also means it's no good.

After 4 months test your salami for doneness. There are all kinds of gadgets and gizmos you can buy to help you know when the salami is ready, but we do it the old-world way—we just cut into one side of it. It should be firm on the outside with not too much give to it. Old-school Italians like their salami really firm and hard, but we prefer it a little softer and more supple.

When the salami is ready to eat, combine the water and vinegar in a large mixing bowl. Swab the salami with the solution. Pat the salami dry with paper towels and set it on a cooling rack to dry completely. Slice and serve. Once cut into, the salami will keep in the fridge for up to 6 months.

Makes 1
[5 to 5 ½-pound] salami

4.5 ounces kosher salt

1.3 ounces dextrose

1.28 ounces curing salt #2

8 pounds coppa or fat-on pork loin (roughly 2 coppas or pork loins), cut into 1- to 2-inch cubes

Lonza Rub

25 grams fennel seeds

27 grams dried Mexican oregano

14 grams red pepper flakes

8 grams freshly ground black pepper

½ cup water

½ cup distilled white vinegar

pork and duck rillettes

It sounds fancy, but *rillette* is really just an unctuous, flavorful spread made out of long-cooked duck legs and pork shoulder, stewed in their own fat. The original version of this dish comes from Andre Soltner's *The Lutèce Cookbook*, which my wife gave to me as a birthday present. We made some Publican tweaks, though, adding whiskey—the Frenchies use Armagnac—and *lots* of white wine. And instead of giving it a pulverized, homogenous texture, we keep ours really course and chunky. Then we serve it with jam (often peach preserves) or seasonal fruit on great crusty sourdough bread.

In a small bowl, combine the salt, pepper, sage, thyme, and bay leaves. Season the meat with salt-herb mix. Cover and place in the fridge overnight.

In a Dutch oven, over medium-high heat, brown the duck legs on all sides. Pour off and reserve the fat for adding back later. Remove the legs from the pan and repeat with the pork shoulder and belly.

Return the duck and pork to the Dutch oven, putting the pork in first and the duck legs on top. Add the wine, onion, garlic, and cloves. Cover, bring the liquid to a boil, and then immediately decrease the heat to low and cook at a low bubble for 1 hour.

Check the duck legs for doneness, inserting the tip of a knife into one of the thickest parts. If the meat is becoming tender, cook for 20 more minutes. If the meat is not yet tender, cook for 30 more minutes, or until the meet is falling off the bones.

Transfer the duck legs from the pot to a plate. Carefully pick out all the bones. Return the meat to the pot and add the whiskey. Cook uncovered until all the moisture has cooked off, about 30 minutes.

Mash the pork and duck mixture with the back of a spoon, until it's still coarse in texture. (We like it coarse, though you can mash it until it's smoother if you prefer it that way.) The rillettes should be moist and fatty, so all of the reserved fat over the top. Taste and add more salt, if necessary. Err on the side of salty when the mixture is hot because the rillettes mellow in flavor as the mixture cools.

Serve cold or at room temperature with the peaches and sourdough bread.

Makes about 3 cups

1½ teaspoons salt, plus more as needed

¼ teaspoon freshly ground black pepper

½ teaspoon finely chopped sage leaves

½ teaspoon thyme leaves

½ teaspoon crumbled dried bay leaf

1 pound duck legs

1 pound pork shoulder

½ pound pork belly

2 cups white wine

1 white onion, diced

1 clove garlic

2 teaspoons ground cloves, toasted

1 tablespoon rye whiskey

Macerated Peaches (recipe follows) or fruit preserves

Spence Sourdough (page 282) or other good crusty peasant-style bread, toasted

cont'd.

MACERATED PEACHES

You can use this recipe for any seasonal fruit, and it makes a nice relish that's a little sweet, a little savory.

Makes 1 *or as many as you wish*

Peaches, pitted	**Sea salt**
Extra-virgin olive oil	**Freshly ground black pepper**
Lemon	**Honey (optional)**

Slice the fruit into bite-size pieces. Toss with a splash of olive oil, a squeeze of lemon juice, salt, and pepper. If the fruit is tart, add a drizzle of honey. Serve immediately.

chicken liver pâté

COSMO We were joking around that we wanted to make a pâté called "patasia" and put a bunch of Asian ingredients in it like sambal, rice wine vinegar, mirin, and fish sauce (a ton of fish sauce). We did it, and while it didn't taste "Asian" by any stretch, it did taste pretty spectacular. It has been on the menu for four years, and if we took it off, our customers would revolt.

———————

Add about half the oil to a large sauté pan over high heat, enough so there's a thin layer coating the entire bottom of the pan. Heat it almost to the point of smoking.

Pat dry the livers with a paper towel and carefully add them to the pan in a single layer. Depending on the size of your pan, you might need to do this in two or more batches. Sear them for 1 to 2 minutes until browned, then flip and sear the other side. Remove from the pan and set aside.

Add the onions, garlic, Country Rib "Guts," and 2 tablespoons of the butter to the pan. Cook, stirring constantly with a wooden spoon, until the onions and garlic are caramelized and tender, 5 to 7 minutes. Add the rice wine vinegar, fish sauce, mirin, and sambal. Let the mixture reduce by two-thirds, or until the liquid starts to become slightly thicker and more syrupy, 10 to 12 minutes. Taste the mixture, it should be very tart and sweet. If it's not, add a touch more mirin and rice wine vinegar.

Add the livers back to the pan and mix well. Cook them just long enough to warm, about 2 minutes. Transfer the whole mixture to a large bowl or nonreactive container. While the livers are still warm—they have to be warm or the pâté will come out grainy and discolored—add half the liver mixture plus 3 tablespoons of the butter, 2 tablespoons of the cream, and ⅛ teaspoon of the curing salt. Using an immersion blender, blend on low speed and slowly work your way up to high. Blend on high for 2 to 3 minutes to make sure the mixture is very smooth. Transfer the pâté to a clean large mixing bowl and repeat with the second half of the liver mixture plus the remaining 3 tablespoons of butter, 2 tablespoons of cream, and ⅛ teaspoon of curing salt.

Whisk together both batches and then push the whole mixture through a fine mesh strainer into a nonreactive container. Season with salt to taste. Cover with plastic wrap, pressing the wrap directly onto the surface of the pâté. This will help keep the pâté from oxidizing and discoloring. Refrigerate overnight; serve with crusty bread (especially Hemp Seed Ciabatta, page 285) and pickles. The pâté will keep for up to 1 week in the fridge.

Makes 2 cups

Rice bran oil or other high smoking-point oil such as sunflower, grapeseed, or peanut

1 pound chicken livers, any veins or excess fat removed

½ white onion, sliced

3 cloves garlic, sliced

2 tablespoons Country Rib "Guts" (optional; page 177)

½ cup unsalted butter

¾ cup rice wine vinegar

3 tablespoons fish sauce

¼ cup plus 2 tablespoons mirin

1 tablespoon sambal

¼ cup heavy cream

¼ teaspoon curing salt #1

1½ teaspoons salt

harissa pâté

COSMO The night before we opened Publican Quality Meats, we knew we needed one more pâté for the menu. We'd had no sleep and were delirious, so we attempted a version of this, which was a disaster. Eventually we got the balance right between the chicken liver-yness and our spin on harissa, and people loved it. It's a pâté grand-mère, as opposed to campagna, which is more coarse and offal-based, so it's a finer grind and smoother consistency.

If you don't want to make your own spice paste, just sub in ¼ cup plus 3 tablespoons of store-bought harissa.

———————

To make the spice paste: Place chile powder, chile flakes, caraway, cumin, pimentón, garlic, oil, and wine in a blender and blend on high until smooth. Set aside.

To make the panade: Combine the panko, cream, and egg in a medium bowl until it becomes a paste. Set aside.

To make the pâté: Heat the olive oil in a large sauté pan over medium-low heat. Add the onion and cook, stirring constantly, until it becomes tender and translucent, 8 to 10 minutes. Transfer to a large bowl or storage container and allow to cool completely. Stir in the pork, chicken livers, granulated garlic, salt, pepper, and curing salt. Refrigerate overnight.

Preheat the oven to 400°F.

Fit a meat grinder with the smallest die and grind the meat. Lay the ground meat on a baking sheet and transfer to the freezer for 20 minutes. Repeat and grind a second time.

In a large bowl, combine the mixture with the apricots and panade. Work the mixture vigorously with your hands for about 2 minutes.

Test the mixture to see if it is well mixed: form a quarter–size piece and set it in a small pan. Place the pan in the oven and cook for 5 minutes, or until cooked through. Taste and add salt to the terrine mixture if needed. It should taste slightly salty because the flavor will be muted when served cold.

Makes 1 [10 *by* 2½ *by 3-inch*] *terrine*

SPICE PASTE

3 tablespoons plus 1 teaspoon ground guajillo chile powder

3 tablespoons plus 1 teaspoon Korean chile flakes

¼ teaspoon caraway seeds, toasted and ground

⅓ teaspoon cumin seeds, toasted and ground

½ teaspoon pimentón de la Vera (hot smoked Spanish paprika)

1 clove garlic

3 tablespoons extra-virgin olive oil

Dash of red wine

PANADE

1 cup panko bread crumbs

⅓ cup cream

1 large egg

Decrease the oven temperature to 300°F.

Line a terrine mold with the bacon, making sure the entire inside surface of the mold is covered and that there's about a 1-inch overhang of bacon on the sides. Spoon the pâté mixture into the mold, pressing it in well to avoid air pockets. Fold the bacon over the top and cover with the lid.

Place the terrine mold into a roasting pan and fill it with hot water until it comes three-quarters of the way up the sides of the mold. Carefully transfer the pan to the oven and cook for about 2½ hours, until the internal temperature reaches between 135°F and 140°F on an instant-read thermometer. Start checking the temperature after 1½ hours, and then every 15 minutes thereafter (because overcooked pâté is gross). Remove the pan from the oven and let the terrine cool in the water, about 45 minutes. Once cool enough to handle, remove the mold from the water. When completely cool, refrigerate overnight.

To serve, run a knife around the inside edge of the mold and then invert to demold the terrine. Wrap the terrine tightly with plastic wrap. Refrigerate the pâté overnight again. Slice the terrine and serve with the pickles, mustard, and bread. The terrine will keep in the fridge for up to 1 week.

PÂTÉ

1 tablespoon olive oil

½ white onion, sliced

1 pound pork shoulder, diced into 1-inch cubes

½ pound chicken livers, cleaned

1 tablespoon plus 1 teaspoon granulated garlic

1½ tablespoons salt

1 teaspoon freshly ground black pepper

¼ teaspoon curing salt #1

⅓ cup dried apricots, cut into ¼-inch-thick slices

½ pound bacon, thinly sliced

Pickles, for serving

Whole-grain mustard, for serving

Crusty bread, for serving

Herb Eckhouse, La Quercia Cured Meats

In the early days of my career, I would agree to do events just because I wanted to see different places and things. So when I was invited out to Des Moines, Iowa, in 2002, I was excited to go because I'd heard that they had a pretty incredible farmers' market there. I was hanging out at a stand with Larry Cleverley, one of the founders of the market and an exceptional grower, and Paul Willis, the guy responsible for bringing sustainable hog farming to the Niman Ranch meat company. Paul was busy grilling up some sausages and other cuts—all super delicious—and he and Larry told me there was someone they wanted me to meet. Larry made a call and left a message—the guy was out for a run. About half an hour later, Herb, this skinny, long-haired, hippy-looking guy in a track suit shows up. (Herb admits to not even taking a shower after getting the call that there was a chef in town who wanted to meet him). He had some sliced prosciutto in a cooler in his Volvo station wagon. So there we all were, standing in this parking garage, eating what was hands-down the best prosciutto—imported or domestic—that I'd ever had. It was really fine, not super salty, and had great nuanced flavors. It totally blew me away. And that's how I came to buy prosciutto from a guy named Herb in Iowa.

Herb Eckhouse—Harvard grad, Switzerland ski bum, Iowa rancher, agricultural loan banker, commodity crop and vegetable seed marketer, and self-taught cured-meat maker—was heavily influenced by the food cultures of Berkeley (his wife, Kathy, who he met while hitchhiking out West, is from San Francisco) and Italy (he spent about three years working in Parma, the heart of Emilia-Romagna). He came back from Italy, recognized the amazing bounty of Iowa, and thought *What great foods are we making from this?* Answer: None. And it seemed disrespectful and wrong. He figured he could make something

great, and why not make prosciutto? One thing lead to another and he hooked up with the guys from Niman Ranch, who were looking for someone to partner with to cure their hams. (Herb and his company, La Quercia, have never used confinement hogs and always cure meat from animals that have been raised responsibly and humanely.) Along with a used commercial kitchen fridge and a speed rack, Herb gave himself a master's degree in salting and curing ham.

Now we carry his product in almost every one of our restaurants, but it gets a particular place of honor at The Publican. Just as we showcase our oysters as perfect, unmanipulated product, Herb's prosciutto is at the very top of the meat-focused section of our menu. And now we're lucky enough to have our own Publican–La Quercia partnership, which means that any time Herb tries something new—a new hog supplier or a new breed—we get a head start on serving it. As Herb says, it's all about life, liberty, and the prosciutto happiness.

headcheese

This version of the classic terrine that Brian Huston and I developed, and Melba Ortiz perfected, is like a headcheese taco, seasoned with cilantro and lime. The cilantro and lime help cut the richness of the pig head meat, which we brine, braise, and then bathe in a marinade. Slice it thin—or cube it up—and serve it with mustard and pickles.

———————————

To make the brine: Add 8 cups of the water to a large pot over low heat. Throw in the salt, sugar, curing salt #1, thyme, chile de árbol, and bay leaf and cook until the salt and sugar have just dissolved. Remove the pot from the heat and transfer the mixture to a large nonreactive container. Whisk in the remaining 8 cups of water and let the brine cool, about 20 minutes. When the brine is at room temperatre, add the pig head pieces, cover, and transfer the container to the fridge to brine for 5 days.

To do the braise: Preheat the oven to 275°F.

Transfer the head to a large stockpot and discard the brine. Add enough stock to just cover the head pieces and toss in the thyme, bay leaves, and chiles. Bring the pot to a simmer, then cover and transfer to the oven. Cook for 3 hours and then check the head—the meat should be falling off the bone when pulled. Cook for another 30 minutes, if needed. Remove from the oven and set aside until cool to the touch, 30 to 45 minutes.

Remove the head pieces, thyme, bay leaves, and chiles from the braising liquid. Pick all the meat off the bones, being sure to discard any excess fat or glands from the meat. Set aside.

To complete the bath: While the head meat is still slightly warm, combine it in a large bowl with all the bath ingredients and mix well. By now the braising liquid should be cool and the natural gelatin and collagen from the head will have made it thick. Take 1 cup of the liquid and toss with the head meat mixture to coat. It should just be moistened. Transfer the remaining headcheese-cooking liquid to an airtight container and save to use in the Pork Pies (page 234). The liquid will keep in the fridge for up to 1 week.

Line a 10 by 2½ by 3-inch terrine mold with plastic wrap, leaving an overhang. Pack the meat mixture into the mold and then fold the overhanging plastic wrap over the meat. Refrigerate overnight.

The next day, the terrine will be firm at room temperature. Using the plastic wrap as a sling, lift the terrine out of the mold and onto a cutting board. Unwrap the terrine, slice while cold, and serve. The terrine will keep in the fridge for up to 1 week.

Makes 1 [10 by 2½ by 3-inch] terrine

BRINE

1 gallon water

¾ cup kosher salt

¾ cup sugar

1½ teaspoons curing salt #1

1 sprig thyme

1 chile de árbol

1 bay leaf

1 pork head (about 15 pounds), cut into 3 to 4 pieces by your butcher

BRAISE

2 quarts Pork Stock (page 65, or store-bought) or Chicken Stock (page 114, or store-bought)

1 small bunch thyme

2 bay leaves

2 dried chiles de árbol

BATH

½ bunch cilantro, chopped

1 jalapeño chile, stemmed, seeded, and minced

1 cup minced shallots

1 teaspoon ground cayenne pepper

Zest and juice of 4 limes

Sea salt

pork pies

Makes 4 pies

FILLING

1¼ pounds pork shoulder

5 ounces pork belly

5 ounces bacon

2 teaspoons sea salt

2 teaspoons Vulcan's Fire Salt (available online)

1½ teaspoons whole black peppercorns, toasted and ground

¾ teaspoon mace, toasted and ground

1½ tablespoons chopped thyme

3 tablespoons chopped sage

Pinch of ground bay leaf

DOUGH

¼ cup unsalted butter

½ cup rendered pork lard

½ cup water

½ cup plus 2 tablespoons all-purpose flour

1 large egg

One day Brian Huston and I were talking in our sliver of an office at the restaurant, and he told me that he wanted to add a pork pie to the menu. It made sense—it's one of those ridiculously hearty, quintessentially European peasant foods. And then, randomly, we came across a video of Fergus Henderson judging a pork pie contest, which made us want to do it even more. He'd tap on the pies, smell them, taste them, and used words to describe them like "honest" and "convincing." We fell in love with that. Plus the idea of sitting down in a pub with a mixed-meat pie and a pint of beer seemed like the coolest thing ever. So we had to do it. Brian did research by reading some old English cookbooks, and Melba took our initial chubby-fingered efforts and, like a lot of other things, made them better. But the final piece didn't fall into place until we met a woman at the Green City Market in Chicago. She sold lamb pies that she seasoned with Vulcan's Fire Salt. It's just like it sounds: a spicy salt that's actually the byproduct of making Tabasco. We took the idea and started using it as the main seasoning for our pork pies, which have been on the menu ever since.

———————

Preheat the oven to 400°F.

To make the filling: Cut the pork shoulder, belly, and bacon into ⅓-inch cubes. Combine them in a large mixing bowl with the sea salt, Vulcan's Fire Salt, pepper, mace, thyme, sage, and bay leaf. Continue mixing with your hands for another 5 minutes. (It's very important that this be mixed well.)

Test the mixture to see if it is well mixed: form a quarter-size piece and set it in a small pan. Place the pan in the oven and cook for 5 minutes, or until cooked through. Taste and add salt to the filling mixture, if needed. It should taste slightly salty since the flavor will be muted when served cold. Separate the filling into 4 equal pieces, form into balls, wrap in plastic, and refrigerate for 1 hour.

To make the dough: In a small saucepan over medium heat, combine the butter, lard, and the ½ cup water. When completely melted, remove the pot from the heat. Set aside.

Add the flour to the bowl of a stand mixer fitted with the paddle attachment. Start the mixer on low speed and slowly add the butter-lard mixture. Continue to mix the dough for 3 minutes.

cont'd.

pork pies, *continued*

When the dough is no longer warm to the touch, add the egg. Continue mixing for another 2 to 3 minutes. Measure out four 4-ounce balls of dough and leave the leftover dough in the mixer bowl. On a lightly floured surface, roll out each ball to ¼ inch thick and 8 inches in diameter. Set aside. Gather the remaining dough and roll it out to ¼ inch thick and 5 inches in diameter. Using a 4-inch ring cutter, cut 1 circle out of each of the four 5-inch circles of dough. Then use a ½-inch cutter to cut a circle out of the center of each of the 4-inch dough circles. These circles with small holes will become the pie "lids."

Preheat the oven to 300°F.

Coat four 4-inch springform pans with a thin layer of cooking spray. Gently lay each rolled-out ball of dough in a pan, pushing the dough all the way down into the bottom of the mold and up the sides to extend about ½ inch above the rim. Place a chilled pork ball in each mold and top each one with one of the pie lids. Then, using your thumb and forefinger, crimp together the edges of the bottom crust and lid pieces until the entire pie is completely sealed. Repeat for the other 3 pies.

Make the egg wash: In a small bowl, whisk together the egg and water. Lightly brush the top of each pie with the egg wash. Place the pies on a baking sheet and bake for 3 hours, rotating the pies every hour. Set the pies on a cooling rack and let cool completely. Carefully pour 2 tablespoons of the headcheese-cooking liquid into each of the pork pies through the holes in the lids. Set aside to cool completely. Serve the pork pies cold with the mustard and pickles on the side.

Egg Wash

1 large egg

3 tablespoons water

6 tablespoons cooking liquid from Headcheese (see page 233), warmed until liquid (optional; see note, page 237)

Grainy mustard

Cornichons

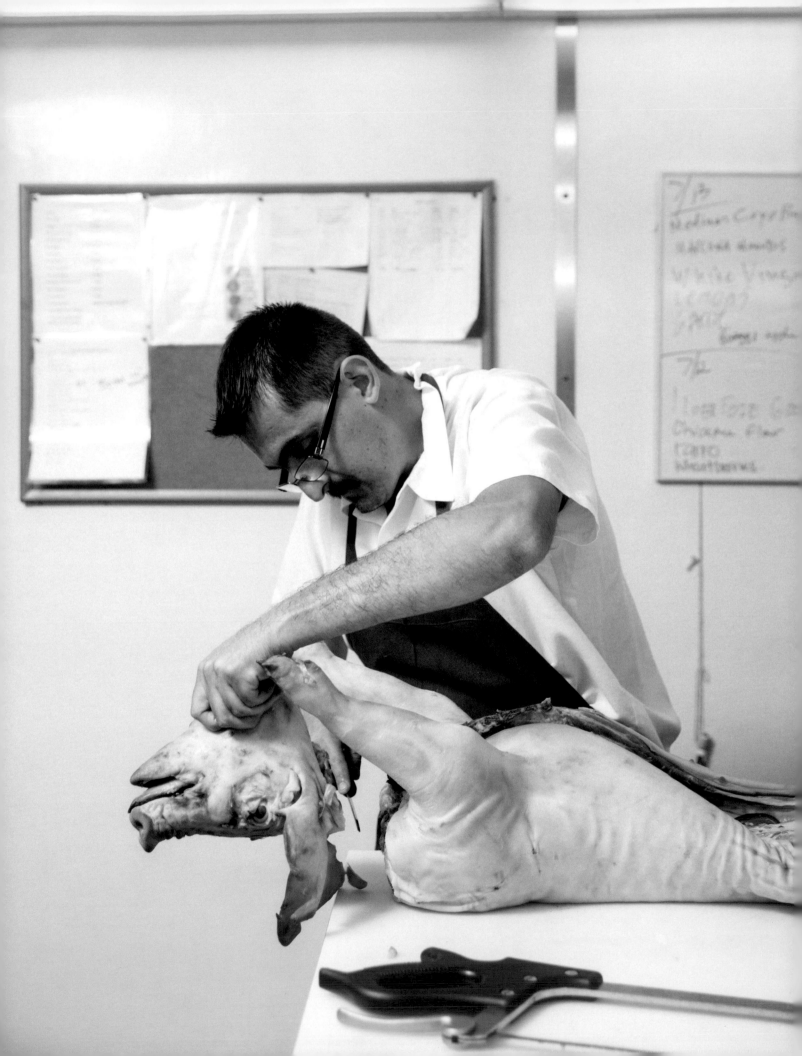

To What's Left Behind:
Offal, Scraps, and Leftover Bits

Shoulders and shanks, knuckles and feet,
      sautéed, deep-fried miracles to eat.
Even slighted scraps, the "What's Left Behind"
—transmuted, parlayed—
      fig. [a]: SCRUMPTIOUS PORK RIND.

Duck Confit

Blood Mort 7-4

Headcheese 7/6

Lonza Cotto 6/14

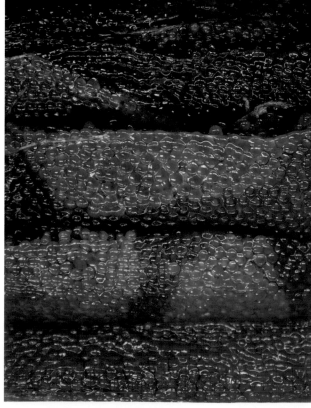

PUBLICAN

Using all the unwanted, usually discarded bits of an animal plays into the original philosophy of The Publican: celebrating the underdogs, reviving things that people don't really eat anymore, and using everything. Juicy, fatty fish collar marinated in roasted garlic marinade; crispy, creamy fried pig's brains that are like the best possible version of McNuggets; ramen-like barbecued tripe with clams—it's all really good stuff. There's just something about offal that's a total mood-changer. It's got so much richness and it's so profoundly delicious that it has the power to literally change your state of mind.

People are always asking what our food costs are. I measure that by how efficient we can be; how close to 100-percent waste free we can get. We're probably at about 98 percent. Take a cow or pig, for example. We use the meat, of course, but what's left? There's the skin that we can use for pork rinds, and the bones that we can use for stock. We save the pig brains and beef hearts until we have enough to run a dish that features them. We take the cow's tallow and pig's lard and render it to use in the fryers. Then we set aside what we can't eat—glands, sinew, etcetera—and have a compost company take it.

We developed a following because of our excitement for making the best possible use of the whole animal. Now people come into the restaurant *expecting* to try dishes like the ones in this chapter. We once got in 7 pounds of duck livers. We figured we had enough to run a special for the weekend. We sold out in four hours. I just sat there wondering, *How on Earth have we sold seventeen orders of grilled duck livers?* Ultimately, it's great for everyone because we're serving exciting dishes that people haven't seen in very many places; we're challenging ourselves to be more and more creative; and we're not throwing away perfectly good food.

smoked trout roe

When I was growing up, my dad would get roe, and we'd cure it. You'd think you have to keep everything cold because that's what you assume with seafood. But actually, putting the roe in slightly warm salted water helps free the eggs from the sacs more easily. And whereas bad roe is really fishy, with this stuff it's more of a pure expression of fish flavor. They're almost like a seasoning component that works really well with something else that's fatty. You could use other kinds of roe—like King salmon—but nothing's quite as tender or perfect as steelhead roe.

COSMO The original idea for this recipe came from a college dorm blog that Erling Wu-Bower found about drinking beer and making salmon roe. Which is crazy; right? Erling kept playing around with the recipe and eventually found a company called BLiS Gourmet, which makes maple syrup–smoked roe. They were the first guys to do barrel-aged B-grade maple syrup aged in bourbon casks. We ran with that and now cold-smoke our roe with maple and dill. We love using it to add a salty-smoky-sweet note to just about anything, from eggs to avocado salads to duck hearts.

Makes 1 ½ *cups*

1 cup kosher salt

3 quarts slightly warm (not cold) water

1 (1-pound) sack uncured roe, trout or salmon

¼ bunch dill

⅓ cup B-grade maple syrup

1 lemon, cut in half

1 lime

Combine the salt and water to create the brine. Once the salt has dissolved, place the roe in the liquid for 30 minutes. Fill a bowl with cold water.

Gently run your fingers through the roe to release it from its membrane. Once all the roe is free and separated, using a strainer transfer the remaining roe to the cold water and reserve the brine. The roe will initially turn cloudy in the cold water, but this is only temporary. Pick through the roe to remove any excess membrane or damaged roe, then transfer it back to the brine for 5 minutes. The roe will again become crystal clear. Strain out the roe once again.

Use a peeler to remove the zest from the lemon and lime. You want big enough pieces that you can easily remove from the marinade mixture later on.

Combine the zest, dill, and maple syrup in a medium bowl and add the roe. Cover and marinate the roe in the fridge overnight.

To cold-smoke the roe, heat your grill to medium-low. Push the coals to one side of the grill and place a pan of ice on the other side. Set the roe on top of the grill grate (in a heat-proof container), cover, and smoke for 20 minutes, making sure you keep the heat at a relatively even medium-low level.

Remove the dill and zest from the roe (to avoid imparting a bitter taste) and set the roe aside to cool. Transfer to an airtight container and refrigerate until ready to serve. The roe will keep in the fridge for up to 3 weeks.

pork rinds with poof powder

We've perfected the process of turning pork skin into super-light, airy puffs: We fry 'em to order and toss them in Poof Powder. If you put one next to your ear, you can hear it still crackling from the fryer. And during hockey season, if you're wearing a 'Hawks jersey and it's game night, your pig skin's on us.

COSMO Malt vinegar and cheddar cheese powder are how we add some acidity to the skins without making them soggy. We add some ground Espelette pepper and together they make our "poof powder," which you can use on anything and everything—popcorn, French fries, what have you. You could also just toss your pork rinds with salt and pepper and they'd be delicious.

Line 2 baking sheets with parchment paper.

Add the skin to a large stockpot and cover with cold water. Bring the pot to a simmer and cook—maintaining a gentle simmer—for about 1½ hours, or until the skin tears when pulled. Remove the skin with a long-handled strainer.

Layer each piece of skin between the sheets of parchment paper. You want to do this while the skin is still warm or the pieces will stick together because of their natural gelatin. Set the skin aside to cool.

Preheat a dehydrator to 200°F or the oven to 200°F (or as low as it will go).

Use a metal bench scraper to scrape any excess fat off the back of the skin. (You could also do this with the back of your knife, which is what we used to do before Chris Cosentino showed us this much faster, easier way of doing it.) Cut the skin into 1½-inch-square pieces.

Arrange the pieces on a roasting rack and place in the dehydrator or oven to dehydrate overnight for 16 hours in the dehydrator or 14 if in the oven. The skin will look like panes of glass when they're done.

Heat a few inches of oil in a large pot to 350°F on a deep-fat/candy thermometer.

Make the Poof Powder: In a small bowl, combine the cheddar cheese powder, malt vinegar powder, and piment d'Espelette. Set aside.

Working in batches of 3 or 4 pieces at a time, fry the skins until they puff into crunchy, pork rind clouds and are about quadruple in size, about 15 seconds. Immediately toss the rinds with a pinch of salt and enough of the poof powder to lightly coat. These are best served right out of the fryer.

Makes 30 to 50 pieces

1 to 2 pounds pig skin

Vegetable oil, for frying

Sea salt

POOF POWDER

3 tablespoons cheddar cheese powder

2 tablespoons malt vinegar powder

1 tablespoon piment d'Espelette

grilled fish collar with roasted garlic marinade and lemon

The best piece of fish I've probably ever had in my life is what's called the "super premium yellowtail collar" at Katsu on Peterson Avenue in Chicago. It's a restaurant run by Katsu Imamura, who has a direct link to a fish market in Japan. He gets these enormous yellowtail, which have a huge collar—like a foot big. He grills it from start to finish and then serves it with a spear of baby ginger and ground daikon and that's it. Collar doesn't need much more than that because it's incredibly oily and delicious. It's pretty much pure gelatin, so it's among the fattiest parts of the entire fish. You could grill it for a year, and it would still be super-moist. I haven't met a collar that wasn't good.

We always save up our fish collars in the freezer so that when we have enough, we run a special. And like Chef Katsu, we don't do much to them other than dunk them in our Roasted Garlic Marinade and grill them until the little bones inside are crispy enough to eat.

Now, you might go to some places that fry their collars. But here's grumpy old man comment #427: This habit of dropping everything in the deep-fryer—meatballs, sweetbreads, pork belly—is rampant. Obviously, you could deep-fry collar, and it would be really good. But for me, these things are more delicate when fried in a pan with oil or grilled as opposed to submerged in fat. People say deep-frying "opens the pores" of a food, but I think it just soaks up all that oil. So for collars, stick to the grill. You'll get a cleaner, tastier dish.

Toss the collars in the marinade and let them sit in the fridge for 1 to 2 hours.

Remove the collars from the marinade. Get your grill hot, season the collars with salt and pepper, and cook them for 7 to 9 minutes, flipping and rotating them every other minute until the collar is cooked through. Add the lemons to the grill, cut-side down. When you think the fish is done, stick a cake tester into the thickest part of the collar. Leave the tester in it for a couple seconds, remove it, and touch it. If it's warm, the collar should be done. Serve with the lemon wedges.

Makes 4 servings

2 yellowtail, striped bass, or sea bass collars

½ cup Roasted Garlic Marinade (recipe follows)

Sea salt

Freshly ground black pepper

1 lemon, cut into wedges

cont'd.

ROASTED GARLIC MARINADE

One of my mom's greatest recipes involves taking a side of white fish and soaking it in Seven Seas Italian dressing. Then she puts it skin-side down in a pan—always lined with aluminum foil so she doesn't have to wash it—broils the fish, and sprinkles it with pimentón. To this day, it's one of my favorite things to eat. Our Roasted Garlic Marinade, which all the chefs in the company use as their mother marinade for fish and birds, especially quail—is our equivalent. We roast garlic in oil and add black pepper, red pepper flakes, and thyme, then use the oil to marinate pretty much everything (in addition to using it to make Garlic Aioli, page 24) because it doesn't mask flavor, just it gives it a lot of depth.

Makes about 2 cups

1 cup rice bran oil

½ cup garlic cloves

2 teaspoons herbs de Provence

1 teaspoon red pepper flakes

½ teaspoon freshly ground black pepper

1 bay leaf

2 teaspoons red wine vinegar

Put the oil in a small pot over low heat. Add the garlic and let the oil start to gently bubble. Pull it off the heat and let it sit for 4 minutes. Bring it back to a bubble again and let it coast for 4 more minutes. The garlic should be tender when pierced. Turn off the heat and let the garlic cool in the oil. When the oil is room temperature, transfer the garlic to a blender along with the herbs de Provence, red pepper flakes, black pepper, bay leaf, and vinegar, and blend until smooth. Store in the fridge for up to 10 days.

doug bigwood's salmon frames

Doug Bigwood is a friend of mine from Minneapolis. I met him through Dave Paulson, a former rock 'n' roll tour manager for a lot of great bands, who loves to cook and throw parties and generally have a good time. After we'd just opened The Publican, Surly Brewing—a Minneapolis brewery run buy a bunch of heavy metal guys—had just gotten a machine that could can tallboys. I really wanted their beer, so I called up Paulson and asked if we could get some. He said, "Yeah, how much do you want?" I said, "Twenty cases." And he said, "Okay, me and Doug will drive it down." It was pretty much against the law, crossing state lines with all that beer to sell, but we did it anyway. And we ended up just giving it away to our customers, so we weren't really doing any wrong. Anyway, that's when I met Doug, who had basically just come down to Chicago to party.

In addition to beer deliveryman, Doug is a fishmonger, and during sockeye salmon season, he and Dave throw a giant crawfish boil. Doug sets aside the sockeye salmon "frames," or, basically, headless fish carcasses with no collar and very little meat. He throws 'em in a baggie with his jerk seasoning and some pesto, and when everyone gets popped up drinking beer and eating crawfish, he starts thowing 'em on the grill and basically just burning them. People lose their minds over the hot, spicy, crunchy, slightly oily frames. I told Cosmo about it, and he interpreted the recipe for the restaurant.

Pour 3/4 cup of the marinade into a large bowl or container with a lid. Reserve the remaining 1/4 cup of marinade for coating the frames after cooking. Add the salmon bones to the bowl and toss to coat. Put them in the fridge to marinate for at least 4 hours, or for best results, overnight.

When you're ready to cook the frames, light your grill and arrange the frames directly over the hottest part of the grill. Grill them for 2 to 3 minutes, until both sides are evenly marked. Really go for it with the char. Dunk the cooked frames into the reserved 1/4 cup of marinade (not the marinade that your raw fish has been soaking in) for 1 or 2 seconds. Transfer them to a serving platter and set aside.

In a medium bowl, combine the mint, dill, basil, and spring onion. Season the mixture with salt and pepper, and then dress it with lime juice and olive oil. Taste the salad and adjust its seasoning as desired, then spread it over the top of the fish. Serve immediately. Eat with your hands.

Serves 4

1 cup of The Marinade (recipe follows)

2 salmon carcasses (about 2 pounds), cut into 4- to 5-inch pieces

1/4 cup minced mint

1/4 cup minced dill

1/4 cup minced basil

1/3 cup slivered spring onion

Sea salt

Freshly ground black pepper

Juice of 1 lime

Olive oil

cont'd.

THE MARINADE

In addition to drizzling this on fish, we love it on pork ribs and chicken wings.

Makes 2 cups

1 cup dried chiles de árbol	¼ cup chopped dill
1 cup fish sauce	3 tablespoons rice wine vinegar
⅓ cup honey	Zest and juice of 16 limes, plus 2 more as needed
2 tablespoons sugar	

Preheat the oven to 450°F. Open some windows.

Add the chiles to an ovenproof sauté pan and transfer to the oven. Let the chiles burn—and we mean burn—until black. Take a deep breath before you open the oven and place the peppers on a plate near a window so they don't make everyone in the house cough.

Once the peppers cool, remove the stems and put the chiles in a food processor fitted with the metal blade or blender. Add the fish sauce, honey, sugar, dill, vinegar, and lime juice. Don't add the lime zest at this point—the agitation of the food processor or blender can make citrus zest and, consequently, the marinade taste bitter). Blend on high for 1 minute. The marinade should be sweet, spicy, and tart. Taste it, and if it's not quite tart enough, add the juice of a couple more limes.

Transfer the mixture to a medium mixing bowl and whisk in the zest. Store, covered, in the fridge for up to 10 days.

A FEW WORDS OF WISDOM

Two things about these frames: 1. Ask your fishmonger for the meatiest ones.
2. When it comes to charring anything, we always say "The darker the better"—and these salmon frames are no exception. We love the flavor that a good char gives to fish. We'll be sure to go over that more in our second book, which we've tentatively titled *It's Not Burnt, It's Charred.*

beef heart and tuna tartare with chermoula

Like most of the offal we serve, beef heart entered the equation because it's inexpensive. But also because it's the most pure expression of beef flavor. It's so beefy; it's incredible. Before The Publican opened, Brian Huston, Erling Wu-Bower, and I went on a food- and drink-driven trip to New York, sleeping in a fleabag motel somewhere on the Lower East Side because we couldn't find a cheap hotel room and eat like five meals a night. One of our stops was Gabrielle Hamilton's restaurant Prune, where we had beef heart. I've had it a million times over the years, but the way she served it so simply—just thinly sliced and grilled—was the best I'd eaten. We've tried to stay pretty true to that standard.

COSMO I was reading a Patagonia chef's book (not Francis Mallmann's), and he was doing tuna tartare with chermoula, a bright, herbaceous sauce. I thought about how we could play with texture, and how the slightly chewy, rich heart would go really nicely with creamy, tender tuna. And the Chermoula would highlight the tunas flavor instead of clobbering it.

Tartare can be finicky because it's all about striking the perfect balance of flavors. We think we do it really well, probably because we're so particular about it. We taste the mixture about ten times every time we make it. And we *always* season it first with gray salt—a really coarse, wet salt—and olive oil and then add the acidic ingredients, so they don't get in the way of tasting the salt.

———————

In a large mixing bowl, combine the beef heart and tuna and season with the salt. Taste the mixture. It should be a touch salty. Add the Charred Onions, Pickled Beets, and olive oil and vigorously mix with a spoon. You want the olive oil to slightly thicken as it whips around the cold meat. Add the Chermoula and lemon juice and stir to combine. The texture should be nice and chunky. Finally, fold in the Fried Shallots. Taste and adjust the seasoning with lemon and salt, if desired.

Spread the tartare on a plate and garnish with the scallion tops. Serve with the toast or crackers.

Makes 4 servings

3½ ounces beef heart, cleaned and diced

3½ ounces tuna, cleaned and diced

Coarse gray sea salt

3 tablespoons Charred Onions (recipe follows)

3 tablespoons Pickled Beets (recipe follows)

2 tablespoons extra-virgin olive oil

3 tablespoons Chermoula (recipe follows)

Juice of 2 lemons

2 tablespoons Fried Shallots (page 56)

⅓ cup scallions, white and light-green parts only, cut on the diagonal

2 tablespoons pumpkin seeds, toasted

2 tablespoons sunflower seeds, toasted

1 stem dill, torn

¼ cup flat-leaf parsley leaves

Toast or Best Homemade Crackers (page 90, or store-bought), for serving

cont'd.

CHARRED ONIONS

These add smoky sweetness to just about anything and are particularly good in salads. As time goes on, we find ourselves using them more and more.

Makes about 1 cup

1 red onion, peeled and sliced into 1½-inch rings

Extra-virgin olive oil

Sea salt

Toss the onion rings with olive oil and season with salt.

Add the onion rings to a large (preferably cast-iron) pan over medium-high heat. Cook for 4 to 5 minutes on each side, until the onions are charred black. Transfer the onions to a bowl and cover with plastic wrap. Let them sit long enough to cool.

Transfer the onions to a cutting board and finely chop. Season with salt to taste and store in an airtight container in the fridge for up to 4 days.

PICKLED BEETS

A great addition to any salad. When making them, you want to half-cook—for lack of a better cooking term—the beets. It'll give them a nice, crunchy, more pickle-y texture.

Makes about 1½ cups

1 pound beets

Sea salt

Freshly ground black pepper

2 teaspoons olive oil

½ cup water, plus more as needed

2 tablespoons champagne vinegar

1 tablespoon fish sauce

1½ tablespoons sugar

Preheat the oven to 350°F.

Rub the beets with salt, pepper, and olive oil. Place them in a small roasting pan with the water—enough to cover the bottom of the pan. Cover the pan with aluminum foil and let the beets roast for 60 to 75 minutes. You want to cook the beets until they are just soft enough to pierce with a fork but not tender all the way through. Remove the beets from the oven and set aside to cool, leaving the foil on.

cont'd.

Once the beets are cool enough to handle, remove the skin. Grate the beets using a box grater or food processor and season with salt, champagne vinegar, fish sauce, and sugar. Taste them. They should be sweet and sour.

Lay the pickled beets on a cutting board and chop them to the point of almost mincing. The pickled beets will keep in the fridge for up to 10 days.

CHERMOULA

This herbaceous mixture is usually used as a marinade in Mediterranean cuisine, but we like it as a vinaigrette or dressing—especially on cooked seafood and gamier meats like lamb and beef heart.

Makes 2 cups

2 cloves garlic

1 serrano chile, stemmed and seeded

1 tablespoon caraway seeds

1 tablespoon coriander seeds

1 tablespoon cumin seeds

½ tablespoon sumac powder

1 teaspoon ground cayenne pepper

1 bunch cilantro, coarsely chopped

½ bunch parsley, coarsely chopped

1 cup olive oil

1 tablespoon pimentón de la Vera (hot smoked Spanish paprika)

¼ cup red wine vinegar

1 tablespoon lemon vinegar

Zest and juice of 2 lemons

1 tablespoon honey

Preheat the oven to 400°F.

Combine the garlic, chile, caraway, coriander, cumin, sumac, and cayenne in an ovenproof sauté pan. Roast in the oven for 4 to 5 minutes, until everything is toasted and golden brown. Transfer the mixture to a mortar and pestle and grind into a paste, making sure none of the spices are left whole and that the paste is nice and smooth. Add the cilantro and parsley to the mixture and beat into a paste with a chunky, pesto-like consistency.

In a small saucepan, heat the olive oil and pimentón over very low heat for about 10 minutes. Cool and strain the liquid through a coffee filter. Mix the infused oil into the herb and spice paste.

Transfer everything to a medium mixing bowl. Whisk in the red wine vinegar, lemon vinegar, lemon zest, lemon juice, and honey. Season to taste with salt. The chermoula will keep, tightly covered, in the fridge for up to 5 days.

grilled duck hearts with homemade butter cheese and pepper jelly

When you're opening a restaurant, you want to use everything that's free. Blackbird had a freezer full of duck gizzards and hearts, so at The Publican we'd confit the gizzards and use them in a salad; and we'd grill the hearts, which are incredibly delicious. Now we get our hearts from a guy who Cosmo thinks sounds like Sebastian the crab from *The Little Mermaid*. ("Can I get some duck hearts?" "But of 'carse!") They're big, like plums, and they're a little sweet, a little roast beef-y and firm, but not too firm. We serve 'em with pepper jelly—because we love all peppers, from sweeter Jimmy Nardellos and Padróns, to hot Cherry Bombs—which is basically a simple syrup that we cook the peppers in and thin out with a little vinegar. You dunk the hearts then grill 'em, so they're sweet, sour, and spicy.

In a large bowl, combine the salt with the water and stir until the salt dissolves. Add the hearts and let them sit in the fridge for 1 hour.

Drain the hearts, pat them dry, and season them with salt. Get a grill or grill pan nice and hot. Sear the hearts over high heat. Cook for 2 to 3 minutes, turning occasionally.

Set aside 2 tablespoons of the pepper jelly for finishing the toasts. Dunk the hearts in the remaining pepper jelly and return them to the grill. Cook for another 2 minutes; the sugars in the jelly will start to caramelize. Remove the hearts from the grill and let them rest.

Spoon olive oil onto the bread, spreading it with the back of a spoon, and then grill the bread on both sides until golden brown and toasty. Evenly spread the butter cheese over the bread and cut each slice in half. Set aside.

To make the salad: In a medium bowl, combine the escarole, onion, dill, and almonds. Toss with olive oil, lemon juice, and a pinch of salt. Taste and adjust the seasoning, if desired.

Cut the duck hearts in half and arrange them over the cut bread. Spread the salad over the top, drizzle the salad with a bit of the leftover pepper jelly, and serve.

BUYING DUCK HEARTS

We like using foie gras duck hearts because they're much bigger than regular duck hearts, as well as richer and sweeter. We get them from a producer in Minnesota called Au Bon Canard, but look for a producer near you. That said, regular duck hearts will work just fine.

Serves 8

2½ tablespoons salt, plus more to taste

1 quart water

1 pound duck hearts

1 cup Pepper Jelly (recipe follows), at room temperature

4 pieces thick-cut sourdough bread

Olive oil

1 cup Homemade Butter Cheese (recipe follows)

SALAD

1 head escarole, cleaned, trimmed, and torn into bite-size pieces

¼ cup slivered red onion

2 tablespoons dill frond pieces

¼ cup coarsely chopped marcona almonds

1 tablespoon olive oil

1 lemon, cut in half

sea salt

cont'd.

PEPPER JELLY

It's best to make this sweet, hot relish at the height of pepper season. We particularly love cherry bomb peppers for heat and then mix them with sweeter peppers, like Jimmy Nardellos and Padróns. But you could make this any time of year with bell peppers and Fresno chiles or only bells. Slather it on pork—we love it on pork—or offal, like grilled hearts or livers.

Shout-out to Vicki Westerhoff of Genesis Growers in St. Anne, Illinois, who not only grows some of the best peppers we get but also is one badass lady. She saved her family's farm (and her own health) by converting to organic practices—and proved just about everyone in her community wrong who thought that women couldn't farm. At sixty-three, she's still out in the field seven days a week, doing the work of three men.

Makes 3½ cups

1 cup sweet peppers, such as sweet Hungarian, Jimmy Nardello, Padrón, or banana peppers, stemmed, seeded, and julienned

½ cup spicy peppers, such as hot cherry bomb, Fresnos, hot Hungarian, or habanero peppers, cored, seeded, and julienned

½ red onion, julienned

¾ cup distilled white vinegar

3 cups granulated sugar

3 tablespoons plus 2 teaspoons powdered pectin

In a wide, shallow saucepot over medium-low heat, add the peppers and onion and stir constantly with a wooden spoon until they're tender and the onion starts turning translucent. Add the vinegar, sugar, and pectin and continue stirring until the sugar has completely dissolved. Taste the jelly—it should be sweet with a great, rich heat. Remove from the heat and set aside to cool slightly. Transfer to a nonreactive container and let it cool completely. Cover with a lid and store in the fridge for up to 3 months.

HOMEMADE BUTTER CHEESE

This is inspired by the store-bought spread. Serve it on its own as a dip, slather it on bread, or add a little dollop to red meat.

Makes 4 cups

2½ cups cream cheese, at room temperature

¼ cup half-and-half

1 clove garlic, minced

1 shallot, minced

½ teaspoon red pepper flakes

1 cup grated Parmesan

¼ cup minced dill

2 teaspoons fresh thyme leaves

8 basil leaves, cut in chiffonade

1 lemon, zested and cut in half

3 tablespoons unsalted butter, at room temperature

Sea salt

Freshly ground black pepper

In a food processor fitted with the steel blade, whip the cream cheese with the half-and-half until smooth. Add the garlic, shallot, and red pepper flakes and pulse until fully incorporated.

Transfer the mixture to a medium bowl and fold in the Parmesan, dill, thyme, basil, and lemon zest. Whisk in the butter and season with pepper and a squeeze of lemon juice. Taste and adjust the seasoning, as desired. The Parmesan will most likely give it all the salt it needs.

Cover and store the cheese spread in the fridge for up to 1 week.

fried pig brains with gooseberry salsa verde

Because we were always having to order extra pig heads at Publican Quality Market—as a result of selling so much headcheese—we started saving the brains. When we'd have 5 or 10 portions, we'd run a brain special. We'd had veal brains on our early menus, but Brian Huston figured out how to take this concept to the next level. He'd bread 'em with flour, coat 'em with egg wash and bread crumbs, and then deep-fry 'em. They're like the creamiest chicken nuggets with a surprisingly light texture. Then we balance them with something sweet and acidic (our version of sweet 'n' sour sauce, I guess). We take gooseberries, which are the tropical fruit of the Midwest, and incorporate their bright flavor into a salsa verde. People are crazy for this dish—there aren't enough pig brains in the world to put on The Publican's menu.

Serves 4

Rice bran oil, or other high smoking-point oil like sunflower, grapeseed, or peanut

1 large egg

2 tablespoons water

¼ cup panko bread crumbs

Sea salt

¼ cup all-purpose flour

½ pound pig brains, cleaned (ask your butcher to do it) and torn into golf ball–size pieces

pulverized salt (see page 40)

½ lemon

¼ cup Salsa Verde (recipe follows)

⅓ cup gooseberries, halved

Start by heating a deep fryer or a pot of the oil to 350°F on a deep-fat/candy thermometer. Line a plate with paper towels.

In a medium bowl, make an egg wash by whisking the egg with the 2 tablespoons of water. Take half of the bread crumbs and put them in a blender. Pulse them into a fine powder and mix them back in with the remaining bread crumbs in a medium bowl. Season to taste with salt.

In another medium bowl, season the flour with salt and pepper to taste. It sounds crazy, but, really, taste the flour; we always do at the restaurant. It should taste seasoned.

Start by tossing the brains in the flour to coat completely. Using your fingers or a fine-mesh strainer, shake off the excess flour. Then dip the brains into the egg wash, again using your fingers or a strainer to remove them from the bowl. Lastly, dredge the brains in the bread crumbs, removing any excess.

Add the brains to the fryer, making sure the pieces are completely submerged so they cook evenly. Once they are golden brown, about 3 to 5 minutes, remove them from the oil and place on the paper towels to blot any excess oil. Season with the pulverized salt and a squeeze of lemon.

Arrange the brains on a platter. Combine the Salsa Verde and the gooseberries and spoon them over the top. Serve immediately.

SALSA VERDE

COSMO Paul likes to call this one of The Publican Mother Sauces. We use it on almost everything—roasted vegetables, grilled meat, poached fish. It's a crazy simple recipe; just mix everything in a bowl. But you'll have to taste and adjust with every batch. Some capers are saltier than others, so you may need more or less salt. Also, a jalapeño's heat can vary depending on the time of year and climate where it's grown. A rule of thumb is "hot nights equal hot peppers." So if you're buying a jalapeño at the farmers' market in the middle of summer, it will most likely be hotter than one you buy at the grocery store in the winter.

Makes 2 cups

8 shallots, minced

¼ cup capers, rinsed and chopped

10 brown anchovy fillets, rinsed and chopped

½ cup champagne vinegar

½ cup extra-virgin olive oil

2 tablespoons honey

1 jalapeño, stemmed, seeded, and ribs removed, minced

Salt

Mix the shallots, capers, anchovies, vinegar, oil, honey, jalapeño, and salt in a bowl. It will keep in the fridge for about 1 week.

sweetbreads with palm sugar butter

Sweetbreads were on the menu when I got my first cooking job, and they're something that I've cooked throughout my entire career. People are always saying how much they love our sweeties, and that has to do with a couple of things. Number one: Use heart sweetbreads, which are from the pancreas of the animal instead of the thymus gland. Number two: We blanch ours in a court bouillon, or flavored broth—which everyone does—but instead of taking them out and plunging them into ice water, we cool the contents of the whole pot. So you undercook the sweetbreads just enough so that they won't overcook while they sit in the court bouillon, which helps a lot with their texture and also lets them absorb more flavor. Then we dredge them in seasoned rice flour—which has little to no gluten—so they don't get gummy.

Over the years we've used a lot of different kinds of butters for the final baste of the sweetbreads, and I like the idea of using something a little sweet like palm sugar butter. The key is to cook the sweetbreads, pull them off the heat to let them cool slightly, then add the butter and baste so the pan isn't too hot and cause the butter to burn or break. It forms a kind of crust on the outside, a little sweet to cut the creamy.

To make the sweetbreads: In a colander, rinse the sweetbreads under cold water for 5 minutes to get rid of any remaining blood in the meat.

Add a thin layer of olive oil to a saucepan over medium heat. Add the carrot, celery, and onion and cook, stirring frequently, for 3 to 4 minutes. Add the bay leaf, chiles, thyme, and peppercorns. Cook until the onion becomes translucent and slightly tender, 5 to 7 minutes. Increase the heat to medium-high and add the white wine. Let the white wine reduce by two-thirds, 5 to 7 minutes. Add the water and bring the mixture to a simmer. Season to taste with a generous amount of salt—the water should taste salty.

Add the sweetbreads to the pot and cook for 8 minutes. Halfway through cooking, stir the pot so that the sweetbreads on the bottom don't start to overcook.

While the sweetbreads are cooking, fill a large bowl or pot with ice. When the sweetbreads are done, pour the hot liquid and sweetbreads over the ice to cool right away. If all of the ice melts, add more as needed to ensure that the sweetbreads keep cooling. Once they are cool enough to handle, peel off the outer membrane and remove any larger veins. The sweetbreads might break apart during this process, and that's okay.

Serves 4

SWEETBREADS

1 pound sweetbreads (all same size)

Olive oil

1 carrot, diced

1 stalk celery, coarsely chopped

1 small white onion, coarsely chopped

1 bay leaf

2 dried chiles de árbol

2 sprigs thyme

1 teaspoon black peppercorns

2 cups white wine

6 cups water

¼ cup sea salt

PALM SUGAR BUTTER

¼ cup palm sugar, at room temperature

½ cup unsalted butter, at room temperature

Salt

½ cup Wondra flour

Rice bran oil

cont'd.

sweetbreads with palm sugar butter, *continued*

SALAD

⅓ cup thinly sliced celery

⅓ cup thinly sliced celery root

⅓ cup thinly sliced carrots

1 teaspoon chopped chives

1 teaspoon chopped parsley

1 teaspoon chopped tarragon

¼ cup Mustard Remoulade (recipe follows)

2 tablespoons celery leaves

1 teaspoon celery seeds

1 lemon, cut in half

To assemble the dish, first make the palm sugar butter: Combine the palm sugar and butter in a food processor fitted with the steel blade or blender and blend on high until smooth, 3 to 4 minutes. Set aside.

Remove the sweet breads from the ice water and pat dry. Season the sweetbreads with salt. In a shallow bowl, dredge them in the Wondra flour.

Add a generous coating of rice bran oil to the bottom of a large sauté pan over medium heat. Carefully place the sweetbreads in the pan and cook them on both sides until they are lightly brown all over, 5 to 7 minutes. Keeping the sweetbreads in the pan, drain off any excess oil and return the pan to the stove, increasing the heat to medium-high. Add ½ cup palm sugar butter to the pan and, using a large spoon, baste the sweetbreads as the butter melts and the palm sugar starts to caramelize, 1 to 2 minutes. The sweetbreads should be golden brown. Transfer them to a serving plate and set aside.

To make the salad: in a small bowl, combine the celery, celery root, carrots, and chopped herbs. Mix with the remoulade and season with salt. Spread the salad over the sweetbreads and garnish with the celery leaves, celery seeds, and a squeeze of the lemon. Serve immediately.

MUSTARD REMOULADE

This is a great replacement for mayonnaise—it's really good with turkey and awesome with fried food.

Makes about 2 cups

1¼ cups Garlic Aioli (page 24)

1 teaspoon Worcestershire sauce

¼ cup minced red onion

2 teaspoons freshly squeezed lemon juice

2 teaspoons minced garlic

½ teaspoon Tabasco sauce

¼ cup plus 1 tablespoon whole-grain mustard

Sea salt

Freshly ground black pepper

In a small bowl, whisk together the aioli, Worcestershire, onion, lemon juice, garlic, Tabasco, and mustard. Season to taste with salt and pepper. Store in the fridge for up to 4 days.

blood pasta with sea beans, fava beans, and mussels

COSMO Six years ago we participated in a charity dinner organized by the guys at Three Floyds Brewing Co from Munster, Indiana. It was called the Dark Lord Dinner because the food was supposed to pair with their Dark Lord imperial stout. We had every chef in the company do a course, and it was all about going above and beyond—chanterelles, foie gras, truffles, chicken cooked inside a pig bladder, dessert with gold leaf. It was pretty meat-heavy, so I wanted to do something with seafood and possibly a pasta. I started thinking about what would happen if I used blood as a binder in pasta instead of egg, and when I realized it could totally work, I got super-excited to tell Paul about it because I thought I invented something awesome. Then I looked it up and, sure enough, San Francisco chef Chris Cosentino had done it two years before. And it's actually very traditional in the area where Italy borders the Alps.

The dough is much wetter than normal pasta dough, and it's beet red. Then as you cook it, the blood coagulates and thickens the pasta, making it firmer—the same way it gives blood sausage texture. We give metric weights here because, just as for pastry and bread making, precise measures are key. Normally we don't use boiling water when making pasta, but in this case—because we're using rye flour, which takes a longer time to cook because it's really dense—we do. As for where to find cow's blood; you can find it in almost any Asian market or ask your butcher. If you haven't tasted sea beans before, the flavor is like a mashup of purslane and capers.

To make the pasta dough: In the bowl of a stand mixer fitted with the hook attachment or on a clean surface with your hands, mix together the flours, egg, beef blood, and salt on low speed. Once fully incorporated, turn out the dough onto a floured surface—if it's not there already—and knead the dough with both hands for another 8 to 15 minutes, until the dough has a nice sheen and an almost waxy feel to it.

Cover the dough with plastic wrap and chill in the fridge for at least 1 hour before using, or up to 4 days.

Flatten the dough into a thick oval. Using a pasta machine set on the widest setting, roll the dough. Fold the ends of the dough to meet in the center and pass it through the rollers, again on the widest setting. Adjust the rollers to the next setting down and pass the dough through, repeating until you have

Serves 4

PASTA DOUGH

5 ounces all-purpose flour, plus more for kneading

5 ounces rye flour

1 large egg

3½ ounces beef blood

½ ounce salt

1 tablespoon extra-virgin olive oil

2 tablespoons minced green garlic

3 tablespoons sliced spring onion

1 teaspoon red pepper flakes

1 pound mussels, scrubbed and debearded

2 tablespoons Fish Stock (page 119, or store-bought) or water

1 cup sea beans or any spring vegetable, such as peas, asparagus, ramps, dandelion greens, or purslane

2/3 cup fava beans, blanched and shucked

3 tablespoons Banyuls vinegar

3 tablespoons unsalted butter

Sea salt

Juice of 1 lemon

3 tablespoons chopped parsley

1/3 cup Bread Crumbs (page 61, or store-bought)

cont'd.

rolled it on the number 3 setting. The pasta might seem *almost* too thick, but don't worry, the thickness makes it easier to get the desired texture after cooking. Cut the pasta into narrow ribbons, like tagliatelle. At this point, you can cook the pasta now, or store it for one more day. Just toss it with a generous amount of flour, lay it on a baking sheet or plate, and cover with plastic wrap.

Fill a large stockpot with water and bring to a boil.

Meanwhile, heat the olive oil in a large sauté pan with a fitted lid over medium heat. Add the green garlic, spring onion, and red pepper flakes and move them around the pan until they start to become translucent, about 3 minutes. Add the mussels and fish stock. Cover the pan with the lid and steam the mussels until they open, 3 to 5 minutes.

While the mussels steam, drop the pasta into the boiling water and cook for about 3 minutes, or until it's slightly al dente. Strain the pasta, making sure to reserve about 1 cup of the pasta water.

Once the mussels have opened, add the sea beans, fava beans, and vinegar to the pan. Reduce the vinegar until almost all the liquid is gone, about 2½ minutes. Add the pasta and butter to the pan. Using tongs, gently mix the pasta with the mussels for 1 minute in order to work the starch out of the noodles and thicken the sauce. If the pasta starts to get too tacky, add a little pasta water.

Season with salt to taste and add a squeeze of lemon juice. Transfer to a serving dish, sprinkle with the parsley, top with the bread crumbs, and serve.

SAVE THE MUSSELS

Since you're essentially manning two pots at once to finish this dish (the pot of cooking pasta and the pan of vegetables and mussels, etcetera), there is a little finesse of timing involved. If your mussels are all steamed and ready to go but your pasta isn't, avoid overcooking them by removing them from the pan and setting them aside while the pasta finishes. Then when you're ready, just add them back to the pan.

barbecued tripe with clams

One time when I was in San Francisco for an event, I went to Bar Tartine with Chris Cosentino. We sat at the bar and had some amazing dishes— beef tartare with crispy bits on top (which I loved and have interpreted for our own menu), smoked sunflower spread—but it was the barbecued tripe that changed my life the most. They served it in a bowl with a deeply flavored broth, almost like ramen. I came back and told Cosmo that we gotta make this. So we asked them how they do it, and they were kind enough to oblige. The secret is getting the texture of the tripe to match the texture of the clams, so it gets blanched, grilled, braised, then fried. It's probably the best surf and turf we've ever done.

Makes 4 to 6 servings

1½ pounds tripe, trimmed (ask your butcher for help with this), cut into palm-size pieces

1½ tablespoons plus 2 teaspoons Mishmish seasoning (see note, page 269)

2 teaspoons green Hatch chile powder

Sea salt

Olive oil

1 yellow onion

1 serrano chile, stemmed, halved lengthwise, and seeded

2 garlic cloves, thinly sliced

1 bay leaf

2 teaspoons fish sauce

1 cup white wine

2 cups Fish Stock (page 119, or store-bought)

2 cups Chicken Stock (page 114, or store-bought)

To remove impurities from the tripe and get a cleaner flavor, you'll want to blanch it first. In a large stockpot, cover the tripe with water and bring to a boil. Decrease to a simmer, remove the tripe, and discard the water. Let the tripe dry for 1 hour.

Preheat the oven to 350°F. Prepare a hot grill.

Season the tripe evenly with 1½ tablespoons of the Mishmash and the chile powder. Sprinkle with salt and lightly rub the tripe with olive oil.

Char the tripe on the hot grill or a cast-iron pan on both sides, about 2 minutes per side. Place the tripe in a braising pan or large stockpot and set aside.

In a medium saucepot over medium heat, heat a thin layer of olive oil. Add the onion, serrano chile, and garlic. Stir with a wooden spoon until the onion starts to become translucent, about 5 minutes. Add the remaining 2 teaspoons of Mishmash, plus the bay leaf, fish sauce, and white wine. Reduce until three-quarters of the liquid has evaporated, 5 to 7 minutes. Add the fish and chicken stocks and bring to a simmer. Pour the mixture over the tripe and cover the braising pan or pot with foil or a lid.

Transfer the tripe to the oven and cook for 2 hours. Check the tripe—it should be tender enough to cut with a dull knife. If it needs a little more time, return it to the oven for 30 more minutes. Remove the pan from the oven and let the tripe cool in the braising liquid, 30 to 40 minutes. Reserve 1 cup of the braising liquid and cut the tripe into ¼-inch-wide strips. Set aside.

To assemble the dish, heat a thin layer of olive oil in a large saucepot over medium-high heat. Add the spring onions and green garlic and stir with a wooden spoon for about 90 seconds. Add the clams and vermouth. Cover the pot with a lid and steam until the clams start to open, 3 to 5 minutes. Add the tripe, reserved braising liquid, and fava beans and bring the mixture to a simmer. Whisk in the vinegar, herbs, and butter. Season with salt and lemon juice to taste. Serve with grilled or crusty bread.

MISHMISH

We buy this blend from Lior Lev's spice shop, La Boite (page 316). It's a sweet-tart mix of crystallized honey, saffron, lemon, and assorted spices. It's great on pretty much everything—from beef to granola—so we highly recommend adding it to your pantry rotation. But you could also loosely substitute 1 tablespoon lemon zest, 1 tablespoon sugar, 1 teaspoon salt, and ½ teaspoon saffron.

2 tablespoons shaved spring onions

1 tablespoon minced green garlic

15 littleneck clams, rinsed and purged

¼ cup vermouth

1 pint fava beans, blanched and shucked

2 tablespoons 12-year-moscatel vinegar

1 teaspoon chopped chives

1 teaspoon chopped parsley

1 teaspoon chopped tarragon

2 tablespoons unsalted butter

Freshly squeezed lemon juice

Grilled bread (see page 286) or crusty bread, for serving (optional)

To Yeast and Flour:
Bread and Everything on It

A Riot of MASH!
A Fight to RISE!
Rolled in a BOULE!
Our Baking JUSTIFIES!

The FONCERS!
The CRIMPERS!
The Kneading DOCKERS!
  of GREASERS!
  and FOLDERS!
Knocking back SOAKERS!

And Q-U-I-C-K:
  "Over your shoulder!!!!!"

The CRUSTS! The CRACKERS!
The LAMES! The SLASHERS!

Forget the JUNGLE!
The Kitchen's A'RUMBLE!

From the inception of The Publican, we knew that we wanted to make most things ourselves—including our bread. It was a daunting plan and one that we got wrong a few times before we got it really, really right. No matter how tough it was, though, it meant that we got a better product using good, locally grown whole grains and a natural process that honors age-old traditions. Initially, we had guys baking bread in the basement of Publican Quality Meats. The bread was good, but we knew it could be better. We started interviewing for head bakers, and that's when we met Greg Wade, a total bread nut who grew up baking with his mother and grandmother. I asked him what he saw himself doing with the bread program, and he said he wanted to focus on natural fermentation, using local whole grains, and making as many different kinds of whole-grain breads as he possibly could. I couldn't have said it better myself.

Initially, we were just making bread for the One Off Hospitality restaurants, so we were able to get really expansive with our product—doing stuff like pretzels and bagels and English muffins. But we were dead in the water because the model just didn't work. We realized that we didn't need to be known for having the best burger buns in the city, just the best bread. So we took a step back, scrapped the nonessentials, and pared down our list to fewer classic, naturally fermented breads, including the ones in this chapter: Spence Sourdough, 1979 Multigrain, Sesame-Semolina Pugliese, and Hemp Seed Ciabatta. They're dark, crusty hearth loaves with soft, yeasty centers that are just as delicious plain as they are slathered with spreads like Cultured Butter, Pimiento Cheese, or Smoked Eggplant Conserva; or as the foundation of our fettuntas—open-faced sandwiches on grilled bread—piled high with things like pan-roasted mushrooms and ricotta or oil-cured sardines and artichokes.

Now that we've gotten more efficient—and our product is better than ever—we supply not only the restaurants in our group but also about forty other restaurants and hotels.

WHAT MAKES OUR BREAD SO GOOD?

Our baker Greg Wade breaks it down to five essential things:

1. **We withhold salt**, at least initially, when we put together our mix. It's an idea borrowed from a French baker, Raymond Calvel, that when you let flour and water sit without salt, the dough can build longer gluten chains. Then, once you hit the mix with salt, it essentially locks up those bonds. This shortens your mixing time, which is gentler on the dough, and in turn, gives you those nice, irregular air pockets inside the loaves.

2. **We use wetter doughs.** The idea is that after we make our initial mix (with just flour and water), we're creating those nice, long gluten chains in a relatively dry dough, locking them up with salt, and *then* we're adding in the hydration. This makes the loaves incredibly soft inside, with large, open, and irregular crumb structures (in other words, those big air pockets you want to see when you break open a loaf). Plus, you're getting more depth of flavor because bacteria thrives in a wet environment. In the case of bread, that means the yeast and lactobacilli can really do their thing, especially because of our bulk fermentation process. This is where we let the dough sit—generally for about 4 hours—before it gets portioned into individual loaves, which gets you a very light, fluffy, workable dough. So even though it's a very wet dough, it will still hold its shape. If our loaves ever turn out flat, the first question we ask is, "How long did it bulk ferment?" If you're cutting your dough—especially the ciabatta—and it's just weeping on the table, then that's a good sign that it should have bulk fermented longer, too. We use linen-lined proofing baskets because, with the dough's high hydration and long fermentation times, the linen helps support the dough as it sits so it doesn't splay out. That way you get volume instead of area. Using a clay baker or cast-iron pot will help your loaves brown evenly while also creating steam as the hydrated dough hits the hot baking vessel.

3. **We use a sourdough starter.** You need to have a healthy starter to make healthy bread. Sourdough starter is basically flour, water, and time. Eventually, it becomes a live culture of (good) bacteria and yeast and is what's used to leaven bread. It also gives bread a ton of flavor. When you eat a piece of bread and it tastes so good but you don't know why—it's the sourdough starter. The organic acids developed through the fermentation process give great aroma and depth of flavor, while also helping to break down phytic acid, which is what makes whole grains difficult to digest.

Plus, a sourdough starter allows for longer fermentation time (so you get really workable dough without adding emulsifiers or conditioners) and acts as a natural preservative. So now you have a shelf-stable, nutritionally available product that doesn't have a bunch of junk in it.

WHAT YOU'LL NEED

Kitchen scale

Stand mixer with dough hook attachment

Bowl scraper

Bench scraper

Round 2-pound linen-lined proofing basket

A sharp knife or double-sided razor

Baking (pizza) stone

6-quart clay baker or cast-iron pot

4. We know our flour. We know that we want bread flour with about 12 percent protein and without enricheners, additives, bromates, or anything like that. The only acceptable additive is malt or enzyme, in which case you're looking for alpha amylase and diastatic barley malt flour (as opposed to nondiastatic, which has been treated with heat). We also know where our whole grains come from. We've partnered with Spence Farms in southern Illinois, where Marty Travis is producing wheat, rye, and some small specialty grains like oats, barley, and amaranth. He's growing these plants with an eye toward natural, sustainable production based on growing conditions and developing good flavor, in stark contrast to commercial producers who are selecting grains for shelf-sustainability, disease resistance, and crop yield. It means we're not only supporting a farmer who is making more responsible choices, but we're also making more flavorful, healthful bread.

When buying flour for your home kitchen, seek out locally grown and milled grains, which you can usually find at the farmers' market. If you need to buy commercial flour, look for brands like King Arthur, Anson Mills, or Bob's Red Mill, which typically don't include conditioners or additives.

5. We measure our ingredients in grams and that goes for the liquids, too. Bread making is edible chemistry—precise measurements make the loaf.

sourdough starter

To make sourdough starter, you just mix high-quality flour with an equal amount of water by weight, let it sit at room temperature for 24 to 36 hours, and you see all kinds of fermentation activity because of the wild yeast left on the grain at harvest. It's one of my favorite smells in the world, and that aliveness comes through in the bread. The amounts given for flour and water are what you need to establish the starter and then you'll use more, in equal quantities, to feed and develop it for a week before you start baking.

Makes 900 grams starter

450 grams flour, plus more for twice daily feeding

450 grams water, plus more for twice daily feeding

Handful of organic grapes

In a bowl, mix together the flour and water.

Wrap the grapes in cheesecloth and gently squeeze them to release some of the juice into the flour mixture. Then bury the cheesecloth bundle in the flour mixture. Let the starter sit, loosely covered with a clean kitchen towel, at room temperature for 24 hours. It should start to bubble. Remove the grapes and discard. Then pour out and discard half of the starter. Add 200 grams of flour and 200 grams of water to the remaining starter.

Repeat this process twice a day, morning and evening, for 7 days, after which time it will be ready to use. Transfer the starter to a jar with a lid and store it in the fridge, discarding half and replenishing (feeding) it once a week as directed. If you maintain this routine (or enlist someone else to fill in for you whenever you can't), it will keep indefinitely.

FOR BEST RESULTS

There are two measures you can take to ensure the best rise in your bread:

Do a "float test" before using your starter. A healthy, active starter should float in water. Take a pinch of starter, drop it in water, and if it floats, it's ready to use. If the starter sinks, let it ferment a few more days before using and then repeat the test.

Remember: activation before refrigeration. The amount of time you should leave your dough out before refrigerating overnight is going to be dependent on the dough and room temperature. If you're not getting much rise out of the dough—because the dough or your room, or both, are on the cooler side—let the dough activate longer before refrigerating it overnight. Cover it with a kitchen towel to make sure it doesn't dry out while proofing.

FRIENDS OF THE PUBLICAN
Marty Travis, Spence Farm

I met Marty about thirteen years ago, when he'd invited Chicago chefs to come out to Fairbury, Illinois, and dig for ramps. He was one of the only people growing 'em, part of an effort to restore and revive his family-owned, 186-year-old farm from the soybean and corn that had been conventionally grown there. We'd all go out for the ramps and end up begging him to grow us just about anything else because his practices were so conscientious and the land was pretty incredible. He started planting all kinds of heirloom-variety vegetables, but it was a couple years later, when he started growing wheat, that he really became part of The Publican family. Because that's when he met Greg Wade.

As Greg tells it, he was in the kitchen at Girl & the Goat, here in Chicago, and Marty came by to drop off an order. Marty introduced himself, said, "Hey, I grow wheat." Greg said, "Hey, I make bread," and it was love after that. Nobody was doing local, organic grains at that time, and they certainly weren't growing the varieties that you could get from Marty, like einkorn or Sonora wheat. By the time Greg took over our bread program, he was buying almost 100 percent of what Marty was harvesting and milling—six varieties of wheat, four varieties of corn, plus barley, rye, sorghum, and pretty much anything else he or Marty could dream up.

Now Marty, his wife Kris, and their son Will are helping other local farmers find their footing. They represent a cooperative of about thirty family farms in Illinois—many owned by kids no older than eighteen—helping them with distribution and marketing. Just this year alone, Marty, Kris, and Will have turned down fifteen to twenty restaurants who want their product, but they are able to direct the chefs they can't supply to other farmers in the co-op who have the same passion for sustainable growing practices and creative cultivation. As Marty says, "We'd much rather work with just a few individuals and do a really good job." Can't argue with that.

spence sourdough

When you buy a loaf of sourdough from the grocery store, it's probably fermented for about 8 hours. Ours, on the other hand, has sat for about 60 hours in cold fermentation (or in your case, letting it sit in the fridge overnight), allowing it to develop even more flavor. The result is an incredibly soft, chewy bread with deep, sour flavor. You'll find the cracked whole grains for the Soaker at natural foods markets, farmers' markets, or online.

Makes 2 loaves

SOAKER

25 grams cracked whole wheat

25 grams cracked whole rye

50 grams lukewarm water (about 80°F)

LEVAIN

50 grams sourdough starter

50 grams bread flour

50 grams lukewarm water (about 80°F)

FINAL MIX

445 grams bread flour

345 grams lukewarm water (about 80°F)

15 grams salt

On day one, prepare the Soaker: Combine the whole wheat, whole rye, and lukewarm water in a large bowl and mix by hand until fully blended. Let the mixture sit in a large airtight container at room temperature (about 72°F) for 12 hours, until it has doubled in volume.

On day two, prepare the Levain: Combine the sourdough starter, bread flour, and lukewarm water in a large bowl and mix by hand until fully blended. Let the mixture sit in a large airtight container at room temperature for 3 hours, until it has doubled in volume.

To complete the Final Mix: Combine the Levain, Soaker, and the bread flour and water for the Final Mix in a large bowl and mix by hand until the dough is fully mixed with no pockets of flour. Let the dough rest, uncovered, at room temperature for 20 minutes.

Sprinkle the salt over the dough and squeeze it into the dough by hand until fully incorporated.

To complete the bulk fermentation: Cover the dough and set aside to ferment at room temperature for 45 minutes. Give the dough its first fold by scooping your hands underneath each side of the dough and pulling the underside up and over the top. Let the dough sit in the mixing bowl, loosely covered with a clean kitchen towel, at room temperature for another 45 minutes and then fold it a second time. Replace the kitchen towel and let the dough ferment at room temperature for another 2 hours, until it is very light and has doubled in volume.

To shape the dough: Turn out the dough on a floured surface, containing it to keep it from spreading. Sprinkle flour on top of the dough, which will help make it easier to work with. Using a bench scraper, cut the dough in half. Take each half and gently tug it into a square. Fold opposite sides of the dough to meet in the center. Repeat for the other square of dough. Flip the dough pieces over so they are now seam-side down. Gently form each loaf into a round by shaping the sides in a circular motion. Cover loosely with the kitchen towel and let rest for 20 minutes.

Turn the loaves over so they're now seam-side up and repeat the shaping process—refolding the dough over itself from each side, turning the loaves over so they're seam-side down, and rounding the loaves by turning them on the table in a circular motion. Transfer the loaves, seam-side up, to the floured proofing baskets. Let the loaves proof, uncovered, for 30 minutes at room temperature, then transfer them to the refrigerator to rest overnight.

Preheat the oven to 500°F with a pizza stone and clay baker or Dutch oven on the middle rack of the oven.

Take one loaf out of the fridge and turn it out gently onto a lightly floured surface. Score the bread as desired (description follows). Carefully transfer the loaf to the hot baker or pot and cover with the lid. Bake for 20 minutes, then remove the lid and place it on another rack of the oven to keep it hot. Bake for another 20 minutes, until the bread's crust is deeply browned. Transfer the loaf to a cooling rack. Add the second loaf to the pot, cover with the lid, and repeat to bake the second loaf.

SCORING BREAD

When scoring bread, you're doing a few things: First, you're preventing the loaf from bursting by cutting the weakest part of the gluten structure. Second, you're giving the bread more surface area to fully expand. Third, by allowing the loaf to expand, you're going to get a lighter piece of bread out of it. And lastly, it's aesthetically pleasing. It's a way for the baker to "sign" the loaf. It's actually how, back in the day, European families using communal ovens could make sure they were bringing home their own loaves. Using a sharp knife or a double-sided razor (which I prefer because it's smaller, thinner, and more maneuverable), cut about ¼ inch into the dough. From there, feel free to get creative—make a grid, diagonal lines, a diamond pattern, etcetera. Just make sure your incisions are as evenly spaced as possible so your bread rises evenly, resulting in a uniformly shaped loaf.

hemp seed ciabatta

Ciabatta means "light as a slipper" in Italian and is essentially an Italian white bread. Our goal is to make a loaf that still has the signature open-hole structure of our other breads, but with a much lighter texture. This is not a sour-leavened bread, meaning you don't use your sourdough starter for it. Instead, you will use only a mix of flour, water, and a little yeast that you let sit overnight. So you get a little bit of yeasty flavor. We add honey for a bit of sweetness (honey is our go-to sweetener—we never use refined sugar in our breads—and we always make sure to use local or, at the very least, domestic honey), plus hemp seeds, which are a flavorful cross between a peanut and a sesame seed and are also very rich in omega-3 fatty acids. Healthful for you and tasty—just like this bread.

On day one, make the Preferment: Combine the ingredients in a large bowl and mix by hand until fully blended. Let the mixture sit in a large airtight container at room temperature (about 72°F) for 12 hours, until the dough has doubled in volume.

On day two, make the Soaker: Combine the ingredients in a large bowl and mix by hand until fully blended. Let the mixture sit in a large airtight container at room temperature (about 72°F) for 12 hours, until the dough has doubled in volume.

To complete the Final Mix: Transfer the preferment and soaker to the bowl of a stand mixer fitted with the dough hook attachment. Add the bread flour, water, and honey. Mix on the lowest speed for 2 minutes, until the dough is smooth, shiny, and strong. Stop the mixer and scrape the sides of the bowl and under the dough with a bowl scraper. Add the hemp seeds and mix for 1 more minute, until the dough is fully mixed with no pockets of flour. Cover the mixer bowl loosely with a clean kitchen towel and let the dough rest at room temperature for 15 minutes.

Sprinkle the yeast and salt over the dough and mix on very low speed for 1 minute. Once they're fully incorporated into the dough, increase the mixer speed to 5 and mix for 12 minutes. The dough should become smooth and shiny and pull away from the sides of the mixing bowl.

To complete the bulk fermentation: Remove the bowl from the mixer and cover it with the kitchen towel. Let the dough ferment at room temperature for 45 minutes. Give the dough its first fold by scooping your hands underneath each side of the dough and pulling the underside up and over the top. Replace the kitchen towel and let the dough sit in the mixing bowl at room temperature for another 45 minutes. Fold the dough a second time. Re-cover and set aside

Makes 2 loaves

PREFERMENT

175 grams bread flour

1 gram pinch of active dry yeast

175 grams lukewarm water (about 80°F)

SOAKER

43 grams whole-wheat flour

43 grams whole rye flour

86 grams lukewarm water (about 80°F)

FINAL MIX

650 grams bread flour

465 grams lukewarm water (about 80°F)

55 grams honey

65 grams hemp seeds

3 grams active dry yeast

25 grams salt

cont'd.

to ferment for 1 more hour, until the dough is very light and has doubled in volume.

To shape the dough, turn it out on a floured surface. Sprinkle some flour on top of the dough, which will help make it easier to work with. Using a bench scraper, cut the dough in half. Take each half and gently tug it into an 8 by 12-inch rectangle, keeping the dough contained so it doesn't spread.

Lightly flour a piece of baker's linen.

Position the first dough rectangle so its long edge is facing you. As if you're folding a letter, take the left edge of the dough and fold it over one-third of the way. Repeat with the right side, so you end up with a roughly 5 by 12- inch rectangle. Place the dough seam-side up on the baker's linen. Repeat the process with the second rectangle of dough, then place the folded dough on the baker's linen, leaving 4 inches between the two loaves. Pinch the linen between the two loaves and draw them together so that the loaves are now directly next to each another with a thin margin of linen separating them. Wrap the sides of the linen around the dough just tightly enough to help the loaves keep their shape. Let the dough proof at room temperature for 1 hour.

Preheat the oven to 500°F with a pizza stone and clay baker or Dutch oven on the middle rack of the oven.

Gently place one of the loaves seam-side down directly onto the baking stone. Carefully invert the clay baker over the dough, covering it. Place the remaining loaf of bread, still in the linen, in the fridge while the first loaf bakes. Bake for 20 minutes, then remove the clay baker, but leave the baker in the oven so it stays hot. Bake for 20 more minutes, or until the bread's crust is deeply browned. Repeat for the second loaf.

THE VIRTUES OF GRILLING BREAD

For as long as I can remember, I've thought that anything served with grilled bread was that much better. It's like garlic bread—remember getting giddy about it as a kid? That flavorful, oily, almost gooey inside with a crusty outside? When you take really good bread—like Greg Wade's—add olive oil, salt, and pepper and grill it, it's got that same thing going on. At The Publican we look at just about any dish and think, *Man, that'd be awesome with grilled bread.* So if you have a grill lit and you have bread, grill it. Period.

1979 multigrain

When we were developing this recipe, my friend Gil—a sixty-five-year-old guy who used to work for me in another kitchen—took a bite and declared, "This tastes like nostalgia, like fuzzy home movies and Super 8 film—like 1979. That was a good year." And the name stuck.

A lot of people hear "multigrain" and think "healthy" or "Tastes like cardboard," but this is just not that bread. This five-grain, five-seed bread is totally representative of our bread program because it serves our mission of showcasing healthful whole grains and natural fermentation while also being incredibly tasty.

We've included a much larger batch of the seed mix than you'll need because it's less tedious than measuring out teeny amounts of each seed and the mix can last for months in a sealed container at room temperature, so you'll be all set to make this bread whenever the mood strikes.

————————

On day one, make the Soaker: Combine the ingredients in a large bowl and mix by hand until fully blended. Let the mixture sit in a large airtight container at room temperature (about 72°F) for 12 hours, until the dough has doubled in volume.

One day two, make the Levain: Combine the sourdough starter, bread flour, and lukewarm water in a large bowl and mix by hand until fully blended. Let the mixture sit in a large airtight container at room temperature for 3 hours, until the dough has doubled in volume.

To complete the Final Mix: Combine the Levain and Soaker in a large mixing bowl. Add the bread flour, honey, pumpkin seeds, sunflower seeds, and water. Mix by hand until the dough is fully mixed with no pockets of flour. Cover the bowl with a clean kitchen towel and let it rest at room temperature for 30 minutes. Sprinkle the salt over the dough and then, using your hands, squeeze it into the dough until fully incorporated.

To complete the bulk fermentation: Cover the bowl with the kitchen towel and let the dough ferment at room temperature for 45 minutes. Give the dough its first fold by scooping your hands underneath each side of the dough and pulling the underside up and over the top. Replace the kitchen towel and let the dough sit at room temperature in the mixing bowl for another 45 minutes and then fold the dough a second time. Re-cover the bowl and set aside to ferment for another 2 hours, until the dough is very light and has doubled in volume.

Makes 2 loaves

SOAKER
40 grams
whole-wheat flour

20 grams
whole-rye flour

65 grams Seed Mix
(recipe follows)

125 grams lukewarm
water (about 80°F)

SEED MIX
410 grams flax

400 grams millet

370 grams
cracked wheat

340 grams
sesame seeds

330 grams poppy seeds

475 grams rolled oats

LEVAIN
40 grams sourdough
starter

40 grams lukewarm
water (about 80°F)

40 grams bread flour

FINAL MIX
345 grams bread flour

45 grams honey

40 grams toasted
pumpkin seeds

40 grams toasted
sunflower seeds

120 grams lukewarm
water (about 80°F)
water

10 grams salt

cont'd.

To shape the dough, turn it out on a floured surface, containing it to keep it from spreading. Sprinkle some flour on top of the dough, which will help make it easier to work with. Using a bench scraper, cut the dough in half. Take each half and gently tug it into an 8-inch square. Fold the opposite sides of the dough to meet in the center. Repeat for the other square of dough. Flip the dough pieces over so they are now seam-side down. Gently form each loaf into a round by shaping the sides in a circular motion. Loosely cover the rounds with the kitchen towel and let rest for 20 minutes.

Flour the inside of two proofing baskets. Turn the loaves over so they're now seam-side up and repeat the shaping process—folding the dough over itself from each side, turning the loaves over so they're seam-side down, and rounding the loaves by shaping the sides in a circular motion. Transfer the loaves, seam-side up, to the proofing baskets. Let the loaves proof at room temperature for 30 minutes, then cover them with the kitchen towel and transfer them to the refrigerator to sit overnight.

Preheat the oven to 500°F with a pizza stone and clay baker with a lid or dutch oven on the middle rack of the oven.

Take one loaf out of the fridge and turn it out gently onto a lightly floured surface. Score the bread as desired (see page 283). Carefully transfer the loaf to the hot clay baker or pot and cover with the lid. Bake for 20 minutes, then remove the lid and place it on another rack of the oven to keep it hot. Bake for another 20 minutes, until the bread's crust has deeply browned. Transfer the loaf to a cooling rack. Add the second loaf to the pot, cover with the lid, and repeat.

sesame-semolina pugliese

This is a style of bread made in Puglia, Italy, and it's the only loaf we make that's very dense in cell structure—so no big air pockets—with a flat, open face and light, fluffy texture. It's traditionally made with only semolina and bread flour, but we add some whole-rye flour, honey, and olive oil to pack in even more flavor. Then we coat the whole thing in sesame seeds, so while we tend to bake our breads really dark compared to a lot of bakeries, this is one exception because if you take a sesame seed too far, it just tastes bitter.

On day one, make the Soaker: Combine the ingredients in a large bowl and mix by hand until fully blended. Let the mixture sit in a large airtight container at room temperature (about 72°F) for 12 hours, until the dough has doubled in volume.

On day two, make the Final Mix: Transfer the soaker to the bowl of a stand mixer fitted with the dough hook attachment. Add the bread flour, semolina, water, honey, and olive oil. Mix on the lowest speed for 3 minutes. Stop the mixer and scrape the sides of the bowl and underneath the dough with a bowl scraper. Mix for 1 more minute. The dough should be fully mixed with no pockets of flour. Let the dough rest in the bowl of the mixer at room temperature for 20 minutes.

Sprinkle the salt and yeast over the dough and mix on the lowest speed for one minute. Once the salt is incorporated, increase to medium speed and mix for 10 minutes. The dough should become smooth and shiny and pull away from the sides of the mixing bowl.

To complete the bulk fermentation: Remove the bowl from the mixer and cover it. Let the dough ferment for 45 minutes at room temperature. Give the dough its first fold by scooping your hands underneath each side of the dough and pulling the underside up and over the top. Let the dough sit at room temperature in the mixing bowl for another 45 minutes and then fold the dough a second time. Ferment for another 2 hours. The dough should be very light at this point and doubled in volume.

To shape the dough, turn it out on a floured surface, containing it to keep it from spreading. Sprinkle some flour on top of the dough, which will help make it easier to work with. Using a bench scraper, cut the dough in half. Take each half and gently tug it into a 10-inch square. Fold the opposite sides of one square of dough to meet in the center. Repeat for the other square of dough. Flip the dough pieces over so they are now seam-side down. Gently

Makes 2 loaves

SOAKER

195 grams semolina

85 grams whole-rye flour

220 grams lukewarm water (about 80°F)

FINAL MIX

215 grams bread flour

95 grams semolina

125 grams lukewarm water (about 80°F)

30 grams honey

25 grams olive oil

15 grams salt

5 grams dry active yeast

50 grams sesame seeds

cont'd.

form each loaf into a round by shaping the sides in a circular motion. Loosely cover the rounds with the kitchen towel and let rest for 20 minutes.

Turn the loaves over so they're now seam-side up and repeat the shaping process—refolding the dough over itself from each side, turning the loaves over so they're seam-side down, and rounding the loaves by shaping the sides in a circular motion

Flour 2 proofing baskets. Lightly mist the loaves with water and roll them in the sesame seeds so the dough is well coated. Place the loaves seam-side up in the proofing baskets. Let the loaves proof for 30 minutes at room temperature, then cover them with a clean towel and transfer them to the refrigerator to sit overnight.

Preheat the oven to 500°F with a pizza stone and clay baker with a lid or a Dutch oven on the middle rack of the oven.

Take one loaf out of the fridge and turn it out gently onto a lightly floured surface. Score the bread as desired (see page 283). Carefully transfer the loaf to the hot baker or pot and cover with the lid. Bake for 20 minutes, then remove the lid (and put the lid on another rack of the oven to keep it hot). Bake for another 20 minutes, until the bread's crust is deeply browned. Transfer the loaf to a cooling rack. Add the second loaf to the pot and cover with the lid and repeat to finish.

COMMERCIAL YEAST

Commercial or instant yeast has its place in the bakery, in addition to a sourdough starter. It's perfect for when we want very light textured bread, like this pugliese or the ciabatta. We're still able to develop some good organic acids, flavors, and textures; they just aren't as deep or pronounced as with a sourdough starter.

cultured butter

We got the idea to serve cultured butter with our bread before we even started our own bread company. We did a book dinner with the amazingly talented chefs Nick Balla and Cortney Burns when they were at Bar Tartine, and they did a cultured kefir butter. Up until then we always thought the Wisconsin butter we got was the best—in the same way that Heinz makes the best ketchup. But after trying their tangy, rich butter—which is just good cream, good yogurt, and salt—we were converts.

Because making butter is simple and only involves three basic ingredients, it's important to use the best possible quality you can find. We use an organic cream so rich and thick it pours like gravy.

When making this recipe, you also end up with buttermilk as a byproduct. Save it to use in a salad dressing or for baking. It'll be slightly thinner than you're used to using, so if you want a thicker consistency like the kind you get from the store, just re-culture it by adding ½ cup of yogurt, covering it with cheesecloth, and letting it sit out overnight.

Makes 4 cups

2 quarts high-quality heavy cream

1 cup high-quality Greek yogurt

Salt

In a heavy saucepot over medium heat, slowly heat the cream until it reaches 100°F on an instant-read thermometer. (It's important to use a thermometer for this because too much heat will kill the culture.) Whisk in the yogurt, remove the pot from the heat, and transfer the mixture to a nonreactive container and cover with a cheesecloth. Leave it out to culture at room temperature for 14 to 16 hours in a spot that doesn't get a lot of light. Once it has cultured, put the container in the fridge and cool for at least 6 to 8 hours or up to overnight.

Add the butter to a stand mixer fitted with the paddle attachment. Paddle on low speed until it starts to separate into butter and buttermilk, 10 to 12 minutes, and let it keep mixing for another 30 seconds. Pour the butter and buttermilk through a fine-mesh strainer, reserving the buttermilk. Add the butter back to the mixer and beat again on low speed. Add a healthy pinch of salt and mix for another minute or two. You'll notice that more buttermilk will release from the butter. Scoop the butter out of the mixer, wrap it in a cheesecloth, and squeeze it with your hands to remove any excess buttermilk that may be in or on the butter. (If you skip this step, the butter will spoil really quickly.) Reserve the buttermilk. Serve the butter with good, warm bread and store any leftovers in a covered container in your fridge. It will last for a couple weeks.

date muhammara

Makes 6 cups

4 red bell peppers

½ cup olive oil

2 teaspoons whole black cumin or regular cumin

1 teaspoon caraway seeds

2 teaspoons Aleppo pepper

1 fresh bay leaf

1 red onion, sliced

3 cloves garlic, sliced

1 cup piquillo peppers

1 Fresno chile, stemmed and coarsely chopped (with seeds)

⅔ cups pitted dates

¼ cup champagne vinegar

1 teaspoon pimentón de la Vera (hot smoked Spanish paprika)

1 teaspoon sumac

½ teaspoon ground cinnamon

¼ cup date or pomegranate molasses

1 teaspoon black lime zest

2 lemons, juiced

¼ cup chopped mint leaves

¼ cup chopped cilantro leaves

2 tablespoons chopped oregano leaves

Sea salt

COSMO Muhammara is a traditional Turkish hot pepper dip, though this is by no means a traditional recipe. The idea came to us when we got some incredible, super-rich date molasses from Rod at the Rare Tea Cellar here in Chicago. The only thing we could think of that you make with it is this dip, which usually calls for pomegranate molasses. We subbed in the new ingredient, and the rest is history.

To make this sweet-spicy-sour dip—which is also great as a sauce with oily fish like mackerel or root vegetables, especially roasted beets—start with the best dates you can find. We get really incredible barhi dates from California's Duvall Valley that taste like butterscotch, but medjool dates from the grocery store will work just fine. We also prefer using fresh bay leaves to dried—they have SO much more flavor—but if you can't find them, just triple the amount and don't toast them.

Roast the bell peppers over a gas flame or under the broiler, transferring them to a bowl when their surface has blacked on all sides and they small fragrant. Cover with plastic wrap and set aside for 10 minutes. Peel the charred skin off the peppers, then stem and seed them. Set aside.

Add the olive oil to a large, heavy stockpot over medium heat. Add the cumin, caraway, Aleppo pepper, and bay leaves and toast for about 1 minute. Add the onion and garlic and sweat them down until the onion starts to become translucent, 4 to 5 minutes. Add the roasted peppers, the piquillo peppers, Fresno chile, and the dates and cook for another 3 to 4 minutes. Pour in the vinegar and bring the pot to a simmer. Stir in the pimentón, sumac, and cinnamon, and cook for another 5 to 6 minutes, until everything starts to get tender. Remove the pot from the stove and let the mixture cool to room temperature.

Add the mixture in batches to a food processor fitted with the steel blade and pulse into a chunky paste. Transfer it to a large bowl and add the molasses, black lime zest, lemon juice, and chopped herbs. Mix well and season with salt to taste. Store in the fridge, covered, for up to 1 week.

BLACK LIMES

Black limes are dried limes that have turned black. They are commonly used in Persian dishes to add bright, sour acidity with a little bit of fermented funk. You can buy them online if you can't find them in a local store.

pimiento cheese

We think just about anything dipped in this would be great—raw vegetables, toasted bread, even ham. We use Hook's 4-year-aged white cheddar, which has a nice tang. That, plus the cayenne and black pepper—which we actually give a measure for instead of "to taste" so it'll definitely be peppery—is something else.

Makes 4 cups

1 teaspoon cayenne pepper

1 tablespoon cracked black pepper

1½ cups mayonnaise (we like Hellmann's/ Best Foods)

½ cup diced pimento peppers

2 cups grated aged white cheddar

Sea salt

In a large metal mixing bowl, whisk together the cayenne, black pepper, and mayonnaise. Add the pimento peppers and gently fold in the cheese until everything is evenly mixed. Season to taste with salt.

smoked eggplant conserva

COSMO This spread is bright, tangy, silky smooth, and surprisingly rich for a dish made without any kind of dairy. We like serving this over roasted root vegetables, such as sweet potato or squash (a great vegan option), or with game birds like duck and guinea hen. At the restaurant, we smoke the eggplant for two hours after roasting it. If you don't have a way to smoke at home, skip this step. It will still be delicious.

Preheat the oven to 375°F.

Using the tip of your knife, score the entire length of the flesh diagonally at 1/2-inch intervals on one of the eggplant halves. Rotate the eggplant and repeat to make a crosshatch pattern. Salt liberally. Repeat for the other eggplant half. Repeat for the remaining 5 eggplants.

Rub the eggplant halves with about 2 tablespoons of the olive oil and season all over with salt and pepper. Use a fork to poke the eggplant repeatedly all over the skin and flesh. Place the eggplant in a roasting pan and transfer to the oven. Cook for 20 minutes, uncovered. The eggplant should be tender to the touch. If it's not, cook for another 5 to 6 minutes. Alternatively, prepare a smoker and smoke the eggplant for 2 hours.

Let the eggplant cool, scrape the flesh into a bowl, and set aside.

Add the remaining 1/4 cup olive oil to a wide, shallow pan over medium heat. Add the onions, garlic, red pepper flakes, and bay leaf. Stir constantly until the onions start to become translucent and tender, 6 to 7 minutes. Stir in the eggplant flesh and oregano and cook for 4 to 5 minutes. Add the sherry vinegar, balsamic vinegar, and honey and cook for another 3 minutes. Turn off the heat, remove the bay leaf, and let the mixture cool for 5 minutes.

In a blender or food processor fitted with the steel blade, puree the eggplant mixture in batches while slowly adding the grapeseed oil. Blend until completely smooth. Pass the mixture through a chinois or fine-mesh strainer into a bowl. Whisk in the Sriracha and lemon juice, then season with salt and pepper to taste. Transfer to a container with a lid and store in the fridge for up to 10 days.

Makes 8 cups

6 globe eggplants, halved lengthwise

1/4 cup plus 2 tablespoons olive oil

Salt

Freshly ground black pepper

2 onions, sliced

6 cloves garlic, sliced

1/4 teaspoon red pepper flakes

1 bay leaf

2 tablespoons chopped oregano

1/4 cup sherry vinegar

1 tablespoon balsamic vinegar

1 tablespoon honey

1/2 cup grapeseed oil

1 teaspoon Sriracha

Juice of 2 lemons

chickpea hummus

COSMO Our hummus is all about the tahini. We like to use Soom Tahini, which we were turned onto by chef Michael Solomonov, who has this amazing hummus restaurant called Dizengoff in Philly. I'm not sure our version will ever be as good as his, but we're trying.

Makes about 6 cups

1½ cups dried chickpeas, soaked overnight in cold water

2 teaspoons baking soda

½ cup Garlic-Lard Confit (recipe follows)

4½ lemons

2 cups tahini

¼ cup water

1 teaspoon cumin seeds, toasted and ground

½ teaspoon sumac

2 teaspoons neonata (see page 28)

2 teaspoons kosher salt

Sea salt

Fish sauce

In a heavy stockpot, cover the soaked chickpeas with cold water. Bring the pot to a simmer and add the baking soda. Cook the chickpeas for 1 hour, skimming the pot occasionally. Once the chickpeas are tender and beginning to fall apart, cook them for another 10 minutes. Strain and reserve.

In a blender, puree the Garlic-Lard Confit and the juice of 4 of the lemons. Strain the puree through a fine-mesh strainer set over a large bowl. Slowly whisk in the tahini and the water.

The mixture should now be light in color and slightly fluffy. Season with the cumin, sumac, neonata, and kosher salt. Set aside.

In a blender, blend the chickpea and tahini mixture until smooth. Stir in the sea salt and taste the hummus. It may need a squeeze of lemon juice from the remaining ½ lemon and/or a dash of fish sauce for some umami.

Strain the hummus again (a pain, but totally worth it for nice, creamy texture) and store it in the fridge for up to 1 week.

GARLIC-LARD CONFIT

Garlic cooked gently in lard gets tender, subtle, and sweet. Use both the garlic and the garlic-infused fat for hummus, aioli, and marinades. The lard, which is a great healthy fat for cooking, when it is rendered from a sustainably raised animal, is also great for roasting vegetables.

Makes ½ cup

¼ cup pork lard   **¼ cup garlic cloves**

In a heavy pot, slowly heat the lard over low heat until melted. Add the garlic and cook until it's tender, 8 to 10 minutes. Let the garlic cool in the lard and then transfer to a container with a lid. Store the garlic in the lard. It will keep about 1 week in the fridge.

FETTUNTAS

The idea for doing these started after I did an event in Philly with Nancy Silverton from Mozza out in Los Angeles. Everyone out there is obsessed with all things modern and cool, and then there was Nancy, doing her fettuntas with tomatoes roasted on the vine, mozzarella and basil, some beautiful salt, and of course, the bread she makes. (In a perfectly curated outfit with great sunglasses, too. I just love her—she has provided so much inspiration for me.) I asked her what a fettunta was, and she explained that it's like bruschetta but in a Tuscan dialect. It literally translates to "greasy garlic bread" or bread that has been grilled to the point of almost burnt, rubbed with garlic, and soaked with more olive oil than most Americans are comfortable with. It's essentially just a vehicle to put great stuff on.

Something to keep in mind with fettuntas is that if you're putting a bunch of ingredients on bread, you're telling people how to eat it. So every bite needs to have a little bit of everything. It also means that you need a kind of "glue" that holds the components to each other and to the bread. Our biggest criticism of a fettunta—or any dish—is that it can sometimes eat "piecemeal-y." If a dish is just a collection of bits, it's no fun to eat. So now we have a kind of fettunta formula where there's always going to be some kind of schmear that holds everything together, whether it's a puree, rillettes, fresh mozzarella, or whipped egg.

pan-roasted mushroom and turnip fettuntas

Serves 4

Extra-virgin olive oil

2 pounds oyster mushrooms or shiitake, hen of the woods, chanterelle, or other good, fresh mushrooms, cleaned

¼ cup unsalted butter

2 tablespoons thyme leaves

2 tablespoons red pepper flakes

4 cloves garlic, minced

Sea salt

Freshly ground black pepper

2 large turnips, 1 quartered or diced into bite-size pieces and 1 thinly shaved

½ teaspoon sugar

4 (1-inch) thick slices good, crusty bread

¼ cup good ricotta

SALAD

¼ cup chopped mint

¼ cup chopped parsley

¼ cup torn basil leaves

1 cup chopped dandelion greens

1 lemon, cut in half

Saba or aged balsamic or vincotto

COSMO We get our mushrooms mainly from two guys: There's Nick Stama, a retired police officer who grows oyster mushrooms in Baroda, Michigan, and Joe Doherty, a prison warden turned mushroom hunter in the Pacific Northwest. Their prices are great, and their dedication to quality is insane—they'll never send you something that's not perfect. We sauté the mushrooms in olive oil with red pepper flakes and thyme, then finish them with a little butter. We mound them and some shaved raw turnips on ricotta that we slather on our super-hearty 1979 Multigrain.

———————

Preheat the oven to 350°F. Line a plate with paper towels.

Add a thin layer of olive oil to a large sauté pan over high heat. When the oil is almost smoking, make a single layer of mushrooms in the pan. Move the mushrooms around the pan as they cook. You'll notice that they'll start to soak up the oil—as the pan gets dry, add a tablespoon of the butter, along with a pinch each of thyme, red pepper flakes, and garlic. Continue moving the mushrooms until they're golden brown. If the mushrooms release some water at this point, just keep cooking until the water has cooked out and the pan is dry again. Taste and season with salt and pepper, then transfer the cooked mushrooms to the paper towel–lined plate to drain any excess water or oil. Repeat this process until all the mushrooms are cooked.

Wipe the pan clean and add a thin layer of olive oil over high heat. When the oil is almost smoking, throw in the diced turnips and decrease the heat to medium. Sauté the turnips until they begin to get tender and turn golden brown. Sprinkle in the sugar. (We do this with all root vegetables to get a little of the bitterness out of them.) Add the cooked mushrooms back into the pan and remove from the heat. Set aside.

Lightly oil the bread and toast oil-side down on a hot cast-iron grill pan until golden brown. Set aside.

In a small bowl, combine the ricotta with a pinch of salt and a few grinds of pepper. Set aside.

In another bowl, make the salad: Combine the shaved turnips and the mint, parsley, basil, and dandelion greens. Season with salt, pepper, a squeeze of lemon juice, and just enough olive oil to coat. Set aside.

Smear each piece of toast with the seasoned ricotta, cut it into thirds, then reassemble the pieces so it still looks like one whole piece of bread. Spoon the mushroom and turnip mixture over the toast, then top with a handful of the salad. Finish with the saba and serve.

cured sardine fettuntas

COSMO Whenever I'm placing my order with a fisherman, there's always an impulse buy. There's always an, "I also caught this"—*"I'll take that!"* moment. So when I bought too many sardines from Monterey, which is an issue because they're good for like a day, I decided to cure them. I butterflied them, cured them with salt and sugar, dunked them in vinegar, and then marinated them overnight in a roasted garlic-thyme-chile oil with a little citrus zest. It preserved their texture and all their oily goodness, and it's now one of my favorite ways to cure. To make a perfectly balanced fettunta, we layer up the cured sardines over a fresh fava bean puree, artichokes sott'olio, which are pickle-y and oily in all the right ways, and some endive to add a pleasantly bitter note.

Serves 4

Olive oil

4 (¾-inch) thick slices Spence Sourdough (page 282, or store-bought)

½ cup Fava Bean Puree (recipe follows)

4 Cured Sardines (recipe follows)

1 head endive, cut into bite-size pieces

½ cup Artichokes Sott'olio (recipe follows)

1 teaspoon chopped parsley

1 teaspoon chopped tarragon

1 teaspoon chopped chives

Sea salt

Freshly ground black pepper

1 lemon, cut in half

Generously drizzle olive oil on both sides of each slice of the bread. Place the bread in a cast-iron pan over medium heat and weigh it down with a bacon press. If you don't have one, a small sauté pan also works. Press the bread for 1 to 2 minutes per side, until golden and toasted.

Spread the fava bean puree onto each slice and then place a sardine on each piece of bread. Cut each piece of bread in half.

In a medium bowl, toss together the endive and artichokes, along with some of their oil. Season the mixture with the herbs, salt, pepper, and a squeeze of lemon. Spread the salad evenly over each fettunta and serve.

FAVA BEAN PUREE

This is almost like a fresh fava bean hummus. We add tahini because we love the bitter flavor of the sesame and the sweetness of favas (or English peas or fresh chickpeas—which would work here, too). You could also serve this as a dip for bread or pita.

Makes 1½ cups

1 cup blanched and shucked fava beans

1½ tablespoons tahini

1 teaspoon cumin

2 cloves Garlic Confit (page 28)

Zest and juice of 2 lemons

3 tablespoons oil from Garlic Confit (see page 28)

Sea salt

Combine the fava beans, tahini, cumin, Garlic Confit, and lemon juice in a food processor fitted with the steel blade. While the food processor runs, slowly add in the Garlic Confit oil.

Once fully incorporated, transfer the mixture to a medium bowl and whisk in the lemon zest (we do this because the agitation of food processors and blenders can make citrus zest taste bitter.) Taste. Depending on the tahini you use, you may need a touch more zest to lighten it up. Season with salt to taste. The puree will keep in the fridge for up to 1 week.

CURED SARDINES

These are just as good on their own as they are on toast. Ask your fishmonger to clean your sardines for you because it can be tricky. Also, this process is for smaller sardines, so if you're working with ones that are larger, just add 2 to 3 minutes to each step.

Makes 4

3 tablespoons salt

2 teaspoons sugar

½ cup champagne vinegar

2 tablespoons 12-year-aged moscatel vinegar

1½ cups extra-virgin olive oil

Zest of 1 lemon

2 teaspoons red pepper flakes

1 small bunch basil, chopped

1½ tablespoons chopped thyme

2 cloves garlic, slivered

4 small sardines

Combine the salt and sugar in a medium bowl and set aside.

Combine the vinegars in a separate medium bowl and set aside.

Combine the olive oil, lemon zest, red pepper flakes, basil, thyme, and garlic in a medium bowl and set aside.

Spread the salt-sugar mixture evenly over and under the sardines, letting them sit for 10 minutes. Rinse the fish and place them in the vinegar mixture for 20 minutes before submerging them in the flavored oil. The cured sardines will keep in the fridge for up to 10 days.

cont'd.

ARTICHOKES SOTT'OLIO

This preparation is an Italian pickling method where you first pickle a vegetable and then store it in cold oil. If you've ever seen sundried tomatoes or mushrooms or artichokes in a jar of oil in the grocery store— that's what we're making. At the restaurant, we use this for all kinds of veg—mushrooms, beans, squash, tomatoes—which you can easily sub in for artichokes. Just pay close attention to the time they spend simmering in the pickling liquid so they don't overcook.

Makes 2 cups

1 cup red wine vinegar

⅓ cup sugar

1 teaspoon red pepper flakes

1 bay leaf

2 sprigs thyme

Sea salt

⅔ cup water

2 cups cleaned, trimmed baby artichokes, quartered

2 cups olive oil, chilled in the freezer for 1 hour

In a small saucepan, combine the vinegar, sugar, red pepper flakes, bay leaf, thyme, and a pinch of salt. Add in the water. Bring the liquid to a simmer and taste. It should be a well-balanced pickling liquid.

Drop the artichokes into the saucepan and let them simmer until they become tender and the liquid has penetrated them to the center, 2 to 4 minutes. Strain the artichokes from the pot and plunge them into the freezing oil. Let the artichokes cool, then transfer them and the oil to a container with a lid. The artichokes will keep in the fridge for up to 10 days.

pickled beef tongue fettuntas

COSMO Have you ever had a scallop dynamite roll at a sushi restaurant? It's basically shellfish and spicy mayonnaise and they use a pastry torch to sear the top of it so the mayonnaise gets all bubbly and caramelized. Well, I thought about how we could get those same sort of flavors and ended up with this fettunta (see page 301), which is a dish that we're always making for events—especially when we're feeding other chefs.

First we pickle beef tongue, dice it, and crisp it up. Then we put that on top of our Sesame-Semolina Pugliese bread (page 291), which is essentially what you'd get if white bread and semolina had a baby. You can grill it a ton and it's still really supple. Then we make a Calabrian Chile Aioli (page 309) that we mix with some Smoked Trout Roe (page 242) and mound it on top of the tongue. Then we torch it. After that it gets some scallions, some sesame seeds, and mushrooms sott'olio, which are cooked mushrooms that have been dropped into very cold olive oil with red wine pickling liquid. The overall effect is that you get the room-temperature tongue, hot roe, and the cold bits all together. It's pretty insane.

We'll admit this recipe takes a long time to make (it takes 8 days just to brine and braise the tongue), and there are a lot of components. But if there was ever a dish was worth it, this is it.

———————

To make the Brine: Combine the salt, granulated sugar, brown sugar, Insta Cure #1, garlic, and pickling spice in a large pot along with the water. Heat over medium-high heat and cook until the pot comes to a simmer or all the sugar and salt have dissolved. Let cool.

Using a brining needle or injector, pierce the tongue evenly, about 8 times. In the same pot that you used to make the brine or in a covered container, submerge the tongue in the brine, cover, and transfer to the fridge for 1 week.

To make the Braise: Preheat the oven to 350°F.

Remove the tongue from the brine and give it a rinse. Add the sherry vinegar, sherry, fish sauce, sambal, bay leaves, oregano, thyme, and stock to a large braising pan or saucepot and bring to a simmer. Submerge the tongue in the braising liquid, cover with aluminum foil, and transfer to the oven for 3 hours. Check the tongue—it should be fork-tender. If not, continue cooking, checking every 15 minutes. Remove the pan from the oven, remove the foil, and set aside to let the tongue cool completely in the braising liquid.

Makes 6 to 10 servings

BRINE

⅓ cup kosher salt

2 tablespoons granulated sugar

2 tablespoons brown sugar

1½ teaspoons Insta Cure #1

3 cloves garlic

2½ tablespoons pickling spice

8 cups water

1 cow tongue (your butcher can order one for you)

BRAISE

1 cup sherry vinegar

1 cup sherry

1 cup fish sauce

½ cup sambal

4 bay leaves

4 sprigs oregano

4 sprigs thyme

1 quart Pork Stock (page 65) or Chicken Stock (page 114, or store-bought)

cont'd.

When the tongue is cool enough to handle, you'll need to remove its outer layer, which is rubbery and inedible. It should peel off very easily. Place the tongue back in the braising liquid, cover, and refrigerate for at least 1 day and up to 6 days.

Cut the tongue into ¾-inch cubes. In an extra-large sauté pan or two medium pans over medium-high heat, heat a thin layer of rice bran oil. Add the beef tongue, moving the cubes around the pan every 30 seconds to caramelize on all sides, 5 to 8 minutes.

Pour out any excess oil and add the butter. Decrease the heat to medium and, using a large spoon, baste the tongue with the butter for about 30 seconds. Spoon the tongue over the bread slices and set aside.

In a small bowl, combine the aioli and smoked roe and spread evenly over the 4 bread slices. If you have a kitchen torch, give the aioli a couple passes until it just starts to bubble and brown.

Drain the mushrooms sott'olio of any excess oil and sprinkle them over the top of the toasts. Follow with the sesame seeds and scallions and serve immediately.

Rice bran oil or other high smoking-point oil such as sunflower, grapeseed, or peanut

¼ cup unsalted butter

1½ cups Calabrian Chile Aioli (recipe follows)

1 cup Smoked Trout Roe (page 242)

4 (1-inch) thick slices of pugliese bread (page 291, or store-bought), toasted

1 pint cleaned royal trumpet mushrooms, cooked as for Preserved Mushrooms (see page 129)

4 teaspoons toasted sesame seeds

½ cup diagonally sliced scallions, white and green parts

CALABRIAN CHILE AIOLI

Consider this a spicy, creamy, not-so-fancy mayonnaise that you just made yourself. Now slather it on pretty much everything.

Makes 2 cups

2 large egg yolks

Zest and juice of 1 lemon

1 teaspoon grated garlic

2 teaspoons Calabrian chile paste

2 teaspoons Sriracha

1 tablespoon sugar

1½ cups grapeseed oil

Sea salt

In a large bowl, vigorously whisk together the egg yolks, lemon zest, lemon juice, garlic, chile paste, Sriracha, and sugar. Once everything is well-mixed, slow down the whisking and slowly stream the oil into the bowl. The mixture will start to thicken as the oil and yolks emulsify. If the mixture starts to get too thick, add a little water. Continue to add the oil until it's all incorporated. The aioli should be a little looser than store-bought mayonnaise. Season with salt to taste. Store in a covered container in the fridge for up to 10 days.

smoked fish toasts with deviled egg puree

The reason we serve smoked fish at The Publican is because I grew up in the smoked fish business. In fact, my earliest food memory was from my dad's shop, a little place called Village Fishery in Rogers Park, up at the northernmost tip of Chicago. When I was about thirteen or fourteen, I'd go out with one of the guys in a van to Port Washington, Wisconsin, and pick up chubs, a lake fish that you can't find anymore because the alewives killed them all off. We'd have like eight barrels of chubs sloshing around in the back of the van, which we'd pour into enormous stainless-steel tubs to brine, then skewer them on these giant racks. We'd wheel them into the smokehouse, an old wooden room with soot-coated walls. My dad would light a pile of straw, which would smolder overnight and smoke the fish. I remember so clearly the first time I was there in the morning to open that door—the smoke came billowing out and all the fish had gone from silver gray to golden bronze. My dad tore a chub off the rack, took the head off, peeled back the belly flesh, and used his fingers to scoop the meat into his mouth, the oil dripping down his chin. Then he handed me one and said, "Do it, kid"—he was a man of few words—and I did the same. It was warm, succulent, super-rich, freshly smoked, never-chilled fish. Incredible. To this day it's my benchmark for smoked fish.

It's tough for us to serve never-been-chilled smoked fish at the restaurant, but we still make it work on a Smokey Joe Grill with wood chips (something Cosmo figured out after I told him I'd served freshly smoked fish at an event once with like twenty smokers going at once). We found that the one fish that's consistently mind-meltingly delicious when smoked is black cod. Serve it on beautifully toasted bread with some fromage blanc or other creamy cheese—maybe a beer—and call it a day. It's also super good with this Deviled Egg Puree (which you can pair with roasted beets, bread, or any other smoked fish) plus some Bread-and-Butter Pickles (page 19), radishes, celery, and celery leaves.

Serves 4

DEVILED EGG PUREE

½ cup hardboiled egg yolks (see page 99)

¼ cup mayonnaise (we like Hellman's/ Best Foods)

1 tablespoon Dijon mustard

To make the Deviled Egg Puree: In a blender, combine the egg yolks, mayonnaise, Dijon, and hot sauce and blend until smooth. Season to taste with salt and pepper then fold in the shallot. Store in an airtight container in the fridge until you're ready to serve or for up to 4 days.)

To make the smoked fish: In a large stockpot over medium-low heat, combine the salt, sugar, pickling spice, onion and garlic powders, honey, and 4 cups of the water to start the brine. Stir until the sugar and salt have dissolved.

Remove the pot from the heat and whisk in the remaining 4 cups of water. Let the brine cool completely and either transfer it to a large plastic container or keep it in the pot. Place the sablefish in the brine and refrigerate for 2½ hours.

Remove the fish from the brine and lay it on a metal cooling rack. Refrigerate, uncovered, overnight.

The following day, in a smoker filled with wood chips of your choice, smoke the fish over medium heat, covered, for 15 to 20 minutes. The flesh of the fish should turn porcelain white and should no longer be opaque. Let the fish cool just slightly and either serve right away or store it, covered, in the fridge for up to 1 week.

In a small bowl, combine the olive oil, capers, onion, radish, and celery leaf. Season with the lemon juice, salt, and pepper.

Spread the deviled egg puree evenly over all 4 pieces of toast. Cut each slice into thirds and evenly flake the warm fish over each piece. Top with the salad, garnish with the dill and parsley, and serve immediately.

1 tablespoon hot sauce (we like Tapatío)

Sea salt

Freshly ground black pepper

1 large shallot, haché (see note, page 178)

SMOKED SABLEFISH

6 tablespoons kosher salt

2 tablespoons sugar

1 tablespoon pickling spice

1 teaspoon onion powder

½ teaspoon garlic powder

1 tablespoon honey

8 cups water

1 pound sablefish

5 tablespoons extra-virgin olive oil

2 tablespoons capers, rinsed

2 tablespoons thinly sliced red onion

2 to 3 English Breakfast radishes, sliced

2 tablespoons celery leaf

Juice of 1 lemon

Sea salt

Freshly ground black pepper

4 (1-inch) thick slices Spence Sourdough (page 282, or store-bought)

1 tablespoon minced dill

2 tablespoons minced parsley

bone marrow toasts

COSMO We love bone marrow. We get our wood oven really hot, pop out all the marrow from the bone, season it with salt and sugar, and cook it just until it starts to melt so we can schmear it on toast. The Onion Marmalade and Horseradish Dressing add sweetness and a little spice that goes so well with the incredibly rich marrow.

Preheat the oven to broil.

Generously spread the olive oil on both sides of each slice of bread. Place the bread on a cast-iron pan over medium heat and weigh it down with a bacon press. If you don't have one, a small sauté pan also works. Toast the bread for 1 to 2 minutes per side, until golden and toasted. Set aside.

Place the marrow bones in a pan or on a baking sheet, cut-side up. Season with salt and pepper then place under the broiler for 6 to 9 minutes, until the marrow is golden brown and starting to melt.

Use a small spoon to scrape the marrow from each bone onto its own piece of toast and spread it evenly. Top the marrow with the marmalade and all but 1 or 2 teaspoons of vinaigrette.

In a small bowl, toss the remaining vinaigrette with the parsley, tarragon, and scallions. Give the herb salad a squeeze of lemon, then spread the mixture over the toasts. Cut each piece in half and serve.

ONION MARMALADE

This mamalade is great on bread or paired with rich things like foie gras, creamy cheeses, and charcuterie.

Makes 4 to 6 servings

Olive oil

4 (¾-inch) thick slices Spence Sourdough (page 232, or store-bought)

4 marrow bones, cut lengthwise

Sea salt

Freshly ground black pepper

5 tablespoons Onion Marmalade (recipe follows)

3 tablespoons Horseradish Dressing (recipe follows)

¼ cup parsley leaves

¼ cup tarragon leaves

¼ cup sliced scallions, white and light-green parts

1 lemon, cut in half

Makes 1½ cups

¼ cup olive oil

1½ red onions, sliced

2 cloves garlic, slivered

2 teaspoons red pepper flakes

1 sprig rosemary

⅓ cup firmly packed dark brown sugar

⅔ cup red wine

½ cup balsamic vinegar, plus more as needed

Sea salt

Pour the olive oil into a thick-bottomed sauté pan over medium-low heat. Add the onions, garlic, red pepper flakes, and rosemary. Stir constantly for 10 minutes, or until the onions are translucent. Add the sugar and continue to cook for 3 to 4 minutes.

Increase the heat to medium and add the wine and vinegar. The liquid should simmer. Cook for about 10 minutes, or until almost all the liquids have evaporated and the onions are cooked down and jammy. Season the marmalade with salt to taste. If you like your sauce tart, like we do, add a tablespoon of balsamic vinegar to finish it off.

Let the mixture cool, and then place it in a covered container. It will keep in the fridge for up to 1 week.

HORSERADISH DRESSING

This dressing-sauce is just as good on red meat as it is tossed with spring vegetables, such as peas and fava beans. We use a good amount of pepper because it's such a tasty combo with horseradish.

Makes about 2 cups

2 teaspoons Worcestershire sauce

¼ cup shallots, haché (see note, page 178)

¼ cup rice wine vinegar

2 teaspoons honey

2 teaspoons grainy mustard

½ teaspoon Dijon mustard

½ cup fresh horseradish, grated on a Microplane

1 teaspoon caraway seeds, toasted and ground

¾ cup olive oil

Sea salt

Freshly ground black pepper

In a medium bowl, whisk together the Worcestershire sauce, shallots, vinegar, honey, both mustards, horseradish, caraway seeds, and olive oil. Season the dressing with salt and pepper to taste. Store in an airtight container in the fridge for up to 1 week.

the publican waffle with honey butter

Getting to the dessert portion of our menu is a challenge for a lot of our diners. We get it—it's hard to take down a bowl of mussels plus a 25-ounce pork chop, a bunch of veggie dishes, and a few beers and still have room for something sweet (much less stay awake). But if there's one dessert that's gone the distance at The Publican, it's The Publican Waffle. It was on the menu from the start, and people are still talking about it.

There's essentially two styles of waffles: Bruges-style, which is yeasted, thick, and fluffy, and Liege-style, which is thinner and has a gooey, sugary shell. We broke the rules and combined the two—taking a yeasted batter and sandwiching it with pearl sugar, which caramelizes as the waffle cooks. Then we always serve them with a scoop of honey butter and jam. The trick to these waffles is having the right waffle iron—you want the kind that flips so it distributes the batter evenly.

To make the waffles: Place the butter, milk, and water in a medium pot. Warm the mixture over medium-low heat, just until the butter is completely melted. Whisk well to combine. Set aside.

Combine the flour, yeast, granulated sugar, and salt in the bowl of a stand mixer fitted with the whisk attachment or in a large mixing bowl. Stir to combine, then slowly add in the eggs, mixing on low speed.

Continuing to mix on low, slowly add the warm milk mixture. Stop the mixer and scrape down the sides of the bowl, making sure to also scrape the bottom of the bowl. Immediately place the waffle batter in a large storage container. Only fill the container halfway full; this batter loves to rise. The batter can sit at room temperature until ready to cook for up to 1 hour or in the fridge for up to 2 hours.

To make the Honey Butter: combine the butter, honey, and salt in a small bowl and stir until well combined. Set aside.

Heat the waffle iron according to the manufacturer's instructions. Place a large scoop of waffle batter in the iron, spreading it to the edges of the iron and top with a sprinkle of the pearl sugar. Cook until golden brown.

Serve the waffles warm with the powdered sugar sifted over and topped with the Honey Butter and the jam.

Makes 4 servings

WAFFLES

¾ cup unsalted butter, softened

1⅓ cups whole milk

1⅓ cups water

2¾ cups plus 2 tablespoons all-purpose flour

1½ teaspoons active dry yeast

1½ tablespoons granulated sugar

1¼ teaspoons kosher salt

3 whole eggs, at room temperature

HONEY BUTTER

½ cup unsalted butter, softened

1½ teaspoons honey

¼ teaspoon sea salt

Belgian pearl sugar (optional)

Powdered sugar (optional)

Jam (optional)

sources

Anson Mills: www.ansonmills.com

Bellwether Farms: www.bellwetherfarms.com

Blain Farms: info@blainfarms.com

Day Boat Fresh Seafood and Buxton Boats LLC: buxtonboats@gmail.com

Geechie Boy: www.geechieboymill.com

Great Ciao: greatciao.com

IMP Foods: ordersfo@impfoods.com

Island Creek Oysters: www.islandcreekoysters.com

La Boîte: laboiteny.com

La Mozzarella: lamozzarellachicago.com

La Quercia: laquercia.us

Maine Coast Sea Vegetables, Inc.: www.seaveg.com/shop

Market Forays: www.marketforays.com

Midwest Roots: www.mwroots.com

Monterey Fish Market: www.montereyfish.com/pages/nav/retail.html

Mud Creek Ranch: www.mudcreeksp.com

Passmore Ranch: passmoreranch.com

Penryn Orchard Specialties: www.penrynorchardspecialties.com

Rancho Gordo: www.ranchogordo.com

Rare Tea Cellar: www.rareteacellar.com

Red's Best: www.redsbest.com/redsbest

Santa Barbara Pistachio Company: www.santabarbarapistachios.com

Trufflebert Farm: www.trufflebertfarm.com/index.html

Water 2 Table Fish Co.: water2table.com

Wulf's Fish: www.wulfsfish.com

acknowledgments

A special thanks to all past, present, and future Publicans, particularly:

Terry Alexander
Tom Carlin
Luke Coan
Dylan Fultineer
Trey Herty
Brian Huston
Justin Large
Kim Leali
James Lehmann
Donnie Madia
Chris Miller
Patrick Mullins
Melba Ortiz
Thomas Schlesser
Eddie Seitan
Jacob Saben
Michael Studer
Ben Truesdell
AJ Walker
Brian Wolfe
Erling Wu-Bower

———

To those whose talent, product, and wisdom inspires us every day:

Jason Allen
Michael Anthony
Kenny Belov
Skip Bennett
Henry Brockman

Nick Balla & Cortney Burns
Sue Buxton
Dave & Susan Cleverdon
Brian Colgate
Joe Conte
Beth & Brent Eccles
Herb Eckhouse
Ed Gast
Suzanne Goin
Sean Hackbart
Katie Harris
Laurence Hauben
Matthew Henderson
Lissa James Monberg & Adam James
Abby Schilling & Mick Klug
Ben Lloyd
Roger Marcotte
Jim Morlock
Nick & Todd Nichols
Michael Passmore
Jeff Rieger
Lior Lev Sercarz
Chris Sherman
Louis John Slagel
Margarita Smith
Robin Smith
Kim Snyder
Trent Sparrow
David Stern
Peter Stocks
Marc Vetri
Jonathan Waxman
Vicki Westerhoff

———

To those who helped craft this book with love and care:

Janis Donnaud
Rachel Holtzman
Lorena Jones
Ashley Lima
Jane Chinn
Lisa Regul
Taylor Peden & Jen Munkvold
Jason Pickleman

———

And, lastly, those who make it all worth it:

Julia Goss
Patricia & Frank Goss
Robert & Aline Kahan
Mary Klonowski

index

Published in the United States by Lorena Jones Books,
an imprint of Crown Publishing Group,
a division of Penguin Random House LLC, New York.

www.crownpublishing.com
www.tenspeed.com

Lorena Jones Books and the Lorena Jones Books colophon
are trademarks of Penguin Random House, LLC.

Library of Congress Cataloging-in-Publication Data
is on file with the publisher.

Hardcover ISBN: 978-0-399-57856-4
Ebook ISBN: 978-0-399-57857-1

Design by Ashley Lima

Printed in China

10 9 8 7 6 5 4 3 2 1

First Edition

PAUL KAHAN is the executive chef–partner of One Off Hospitality Group, which operates The Publican and seven other Chicago restaurants—Blackbird, Avec, Publican Anker, Big Star, Publican Quality Meats, Nico Osteria, and Dove's Luncheonette—and the craft cocktail bar The Violet Hour. Kahan has won three James Beard Foundation awards: 2004 Best Chef: Midwest; 2013 Outstanding Chef; 2014 Who's Who of Food and Drink in America. He lives in Chicago and decamps to the north woods of Wisconsin whenever time allows.

COSMO GOSS trained at Gramercy Tavern and is The Publican's executive chef. He lives in Chicago.

RACHEL HOLTZMAN is a food writer and native Chicagoan.

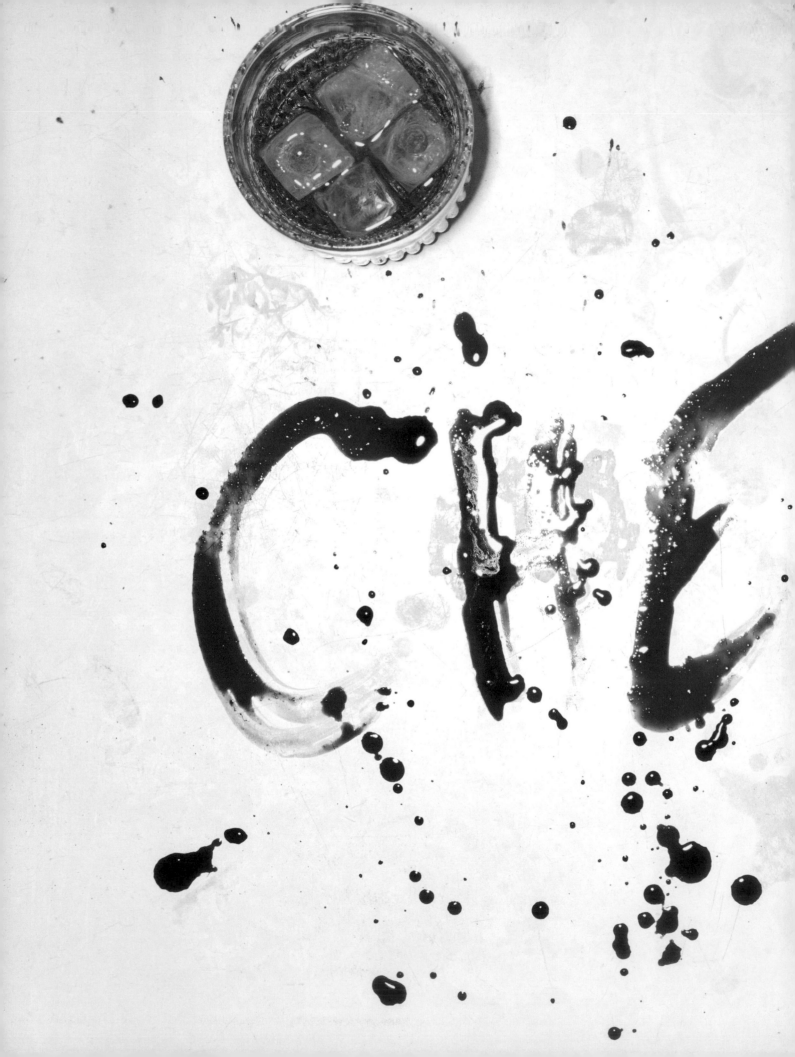